THE MEASURE OF MIND

The Measure of Mind

*Propositional Attitudes
and their Attribution*

ROBERT J. MATTHEWS

OXFORD
UNIVERSITY PRESS

OXFORD

UNIVERSITY PRESS

Great Clarendon Street, Oxford OX2 6DP

Oxford University Press is a department of the University of Oxford.
It furthers the University's objective of excellence in research, scholarship,
and education by publishing worldwide in

Oxford New York

Auckland Cape Town Dar es Salaam Hong Kong Karachi
Kuala Lumpur Madrid Melbourne Mexico City Nairobi
New Delhi Shanghai Taipei Toronto

With offices in

Argentina Austria Brazil Chile Czech Republic France Greece
Guatemala Hungary Italy Japan Poland Portugal Singapore
South Korea Switzerland Thailand Turkey Ukraine Vietnam

Oxford is a registered trade mark of Oxford University Press
in the UK and in certain other countries

Published in the United States
by Oxford University Press Inc., New York

British Library Cataloguing in Publication Data

Data available

Library of Congress Cataloging in Publication Data

Matthews, Robert J.
The measure of mind : propositional attitudes and their attribution / Robert J. Matthews.
p. cm.
ISBN-13: 978–0–19–921115–8 (alk. paper)   1.   Proposition (Logic)   I. Title.
BC181.M38 2007
128'.2—dc22   2007010212

Typeset by Laserwords Private Limited, Chennai, India
Printed in Great Britain
on acid-free paper by
Biddles Ltd, King's Lynn, Norfolk

ISBN 978–0–19–921125–8

1 3 5 7 9 10 8 6 4 2

Preface

This book has been a long time in the writing, much longer than I care to admit. It registers my dissatisfaction with a view of propositional attitudes, and thought more generally, that I once found compelling, but which I now regard as both philosophically indefensible and empirically unsupported. When I entered graduate school at Cornell in 1969, the cognitive revolution initiated by Chomsky in the late 1950s and early 1960s was sweeping behaviorists out of philosophy, linguistics, and psychology, even at Cornell where Wittgensteinian behaviorists such as Norman Malcolm and structural linguists such as Charles Hockett still dominated their respective departments. In the space of a very few years a representationalist view of propositional attitudes, championed primarily by my colleague and friend Jerry Fodor, came to dominate, at least in the East Coast philosophical circles in which I travel. One or another variant of this view has been the Received View of propositional attitudes for the last thirty-five years. Yet notwithstanding my early enthusiasm for this view, over the years I found myself increasingly attracted to a more minimalist view of the attitudes, even as I remained a firmly committed computationalist, and to that extent a representationalist, in matters having to do with cognitive scientific theorizing. This more minimalist view treats propositional attitudes as little more than aptitudes for their characteristic effects both on thought and on behavior, firmly rejecting the notion that common-sense propositional attitude psychology is, as proponents of the Received View claim, a proto-scientific computational cognitive psychology. But it wasn't until I stumbled onto numerical measurement theory in the late 1980s that I began to see a way, a possible way at least, of reconciling this minimalist view of the attitudes with the philosophical, semantic, and empirical psychological considerations that had driven many philosophers of mind to this Received View. I don't claim to have made a compelling case for the measurement-theoretic account of the attitudes and attitude attributions that I lay out in this book, much less for the view of attitudes as aptitudes that I sketch. It will be enough if I succeed in convincing some readers that a measurement-theoretic account is sufficiently promising to merit further work on their part.

Some of the arguments that figure in the book have appeared elsewhere. Portions of Chapter 3.5 are drawn from 'Psychological Reality of Grammars', in A. Kasher (ed.), *The Chomskyan Turn* (London: Basil Blackwell, 1991); portions of Chapter 3.7 and 3.8 are drawn from 'Is There Vindication through Representationalism?', in B. Loewer and G. Rey (eds.), *Meaning in Mind: Fodor and his Critics* (London: Basil Blackwell, 1991). A version of Chapter 4 appeared as 'Logical Form and the Relational Conception of Belief', in G. Preyer and G. Peter (eds.), *Logical Form and Language* (Oxford: Oxford University Press, 2002). A rather unsatisfactory preliminary sketch of the measurement-theoretic account of the attitudes presented in the second part of this book appeared in *Mind* 103 (1994) under the title 'The Measure of Mind'. I thank these publishers and *Mind* for permission to use this material here.

I would like to be able to acknowledge and thank all the various people, including colleagues here at Rutgers, who have helped and encouraged me in this project, but they are too numerous. I would, however, like to offer special thanks to graduate students, many now finished, especially Walter Dean, Kent Johnson, and Matt Phillips, whose discussion in seminar helped me to refine my ideas, to the ZiF (Center for Interdisciplinary Research) at Bielefeld University, for its generous financial support in Spring 1990, to the members of the ZiF's Mind-Brain Group that year (including Ansgar Beckermann, Peter Bieri, Dan Dennett, Jaegwon Kim, and David Rosenthal), which offered me the first opportunity to work out many of the basic ideas of my measurement-theoretic account of the attitudes, to the colloquia audiences at various universities here and abroad where I presented various arguments from the book, and to the two anonymous readers who offered extremely useful comments and criticisms. Finally and most importantly, I want to thank my wife (sailing partner, sounding board, and colleague) Frankie Egan, whose help and support in this and all other endeavors has been invaluable.

Contents

II. A MEASUREMENT-THEORETIC ACCOUNT OF PROPOSITIONAL ATTITUDES AND THEIR ATTRIBUTION

1

A Prospective Introduction

1.1. THE ASCENDANCY OF THE RECEIVED VIEW

The last four decades have witnessed a period of extraordinary activity within the philosophy of mind. It is only slightly hyperbolic to speak of the early years of this period as revolutionary, for in the short space of less than a decade, a well-entrenched behaviorist philosophy of mind was overthrown, replaced by the philosophical view that dominates today. This view, which I shall dub the 'Received View' in recognition of its canonical status in the field, is described in some detail in Chapter 2. The Received View consists of a number of distinct theses, some of which are independent of others, so that what I am calling the Received View is really a cluster of related views, which share a small number of basic commitments, specifically about the nature of propositional attitudes and their role in the production and explanation of behavior and thought. Basically, the Received View holds that common-sense psychology has it right when it takes beliefs, desires, and other propositional attitudes to be the causes of our behavior. Crucially, it identifies propositional attitudes with certain representational states of their possessor, holding that having a propositional attitude (e.g., believing that it's sunny outside today) is a matter of standing in a functional-computational relation to a mental representation, specifically a mental sentence that expresses the propositional content of the attitude (in the present example, a mental representation that expresses the proposition that it's sunny outside today). The view also offers an account of the nature of the molar cognitive capacities (e.g., language comprehension, spatial orientation, face recognition) that scientific cognitive psychology takes it to be its task to explain. Such capacities are said to arise out of the interaction of various constitutive subcapacities, which are them- selves capacities for processing (constructing, transforming, manipulating, etc.) the mental representations that express the propositional contents of a subject's propositional attitudes. Cognitive psychological explanations, it is held, should therefore take the form of an 'intentional functional analysis' that explains molar cognitive capacities in terms of their constitutive subcapacities, and the latter in terms of computational processes defined over these mental representations. In effect, the Received View thus consists in a metaphysical claim about the nature of propositional attitudes, cognitive capacities, and cognition itself, and a normative epistemological claim about the proper form of cognitive psychological explanations.

A number of factors contributed to the emergence and rapid ascendancy of the Received View in the 1960s and early 1970s. First, the collapse of both methodological behaviorism in empirical scientific psychology and logical behaviorism in the philosophy of mind in the late 1950s and early 1960s left psychologists without an explanatory paradigm and philosophers without any reductive materialist account of propositional attitudes and the common-sense explanations that adverted to them. Second, the almost simultaneous collapse of central state identity theory, which proposed to type-identify mental states with states of the central nervous system (e.g., pains with C-fiber firings, as one famous account had it), effectively closed the other major reductionist avenue that philosophers had been pursuing. Yet, and this is a third factor, the newly emerging generative linguistics championed by Noam Chomsky, which so quickly unseated behaviorist learning theory and structuralist linguistics, made wide and unapologetic use of propositional attitude attributions, thereby giving philosophers of mind, most of whom were committed materialists, strong incentive to establish the materialistic and causal explanatory *bona fides* of propositional attitudes and the explanations in which they figured.

These philosophers were only too eager to take up this vindicatory challenge, because, fourth, the notion that explanations in scientific cognitive psychology might legitimately advert to propositional attitudes promised not only a vindication of common-sense belief-desire psychology, a project which had long interested philosophers of mind, but also new employment possibilities, or at least a new job description. Quine's famous critique of the analytic/synthetic distinction had left the very practicability of a priori philosophical analysis in serious doubt. If, as he argued, the distinction was untenable, then such analysis was impossible, and what philosophers presented as a priori analyses were in fact a posteriori empirical claims, albeit of a rather abstract, foundational sort. The newly emerging role for propositional attitudes in cognitive psychological explanations offered philosophers a role within cognitive psychology as Lockean 'underlaborers' whose job it was to vindicate the foundations of scientific cognitive psychology by establishing the materialistic *bona fides* of the propositional attitudes to which cognitive psychological explanations often adverted. Philosophers stood a real chance of gaining admission to their local cognitive science centers if only they could successfully sell their colleagues in these centers on the idea that propositional attitudes needed vindication and they, philosophers, had a plausible account of how this vindication might be effected.

The proposed vindication strategy that proponents of the Received View eventually hit on emerged out of, fifth, concurrent developments in computer science, specifically out of the theory of universal (Turing) computation. With the collapse of logical behaviorism and central state identity theory, functionalist theories of mind had swept philosophy of mind in the early 1960s, principally because they avoided both the peripheralism of the former and the neurological parochialism ('chauvinism') of the latter by defining mental states *relationally* in terms of their causal relations to environmental stimuli (inputs), behavior (outputs), and other mental states. Yet, as attractive as these functionalist theories were, they did not establish the materialistic *bona fides* of the mental states. Such theories were fully compatible with Cartesian (interactionist) dualism. Many functionalists embraced a materialist view that they called 'token physicalism', but those concerned with the materialist *bona fides* of propositional attitudes found little by way of vindication in these token physicalist convictions, since token physicalism was silent as regards the physical implementation of these functionally characterized mental states. What was needed was an implementation story, and it was just this that a computational construal of propositional attitudes seemed to promise. For if propositional attitudes could be identified with computational states, then because computational states were not themselves materialistically suspect, the materialistic *bona fides* of propositional attitudes would be established. The proposed solution was doubly attractive because it also promised an account of the intentionality of propositional attitudes, something that functionalism alone seemingly failed to provide. So the crucial idea of the Received View, then, was this: having a propositional attitude is a matter of having an 'explicit' representation—a computational 'data structure'—that expresses the propositional content of the attitude in question and furthermore plays a particular computational-functional role in the computations that are constitutive of thought. Proponents of the Received View might lack an actual implementation story, but thanks to computers and the theory of universal computation that they implemented, these proponents did have something like an existence proof for the needed implementation story.

1.2. TROUBLES WITH THE RECEIVED VIEW

The Received View presents its claims about the nature of propositional attitudes, cognitive capacities, and cognition as being of a piece with reductive claims in the empirical sciences, specifically as being at the very least nomologically, if not metaphysically, necessary truths. On this view, it is not nomologically possible, for example, that a person believe that it's sunny today and that person not bear the specified computational-functional relation to a mental representation that expresses that propositional content, viz., that it's sunny today. The normative epistemological claim about the proper form of cognitive explanation is said to follow as a consequence of these supposed truths.

The standard arguments in support of the Received View are of two general sorts. First, it is argued that if propositional attitudes, cognitive capacities, and cognition were the sort of things (and processes) that the Received View claims they are, then that fact would explain their having the salient properties that they do. Thus, for example, if propositional attitudes were relations to mental representations that express the propositional content of the attitude in question, then that, it is claimed, would explain their being semantically evaluable (e.g., as true or false in the case of beliefs, as satisfied or not in the case of desires). Second, it is argued that the Received View enjoys indirect but nevertheless strong empirical support from cognitive science. Such science, it is claimed, presupposes the Received View, and hence the former's successes provide support for the presupposed view. Thus, for example, for years it was alleged that a speaker's knowledge of language was implemented computationally in the language faculty by an explicit representation of a grammar that expressed that knowledge, and the fact that such knowledge was so implemented was held to provide indirect empirical support for the Received View.

Chapter 3 examines critically these two arguments in support of the Received View's account of the metaphysical nature of propositional attitudes. With respect to the first sort of argument, which I shall dub the 'abductive argument', I argue that the case made by these arguments is actually quite weak. The explanation proposed by the Received View of the seemingly salient properties of propositional attitudes is defective on two counts. First, the proposed explanation fails to offer any explanation whatever of many propositional attitudes that are commonly attributed to subjects by common-sense belief-desire explanations. And, second, even in those cases that are covered by the proposed explanation, the explanation turns out on close inspection to be implausible on computational grounds, and in some cases radically incomplete, indeed incapable of completion. With respect to the second sort of argument, which I shall dub the 'indirect empirical support argument', I argue that the alleged empirical support is largely non-existent: either the computational theories that are claimed to provide indirect empirical support don't presume the Received View, or to the extent that they do, there is little or no empirical rationale, given the little that we know about human computational architecture, for accepting these theories' assumptions about the computational implementation of the propositional attitudes attributed to subjects by these theories. In a number of cases, the implementation story offered by these theories is provably defective on computational grounds and thus provides no empirical support whatever.

The upshot of the problems with these arguments is that the Received View's proposed account of the metaphysical nature of propositional attitudes remains fundamentally unsupported and quite possibly untenable. When viewed from afar and in the absence of the needed implementation details, the account may appear plausible, but when viewed close up, the account can be seen to be more philosophical fantasy than empirical fact. There is little more to this account than a philosophically satisfying picture of what propositional attitudes *might be* in an imaginary world unconstrained by facts about the nature of common-sense belief-desire explanations, about the full range of available computational architectures, and about the constraints imposed by considerations of computational complexity.

1.3. THE PERSISTENCE OF THE RECEIVED VIEW: THE RELATIONALIST CONCEPTION

Proponents of the Received View have been largely unmoved by arguments of the sort presented in Chapter 3 to the effect that the view does not enjoy the empirical support that they claim for it. They think that there are independent reasons for thinking that the Received View is true. Most fundamentally, the view provides an intuitively plausible explanation of many of the salient apparent properties of propositional attitudes and their presumed role in cognition (e.g., causal efficacy, semantic evaluability, inferential involvement, opacity, productivity, systematicity). In the absence of any alternative explanation of these properties, the lack of empirical support from contemporary cognitive science, they argue, is hardly devastating.

This indifference to the lack of empirical support is only as good as the view's claimed explanatory virtues; however, such virtues, I argue in Chapter 3, are really quite negligible, especially once one considers carefully how, and indeed whether, the sketchy explanations that the Received View offers could possibly be fleshed out. Yet, once again, proponents seem largely unmoved by such arguments. This nonchalance may rest on the conviction that there is something like an a priori argument for the foundational relational conception of propositional attitudes that the Received View both presumes and presumes to explain. On this conception, propositional attitudes are *relations*, specifically relations between the possessor of the attitude and a causally efficacious, semantically evaluable mental particular—a mental representation—that is the 'object' of the attitude. The idea seems to be that the Received View is the most plausible, perhaps the only plausible, version of the indisputably relational nature of the attitudes.

The presumed relational nature of propositional attitudes constitutes the basic structuring assumption from which flows the view's proposed explanation of other properties of propositional attitudes. In taking propositional attitudes to be relations, specifically relations to mental representations, the Received View proposes to explain many of the properties of propositional attitudes in terms of properties of the representational objects that are one of the two relata. Thus, for example, the semantic properties of the attitudes, specifically their semantic evaluability, are explained in terms of the semantic properties of their representational objects. The productivity and systematicity of the attitudes, as well as the inferential relations that hold among various propositional attitudes, are explained in terms of the sentential character of these objects.

The assumption that propositional attitudes are relations that relate their possessor to a semantically evaluable particular that is the 'object' of the attitude, an assumption that I am calling the 'relational conception' of propositional attitudes, is in turn grounded in the conviction that the relational nature of propositional attitudes can simply be read off the logical form of the sentences by which we report propositional attitudes. For relationalists, the relational logical form of sentences used to report propositional attitudes reveals the relational form of the attitudes themselves. It is this conviction, I believe, that ultimately gives the Received View its resilience in the absence of both empirical support and significant explanatory power. Because this reading off can seemingly be accomplished a priori, the Received View of propositional attitudes has for its proponents the status of something approaching an a priori necessary truth. One can argue, as proponents have done, about the precise nature of the mental particulars that are one of the relata, with the possible consequence that they are not precisely the sort of representations that proponents of the Received View commonly take them to be; however, protestations to the contrary notwithstanding, proponents are morally certain that the view cannot be fundamentally mistaken in its relational conception of the attitudes.

In Chapter 4, I challenge the presumption that the relational nature of propositional attitudes can simply be read off the logical form of the sentences by which we report propositional attitudes. I argue that while recent work in formal semantics provides good reason to think that the logical form of these sentences is indeed relational, that fact in itself is no reason to suppose that propositional attitudes are themselves relations. The argument goes something like this. The referent of the *that*-clause that figures in attitude attributions of the canonical form *[noun phrase] [attitude verb] that* S cannot plausibly be construed as the causally efficacious, semantically evaluable 'object' of the attributed attitude. At the very least relationalists will need to distinguish, as some relationalists concerned with the semantics of propositional attitude attributions have, semantical from psychological 'objects' of the attitudes, where the former is the referent of the *that*-clause, and the latter is the mental particular to which the possessor bears a particular psychological relation (e.g., believing). But once relationalists are forced to this distinction, they will have to provide some account of how the former 'objects' manage to track the latter. For in the absence of such an account, relationalists will have no account of how propositional attitude attributions manage to be informative. But once relationalists concede the need for such an account, which is effectively an account of the mapping of propositional attitudes into their natural language representations, the relationalists' claim to find support for the relational conception of the attitudes in the logical form of attitude reports is in trouble, since in the absence of such account, relationalists have no justification for reading the logical form back onto the attitude state.

There is, of course, going to have to be *some sort* of systematic mapping of the relation and relata specified in the logical form of attitude attributions onto the attitudes themselves, since otherwise these attributions could carry no information about these states, which obviously they do. But nothing requires that the psychological image of the logical form be a single sort of relation relating a believer to a single sort of object. Consistent with the requirement that attitude reports carry information about the attitudes of their possessors, the logical form of such reports could have as its image any number of different relations, each with a different relatum to which the possessor of the attitude was related, or it could as well have as its image the possession by this individual of one or more monadic properties. The attribution of physical magnitudes (mass, length, temperature, etc.) illustrates just this last possibility, viz., of an attribution with a relational logical form being used to attribute a monadic property, or at least a relation different from that expressed by the logical form of the attribution. Thus, for example, we attribute a mass to an object by relating that object to a number on a scale, but that object's having the mass that it does is not a matter of its standing in a relation to the relatum that figures in the logical form of the attribution. Having a certain mass is a monadic property of the possessor. The binary relations that figure in the logical forms of these attributions simply provide a way of specifying these properties, by relating their possessors to certain abstract entities, viz., numbers on a scale, that are the *representatives* of these properties. Arguably, something similar could be true for attitude reports. Propositional attitude predicates might, like the predicates by which we attribute physical magnitudes, be a kind of measure predicate.

So here, then, is where things stand at the end of the first part of the book (Chapters 2–4): I have argued in that the Received View enjoys neither the abductive nor the empirical support that proponents have claimed for it. I have further argued that the relational conception of propositional attitudes, which the Received View presupposes, is itself unsupported. One simply cannot read relational character of the attitudes off the presumably relational logical form of propositional attitude attributions. For all we know, propositional attitudes might be monadic properties of their possessors; indeed, the predicates by which we attribute propositional attitudes might be a kind of measure predicate, which like numerical measure predicates such as *has a mass of 5 kg* attribute a monadic property to an individual by means of a relational predicate.

1.4. A MEASUREMENT-THEORETIC ACCOUNT OF THE ATTITUDES

A number of philosophers have been struck by the possibility that propositional attitude attributions succeed in attributing an attitude to an individual by relating that individual to an abstract object that is the 'representative' of the attitude in roughly the way that attributions of physical magnitudes such as mass and temperature succeed in attributing such a magnitude to an object by relating that object to a number on a scale that is the representative of that magnitude. The logical form of the sentence used to attribute a propositional attitude expresses a relation, not between the individual to whom the attitude is attributed and some putative psychological object, e.g., a belief, but between the individual and a representative of the attributed attitude state. The task, then, for someone who wants to move from the logical form, i.e., from the semantics, of attitude sentences, to the metaphysics of the attitudes or the psychology of their possessors is to discern the mapping between these representatives and the attitude states they represent. The task, in other words, is to construct for propositional attitudes the analogue of the numerical measurement theory for physical magnitudes. The remaining chapters of the book (Chapters 5–7) undertake to provide, or at least to sketch in some detail, just such a measurement-theoretic account of the attitudes.

Constructing such a measurement-theoretic account is not a simple task. Most of us are tolerably reliable, at least in most normal circumstances, in measuring and reporting the psychological states of fellow humans (this is hardly surprising given our evolved social nature), but our reliability as attitude-measuring instruments does not appear to presume any explicit understanding of the mapping relation by virtue of which we achieve this reliability. Our grasp of this relation, like our grasp of the linguistic principles that underlie our linguistic competence, is largely tacit. In this respect, we are not different from many other measuring instruments, both natural and artificial, which, while reliable, have little or no understanding of the principles that underlie their operation. But presumably our competence in measuring and reporting the propositional attitudes of others (and even ourselves) should be no less amenable to empirical investigation than other cognitive competences.

The basic idea, then, of the proposed measurement-theoretic account of propositional attitudes is that the predicates by which we attribute propositional attitudes to ourselves and others, like the predicates by which we attribute physical magnitudes such as mass and temperature, are a kind of measure predicate. These predicates are relational in form, i.e., they express a relation, but the relation they express is *not* a substantive relation. To say that a subject has a certain propositional attitude is no more to say that the subject stands in a substantive relation to a proposition (sentence, etc.) than to say that an object has a mass of 5 kg is to say that the object stands in a substantive relation to the number 5. Rather, it is to attribute to that subject a certain psychological state or property which is specified by means of its representative's location in a representational domain, in just the way that we specify the mass of an object by means of its representative's location on a numerical scale. Propositions (sentences, etc.), like numbers, are simply abstract entities used to represent certain psychological states or properties of those to whom propositional attitudes are attributed; they are not, as the relational conception would have it, the psychological 'objects' of these states.

The development of the proposed measurement-theoretic account begins in Chapter 5 with an informal presentation of numerical measurement theory for physical magnitudes. The aim here is to introduce the fundamental concepts of measurement theory, including, in particular, the concepts of a formal relational structure, of representation, uniqueness, and meaningfulness which are defined over sets (or classes) of such structures, and of the representation and uniqueness theorems which constitute a solution to the measurement problem for some specified domain of measured empirical properties or relations. Perhaps most importantly, the chapter introduces the wide range of mapping relations that a given representing relational structure might bear to a represented relational structure and still preserve the practical usefulness of the former structure as a representational system, viz., as a system for representing the latter. The discussion emphasizes that nothing about structural representation requires a strict isomorphism of relational structures; indeed, the practical usefulness of representational systems often makes do with, and indeed sometimes demands, a considerably less robust mapping relation.

Numerical measurement theory, e.g., of physical magnitudes, is of interest primarily for the explanation and justification that it can provide for established measurement practices. In particular, it helps us to understand the empirical content of our measurement claims, not in the sense of explaining the intrinsic nature of the properties or magnitudes being measured (length, mass, temperature, etc.)—something that measurement theory alone cannot do—but in the sense of clarifying just what empirical properties (and relations) the measured properties or magnitudes must possess if they are to be amenable to numerical measurement, if they are to support the numerical measurement practice that has evolved. Such, presumably, is the case with propositional attitudes, too. There is, I assume, an established measurement practice that utilizes a particular sort of measuring device, viz., persons like ourselves, to measure and then report by means of propositional attitude attributions certain as yet unspecified properties and relations of ourselves and others. The task here is to determine the represented empirical structure of the properties and relations of propositional attitudes that this measurement practice measures. This is not at all an easy task, because the representation relation that relates representing and represented structures is not given a priori, so empirical evidence and formal considerations must be developed that simultaneously fix both the representation relation and the represented empirical structure. Once this is accomplished, there will still be the further task of determining the intrinsic nature of these properties and relations which figure in this empirical structure. The measurement-theoretic account plays a role in this second task only insofar as the empirical structure of the attitudes constrains the possibilities as to their intrinsic nature. There is, as one might put it, more to a developed empirical science of the attitudes than just a measurement theory.

Determining the intrinsic nature of the attitudes, whether it be specified in computational or neurophysiological terms, is an empirical scientific task that is beyond the ken of philosophical inquiry as we currently understand it; philosophers can only speculate, in the worst sense of that term, on such matters. But they *can* contribute to the development of an account of what I am calling the empirical structure of the attitudes. And arguably, such an account, were it in hand, would be recognized by most philosophers as an account of the metaphysical nature of propositional attitudes, inasmuch as it would specify conditions that any plausible empirical account of propositional attitudes would have to meet.

1.5. THE EMPIRICAL STRUCTURE OF THE ATTITUDES: THE ATTITUDES AS INTENTIONAL APTITUDES

In Chapter 6 I undertake the task of developing a characterization of the empirical structure of the attitudes, using the conceptual resources developed in the previous chapter. I begin by developing a characterization of the 'representing structure' that is presumed to embed an image of the empirical structure of the attitudes. Once this is in hand, I turn to the much more difficult task of developing a characterization of this empirical structure itself. I attempt to accomplish this by bringing to bear both empirical considerations about our everyday use of attitude attributions and formal considerations about the sorts of mapping relations between representing and represented structures that would be necessary to support such use. The strategy that I employ here is analogous to the one that someone might employ in order to figure out just what entities, properties, and relations were represented on a particular type of nautical chart, say a Mercator's projection: one would observe the particular uses to which mariners put such charts (e.g., determining distance and bearing between known points) with an eye to determining the sorts of empirical information that could be gleaned from, and hence is contained in, such charts. The empirical structure of the attitudes is similarly reconstructed from evidence concerning the explanatory and predictive tasks to which propositional attitude attributions are put. The goal is to develop a characterization that is minimalist in the sense that it attributes to the attitudes only such structure as our actual common-sense psychological use of attitude representations actually requires.

The empirical structure of the attitudes, so developed, turns out to be considerably more minimalist in its cognitive architectural commitments than the one presumed by the Received View, which goes beyond just providing a characterization of the empirical structure of the attitudes, offering an empirically unsupported speculation about the intrinsic computational nature of the attitudes. That view takes propositional attitudes to be explicit representations of a very particular sort, e.g., linguistic representations that express the propositional content of the attitude and that figure computationally in a very specific kind of cognitive computational architecture, namely, that characterized by Newell (1980) as a 'physical symbol system'. On the proposed measurement-theoretic account, the empirical structure of the attitudes turns out to be a structure of causally efficacious internal states of their possessors, which I dub 'intentional aptitudes'. They are so dubbed because they are simply states that are *apt*, under the appropriate enabling conditions, both for the production of the intentional behavior, including verbal behavior, that we take to manifest possession of certain propositional attitudes and for the production of other intentional states, including cognitive emotional states, that we take to be the normal concomitants of certain propositional attitudes. Propositional attitudes so characterized are intentional, not in the sense that they are, as the Received View would have it, themselves necessarily representations of some sort, but rather in the sense that they, and the concomitant attitudes that they are apt to produce, are aptitudes for behavior that is intentional in the sense of being directed towards, or modulated and shaped by, certain states of affairs, viz., the states of affairs specified or described in the *that*-clauses of attitude attributions. It is not part of the characterization of the empirical structure of the attitudes to explain why the attitudes should be the aptitudes that they are, i.e., to explain what their intrinsic nature is such that they should have the particular properties (and relations to one another) that they do. It may therefore be an essential feature of the intrinsic nature of propositional attitudes, or of their possessors, that they are, or that they include as constituents, representations (of some as yet unspecified sort) of these states of affairs. Indeed, this seems quite plausible, perhaps even nomologically necessary. For absent representations of some sort, it is difficult to see how the behavior that particular attitudes are apt to produce could be directed towards, or modulated and shaped by, these states of affairs, especially given that the desired states of affairs are at the time of the goal-directed behavior usually non-existent and the believed state of affairs sometimes non-existent. But whatever the role of such representations, they are not constitutive of the attitudes. The point here is not to deny the existence of mental representations or to deny them any role in cognition; nor is it to deny that the intrinsic nature of the attitudes might, as a matter of empirical fact, in some way involve representations. But it is to deny that representations are constitutive of the attitudes, whatever their intrinsic nature. It is neither conceptually nor metaphysically necessary, and for all we know (given our ignorance of human cognitive architecture) not nomologically necessary either. That it has seemed otherwise to philosophers perhaps reflects a common tendency to impute to the attitudes themselves properties of our natural language representations of them.

The absence of any commitment to representations as constitutive of propositional attitudes is part and parcel of a more general minimalism as regards the cognitive architectural commitments of attitude attributions: to attribute a propositional attitude to an individual is simply to attribute a certain aptitude to that individual without saying anything about whatever it is in virtue of which that individual has that aptitude. This minimalism is similar to that which made logical behaviorism so attractive, though without succumbing to the peripheralism that behaviorists thought their minimalism entailed. One can be minimalist about the attitudes and yet still hold that they are causally efficacious internal states. It is this minimalism that explains the strong conviction held by virtually everyone not under the sway of an architecturally extravagant account of the attitudes that the existence of the attitudes is not committed to any particular account of cognitive architecture, and hence not hostage to developments within scientific cognitive psychology, so long as these developments do not impugn the basic truth that our behavior springs from inner causes.

The empirical structure of the attitudes involves not just a domain of states, which are the attitudes themselves. There are also certain properties and relations defined over these states, specifically those properties and relations that have an image in certain of the properties and relations of our natural language representatives of propositional attitudes. But while the properties and relations of propositional attitudes have an image in the properties and relations of their natural language representatives, they do not necessarily share the salient properties and relations of their representatives; for example, they might not have the semantic or inferential properties of their representatives. But the properties and relations that they do have are ones that explain and rationalize our practice of attributing propositional attitudes in terms of such properties and relations. The latter track measurement-theoretically the former. Thus, the semantic properties track the attitudes' aptness for behavior that is either directed towards or modulated and shaped by states of affairs specified in our natural language representations of propositional attitudes. Similarly, the inferential relations track causal or constitutive relations among attitudes. As with predications of numerical measures to physical magnitudes, propositional attitude attributions predicate specific empirical properties and relations, but the properties and relations that they predicate cannot be transparently read off these attributions.

1.6. SOME QUESTIONS ABOUT THE PROPOSED ACCOUNT

The proposed measurement-theoretic account takes seriously, in a way that the Received View does not, the notion that propositional attitude attributions are natural language *representations* of certain causally efficacious internal states of their possessors. Specifically, on the proposed account, these attributions specify abstract representatives of these internal states. The account takes this notion seriously in the sense that it inquires into the nature of the representation relation that relates these representatives to what they represent, and it provides a well-understood theoretic framework, viz., that of measurement theory, for undertaking this inquiry. It does not presume, as Received View does, that the properties and relations of propositional attitude attributions can simply be read back onto the attitudes themselves.

But a number of questions about the proposed measurement-theoretic account remain. First, there is the question of the explanatory adequacy of the account, e.g., how well it explains what having a propositional attitude amounts to, how well it explains the salient properties of propositional attitudes, how well it explains why we should have evolved the sort of attitude predicates that we have, and whether the account can explain the various puzzles about propositional attitudes that have so preoccupied philosophers since Frege. Second, there is the question of what the account implies regarding the intrinsic nature of propositional attitudes. Third, there is the question of what the account entails as regards the import of propositional attitude psychology for computational cognitive scientific theorizing, specifically as regards the computational entailments of propositional attitude attributions. Finally, there is the question of the consilience of the proposed account with certain philosophical views and projects central to contemporary philosophy of mind, e.g., intentional realism, intentional content essentialism, and propositional attitude-based semantic programmes. In an effort to fill out the proposed measurement-theoretic account of the attitudes, Chapter 7 scouts each of these four questions.

1.7. A FINAL ADVERTISEMENT

The book offers what is intended to be a sustained line of argument against what I am calling the Received View and in favor of the view that propositional attitude predicates are a kind of measure predicate and that propositional attitudes themselves a kind of aptitude. But the three theses that are central to this line of argument, namely, that (i) the Received View does not enjoy the empirical support claimed for it, indeed that this view is not plausible on its face; (ii) propositional attitude predicates are a kind of measure predicate; and (iii) propositional attitudes are themselves a kind of aptitude, are logically independent of one another. One could, therefore, accept (ii) and reject (iii). There are a number of options here that I don't explore, much less argue against, but it does seem to me that the view I offer is the most plausible among the options. At the very least, adopting a measurement-theoretic construal of attitude predicates should make one wary of the Received View, whatever one thinks of the proposed minimalist view of propositional attitudes as aptitudes.

PART I

THE RECEIVED VIEW
AND ITS TROUBLES

2

The Received View

2.1. THE BASIC TENETS

A single view of the nature of propositional attitudes and their role in the production and explanation of thought and behavior has dominated contemporary philosophy of mind for almost four decades. This view, which I shall dub the 'Received View' in recognition of its near-canonical status in the field, consists of a small number of basic tenets. It holds that common-sense belief-desire psychology has it right when it takes beliefs, desires, and other propositional attitudes to be the causes of our behavior. Crucially, it identifies propositional attitudes with certain representational states of their possessor, holding that having a propositional attitude (e.g., believing that it is sunny outside today) is a matter of standing in a functional-computational relation to a mental representation that expresses the propositional content of the attitude (in the present example, a mental representation that expresses the propositional content that it's sunny outside today). The view offers a similarly reductive account of the nature of molar cognitive capacities such as language, vision, face recognition, and spatial navigation that scientific cognitive psychology takes it to be its task to explain. Such capacities are said to arise out of the causal interaction of various constitutive subcapacities, which are themselves capacities for processing (constructing, transforming, manipulating, etc.) mental representations that express the contents of a subject's propositional attitudes. Mental processes themselves are said to consist of computational processes defined over these mental representations that express the contents of subjects' propositional attitudes. Given these tenets regarding the nature of cognitive capacities, propositional attitudes, and cognition itself, cognitive psychological explanations, it is held, should take the form of what Cummins (1983) called 'intentional functional analysis' which explains molar cognitive capacities in terms of their constituent subcapacities, and the latter in terms of computational processes defined over these mental representations. The Received View thus consists of reductive metaphysical claims about the nature of propositional attitudes, cognitive capacities, and cognition itself, and a normative epistemological claim about the proper form of cognitive psychological explanations.

There is, as one might expect, some minor disagreement among proponents as to the specific tenets of the Received View, but as I shall understand it, the view consists of the following eight tenets:

(i) *The possession of a molar cognitive capacity consists in the possession of a number of subcapacities whose causal interaction constitutes the molar capacity,*

where

(ii) *The subcapacities in question are capacities for processing computationally certain mental representations,*

where

(iii) *The representations in question are 'explicit' in the sense of being computationally, if not physically, discrete formal structures that have determinate semantic contents,*

and

(iv) *These representations express the intentional contents of (certain of) their possessor's propositional attitudes (and as such express propositions),*[1]

such that

(v) *For any subject S, attitude A, and proposition P, there exists a computational/functional relation R and an explicit (mental) Representation M such that M expresses P, and S has A to P if and only if S bears R to M.*

Furthermore,

(vi) *Thinking, and indeed cognition more generally, which is the exercise of a cognitive capacity (or competence), is an inferential computational process defined over one or more of these Representations that eventuates in the production of either another Representation or a behavior,*

and

---

[1] I shall often follow the majusculating practice of some proponents of the Received View and dub by the term 'Representations' these mental representations that are said to be the computational embodiments of propositional attitudes and thus express propositions, thereby distinguishing them from other sorts of representations that don't express the propositional contents of propositional attitudes, and indeed may not express propositions at all.

(vii) *Representations are quasi-linguistic in form, having both a compositional syntax and semantics; i.e., Representations take the form of sentences in a 'language of thought'.*[2]

Finally, there is the following normative epistemological claim about the proper form of cognitive psychological explanation:

(viii) *Given tenets (i)–(vii), explanations in cognitive science should take the form of a functional analysis that explains molar cognitive capacities in terms of the causal interaction of their constituent subcapacities, these subcapacities in terms of the causal interaction of their constituent subcapacities, and so on, until such point as one is left with certain functionally primitive subcapacities whose operation is explained in terms of inferential computational operations defined over Representations which express the contents of subjects' propositional attitudes. Cognitive explanations should take this form, for otherwise they will fail to capture the true nature of cognition, the true causes of thought and behavior.*

By way of illustration of how these eight tenets interact, consider our mundane ability to navigate a familiar but totally darkened room in order to turn on a light. We cross the room, moving this way and that, avoiding any furniture in our path, until finally we arrive at a desired location on the opposite side of the room, at which point we stretch out our hand and confidently find, with little or no groping about, a light switch on the wall. Common sense would explain such feats of spatial navigation in terms of our knowing where both the light switch on the wall and the room's furniture are located, perhaps mentioning as well our desire or intention to turn on a light by turning the light switch in question. According to the Received View, such feats are instances of the exercise of a complex molar cognitive capacity, where, by tenet (i), the capacity in question consists of a number of constituent subcapacities whose causal interaction constitutes the molar capacity. For the case at hand, these subcapacities would presumably include the subcapacities of, e.g., not only remembering the location of furniture and the light switch, but also knowing at any point during one's trajectory across the room one's instantaneous location in the room and hence the relative location of the light switch and furniture. These subcapacities, by tenet (ii), are capacities for processing computationally certain mental representations—in the case of the subcapacity just mentioned, continually

---

[2] Some proponents of the Received View, e.g., Fodor, would add that the language of thought is innate, but such a claim is not germane to our present discussion.

updating one's mental representation of one's location in the room in response to kinesthetic information. These representations are, by tenet (iii), 'explicit' in the sense of being computationally, if not physically, discrete formal structures that have determinate semantic contents. By tenet (iv), these representations have propositional contents, specifically the contents of propositional attitudes that could correctly be attributed to the subject undertaking this feat, such that, by tenet (v), having the propositional attitudes in question just is a matter of having these mental representations and their playing a particular computational/functional role specified by the attitude type. Thus, our knowing, for example, that the corner of the sofa lies in our path to the light switch will be a matter of our having an explicit mental representation of that fact, where this representation is capable of playing the sort of computational/functional role characteristic of representations of that attitude type. The mental representations in question are said, by tenet (vii), to be sentential in form, which makes it possible that the computational processes defined over these representations could have, as tenet (vi) claims, an inferential character: the representations serve as premises in an argument that has as its conclusion the room-crossing behavior in question, or more correctly has as its conclusion sentences that serve as motor commands for the relevant behavior. And given the nature of these causal interactions that eventuate in the behavior, an explanation of this feat of navigation, this exercise of a molar cognitive capacity, will take the form specified in tenet (viii).

The Received View, as outlined above, has traveled under a number of different aliases, depending upon the particular aspects of the view being emphasized, with what for present purposes are only minor variations in the formulation of its basic tenets. The crucial Received View of propositional attitudes and cognition, specifically tenets (v) and (vi), has variously been called the 'Representational character of mental states' (Harman 1973), the 'Representational Theory of Mind' (Fodor 1987; Sterelny 1990), the 'Computational Theory of Mind' (Pylyshyn 1984), the 'Computational Representational Theory of Thought' (Loewer and Rey 1991), and the 'Computational Theory of Intentionality' (Cummins 1989). The notion, expressed in tenets (i)–(iii), that cognitive capacities arise from the causal interaction of constituent subcapacities, and those subcapacities in turn from the causal interaction of their subcapacities, and ultimately from computational processes defined over Representations, is sometimes referred to a Homuncular Representational Functionalism (Lycan 1981). The Received View of cognitive explanation, i.e., the notion that cognitive psychological explanations of cognitive capacities should take the form given in tenet (viii), has been called 'intentional functional analysis' (Cummins 1983), 'cognitivism' (Haugeland 1978), and 'classicism' (Fodor and Pylyshyn 1988; Fodor and McLaughlin 1990). Tenet (vi), in conjunction with tenet (vii), is often described by proponents as the 'Language of Thought Hypothesis' (Fodor 1975), since it presumes that in order to explain the productivity and systematicity of these mental Representations, which are the attitudes, there must be some sort of language-like medium of mental representation. Critics of the Received View, such as Stalnaker (1984, 1991 [1999]), sometimes label tenets (iv)–(vii) as simply the 'linguistic picture', or the 'sentence storage model', in order to focus attention on the fundamentally linguistic conception of propositional attitudes which the Received View presumes: For on the Received View, propositional attitudes are linguistic entities, and thinking is a kind of inferential process defined over these entities.

It is important to distinguish the Received View from superficially similar look-alikes that aren't instances of the view. What is distinctive and essential to the Received View is the representational-computational construal of propositional attitudes and their role in cognition. There are any number of theoretical views within computational cognitive psychology that endorse the notion that cognitive capacities are composed of constituent subcapacities, that these subcapacities are themselves constituted by various computational processes defined over representations, that these representations are often explicitly represented, that these representations are often linguistic in structure, and that cognitive explanation should take the form of a functional analysis à la Cummins (1983). Yet these views are not instances of the Received View because they do not make any claim about the representational-computational nature of propositional attitudes and their role in cognition. Newell's (1980) well-known 'physical symbol system hypothesis' is just such a look-alike, sharing just the similarities mentioned above with the Received View, but crucially not committed to the Received View's construal of propositional attitudes. Indeed, Newell (1981) explicitly rejects the Received View's reductionist construal of propositional attitudes, arguing that there is no straightforward representational-computational construal of what he terms 'knowledge-level' attributions. Even in the absence of this rejection, Newell's physical symbol system hypothesis could hardly be construed as a version of the Received View, because as he presents the hypothesis, the contents of the representations over which computations are defined are system-internal: symbols refer to register contents, computational operations, and the like, things which cannot plausibly be construed as the contents of subjects' propositional attitudes. The details of this example are not important here; the crucial point, again, is that we must be careful not to confuse superficially similar look-alikes with the Received View. A view without the tenets that spell out the view's representational-computational construal of propositional attitudes and their role in cognition is not the Received View.

There are a number of important questions to be raised about the eight tenets that constitute what I am calling the Received View, specifically about the four tenets (v)–(viii) that are the crux of the view. In particular, there are questions about how the claims are to be understood, specifically, about how certain central notions that figure in the claims, e.g., that of 'explicit' representation, are to be understood. There are also important questions about the epistemological/metaphysical status of these claims and the considerations adduced in their support. Rather than address these questions here, I will defer them until the next chapter, when we take up some of the problems that afflict the Received View. In this chapter I wish only to remind readers of the general outline of this very familiar view.

2.2. THREE ENTAILMENTS

Three important entailments of the Received View deserve mention. First, according to tenet (vi) of the Received View, cognition is a computational process defined over Representations, i.e., over representations of the contents of the possessor's propositional attitudes, while according to tenet (v), having a propositional attitude is just a matter of bearing a particular sort of relation, specifically one that can be specified in functional-computational terms, to such a Representation. These two claims entail that

(ix) *cognitive science is a propositional attitude psychology,*

inasmuch as these two claims entail that cognitive scientific explanations advert to the same causally efficacious internal states as common-sense propositional attitude psychology, viz., to propositional attitudes.[3] Of course, this scientific propositional attitude psychology is presumably considerably more refined and elaborated than its common-sense counterpart.

Second, according to tenet (viii) of the Received View, the explanatory constructs of cognitive explanations should advert to Representational states

---

[3] Fodor (1987) and Sterelny (1990) are quite explicit in their defense of this entailment.

of the subject and to computational processes defined over such states. It follows immediately from this that on the Received View there can be no non-Representationalist cognitive explanations, since such explanations would not have the right form, i.e., would not advert to the right sort of explanatory constructs. This entails that

(x) *cognitive science is explanatorily uniform,*

in the sense that it must explain cognitive phenomena in terms of inferential computations over Representations. This entailment precludes the very possibility of purely neurophysiological or pharmacological explanations of cognitive phenomena, as well as mixed explanations that advert to both Representational states (and computational processes defined over these states) and other non-Representationalist factors. It also precludes the possibility of connectionist explanations of cognition that are a genuine alternative to explanations that conform to tenet (viii) of the Received View. The latter, it is claimed, exhaust the class of cognitive explanations!

Third, according to tenet (viii) of the Received View, explanations of cognitive capacities take the form of an intentional functional analysis. But such analyses cannot, of course, continue indefinitely: it is not, as one might put it, Representational states and computational processes 'all the way down'. At some point, the Representational/computational analysis of cognitive capacities must give way to *implementation explanations* that explain, in presumably neurophysiological terms, how the primitive cognitive capacities of the intentional functional analyses are implemented. But these implementation explanations are not, on the Received View, cognitive explanations, because they do not have the requisite form. A way of putting the point here would be to say that the only inter-theoretic relations recognized by the Received View are *implementation* relations. This entails that

(xi) *cognitive science is autonomous vis-à-vis neuroscience,*

since the explanations of cognitive science will not advert to the implementation of the states that figure in its explanations; it is enough for cognitive science simply that these states have implementations.

These last two entailments, it should be noted, offer proponents of the Received View a ready rationale for adopting an insular view of cognitive science, according to which neuroscience will play only a supporting role, capable only of providing accounts of the implementation of the Representational states, and computational processes defined over these states, that figure in cognitive explanations. The Received View and its entailments also provide a presumptive argument against proposed cognitive explanations that are not of the form sanctioned by the view. The response of so-called 'classicists', i.e., proponents of the Received View, to non-conforming connectionist explanations illustrates the use of such a presumptive argument (cf. Fodor and Pylyshyn 1988). Classicists claim that connectionists cannot explain cognition, more specifically that they cannot explain its pervasive 'systematicity', viz., the fact that certain cognitive capacities are systematically related as a matter of nomological necessity. The claim is not simply that connectionists have thus far been unable to explain the systematic relation between such capacities, though this is indisputably true; rather the claim is that connectionists *cannot* explain (i.e., never will be able to explain) systematicity. The argument for this claim takes the form of a dilemma. Either connectionist explanations of systematicity are consistent with the Received View, or they are not. If the latter, then connectionists cannot explain systematicity, because their explanations will not have the requisite form for a cognitive explanation. If the former, then they may be able to explain systematicity, but their explanations will not be a genuine alternative to classical explanations, since classical explanations just are explanations that are consistent with the Received View. Either way, the connectionist loses; the connectionist can offer no genuine alternative to classical cognitive explanations. At best connectionists can provide connectionist implementation stories for (classical) cognitive explanations.

2.3. HISTORICAL ORIGINS AND DEVELOPMENT

The emergence of the Received View in the 1960s and early 1970s was occasioned by several roughly concurrent developments: (i) the collapse of scientific (methodological) behaviorism, (ii) failure of both behaviorist and central state identity theory reductionist programmes in the philosophy of mind, (iii) Chomsky's development of generative linguistics which proposed to explicate linguistic competence in terms of grammatical knowledge, and (iv) the development both of the theory of universal computation and of physical machines, i.e., computers, that effectively implemented (under relevant idealizations) abstract universal machines.

Scientific behaviorism collapsed in the late 1950s and early 1960s for a number of reasons, the most salient of which for our purposes had to do with its inability to explain complex cognitive behaviors, most notably linguistic behavior (cf. Chomsky 1959). Behaviorism failed in its attempts to explain such behaviors for basically three reasons. First, behaviorist learning theory, specifically the operant conditioning paradigm which most behaviorists embraced, failed to appreciate both the complexity of acquired cognitive competences (such as language) and the specific, apparently innate contribution of the learner. Second, it failed to appreciate the extent to which the causal processes that map a course of experience into a complex cognitive behavior was mediated by the complex interaction of internal states, such that any plausible explanation of such behavior would have to advert to such states. Behaviorists were committed to the proposition that cognitive behavior could be explained without recourse to so-called intervening variables. Third, the methodological strictures on the descriptive resources that behaviorism allowed itself, eschewing as it did all 'mentalistic' (and more specifically, intentional) vocabulary, left it unable even to state the psychological generalizations that were presumably to be explained.

The collapse of behaviorism left cognitive psychologists without an explanatory paradigm. This lacunae was soon filled, first in generative linguistics and then in cognitive psychology proper, by a form of *intentional* explanation modeled explicitly on the explanations of common-sense belief-desire psychology. That linguists and psychologists should have turned to common-sense psychology is hardly surprising, since with the collapse of behaviorism, the explanatory schemes of common-sense psychology were literally, as some would have it, 'the only game in town'.

In the explanations of common-sense belief-desire psychology upon which cognitive explanations were modeled, both what gets explained (the *explanandum*) and what does the explaining (the *explanans*) are characterized in an *intentional* vocabulary: the *explanans* mentions certain intentional states of the subject—propositional attitudes such as beliefs, desires, and the like—that are supposedly causally efficacious in the production of the intentional state or the action (an intentionally characterized behavior) that is the *explanandum* (cf. Graves et al. 1973). Thus, for example, the common-sense explanation of how a speaker was able to respond appropriately to a question posed in French might simply advert to the fact that this individual *knew* French. A common-sense explanation of why this person answered as she did might advert not simply to the fact that she *knew* French, but also *wanted* to be helpful, and furthermore *believed* that by responding as she did she would satisfy her desire to be helpful.

In the hands of linguists and cognitive psychologists, the intentional explanations of common-sense psychology were greatly elaborated and refined. The explanation, for example, of a speaker's competence in responding to a question posed in French was not left simply at the claim that the speaker knew French; rather linguists endeavored to specify just exactly what the speaker's knowledge of French amounted to. A speaker's knowledge of language was held to consist of a grammar, i.e., a set of rules r_1, . . ., r_n and principles p_1, . . ., p_n that constituted what the speaker knew in virtue of knowing a language.

Cognitive explanations so conceived are, of course, fully compatible with a Cartesian (interactionist) dualism: nothing requires that the beliefs, desires, and the like postulated by these intentional explanations as the internal causes of behavior be physical states. Indeed, behaviorist critics of the emerging cognitivist paradigm (cf. Skinner 1985) saw in these intentional explanations the resurgence of the dualism that scientific psychology had fought so hard to reject. To defend themselves against such criticisms, proponents of intentional explanations had to establish the materialistic respectability of these explanations. One strategy for achieving this is to provide a reduction of propositional attitudes in materialistically respectable terms. In the years prior to the 1960s a variety of reductionist programmes were undertaken, but none succeeded. Of these, logical behaviorism and central state identity theory were the two most prominent. Let us remind ourselves of the broad outlines of these two programmes.

Unlike the radical behaviorism of Watson, the early Skinner, and many other experimental psychologists, which presumed to eliminate propositional attitudes as so much excess metaphysical baggage, logical behaviorism proposed to identify propositional attitudes, indeed mental states of every sort, with complex behavioral dispositions. Thus, for example, sentences of the form *S believes that it is raining outside* were said to be equivalent in meaning to a sentence (or conjunction of sentences) of the form *If S were to go outside, he would carry an umbrella*. While perhaps plausible at first blush, the dispositional analyses proposed by logical behaviorists turned out not to stand up to close scrutiny. It proved difficult to construct an analysis of even the most elementary propositional attitude attribution that did not succumb to obvious counterexamples. And where these analyses did not collapse under the slightest pressure, they invariably smuggled in implicit references to propositional attitudes as part of the *analysans*. In particular, they presupposed certain propositional attitudes on the part of the possessor of the attitude under analysis. The suggested analysis of *S believes that it is raining outside* is a case in point: someone who believes this will carry an umbrella only if he *wants* to stay dry, *believes* that carrying an umbrella will assure satisfaction of this desire, *thinks* that carrying an umbrella will have no untoward consequences, and so on. Logical behaviorists often attempted to avoid this problem through free use of *ceteris paribus* clauses: S's believing that it is raining outside, we are told, is for S to be so disposed that if he were to go outside, then *ceteris paribus* he would carry an umbrella. But if we pause to ask about the relevant factors that are to be held equal, it becomes clear that they are just those beliefs, desires, and other propositional attitudes that must obtain if S's belief that it is raining is to eventuate in his carrying an umbrella when he goes outside. At the very least, logical behaviorism would have to go holist.

Logical behaviorists' ardor for dispositional analyses was eventually dampened, not by their inability to provide a compelling analyses of propositional attitude attributions, but rather by the realization that such analyses failed to preserve the seemingly explanatory character of mentalistic attributions: when, for example, we explain a person's drinking behavior by saying that he was thirsty, we single out the putative cause of that behavior, namely, his being thirsty. On a logical behaviorist construal, however, it is unclear in what sense it is the person's being *thirsty* that explains his behavior, for on that construal to say that a person drank because he was thirsty is to say that the person drank because a conditional of the form *If water were available, then* (ceteris paribus) *the person would drink* is true. The proposed behaviorist construal replaces the intended explanation, according to which the person drank because he was in some particular internal state, by another according to which the person drank for a different reason, namely, because a particular environmental stimulus, namely, water, was present. This is clearly a different explanation, as can be seen in the fact that the conditional in question might be true of a person who was not in the least thirsty (perhaps the subject has a gun to his head and has been told to drink any and all water that appears before him).

The construal of propositional attitudes proposed by central state identity theory had the virtue of preserving the explanatory character of propositional attitude attributions, for unlike logical behaviorism, central state identity theory proposed to identify propositional attitudes with certain neurophysiological states of the organism, states that might plausibly be held to produce the behaviors that propositional attitudes are invoked to explain.

Appellation notwithstanding, however, central state identity theory was in fact a programme rather than a theory, for proponents were unable to specify the neurophysiological counterpart of even the most basic of propositional attitudes. But even if we overlook the promissory character of the programme, there were serious problems. Central state identity theory, as many critics noted, is incompatible with the widely held intuition that creatures with physiologies significantly different from our own might nonetheless have certain propositional attitudes, since that theory identifies propositional attitudes with certain states of our central nervous system. The theory is also incompatible with so-called Lashleyian 'equipotentiality', namely, the possibility that one and the same (type of) propositional attitude may be realized in the same individual at different times as tokens of different neurophysiological types. It is this assumption that propositional attitudes are type-identical with neurophysiological states that is the crucial weakness of central state identity theory: there is no reason to suppose that a taxonomy of neurophysiological states would mirror the taxonomy of propositional attitudes. Indeed, there is every reason to suppose that the two taxonomies will, as Fodor (1974 [1981]) puts it, 'cross-classify'. Neurophysiology may well share with propositional attitude psychology the goal of explaining the etiology of behavior; however, given their otherwise divergent explanatory interests, not to mention their differing taxonomies of the behavior to be explained, one would expect their two fields to type-individuate the presumed causes of behavior in very different ways.

Thus, while logical behaviorism and central state identity theory held out the promise of a materialistically respectable construal of propositional attitudes, both proved unsatisfactory: the first because it failed to preserve the explanatory character of propositional attitude attributions, the second because it failed to type-individuate propositional attitudes in a way that would enable it to capture the generalizations that define the explanatory domain of an adequate psychological theory. Materialistic respectability, were it to be had, would have to be found elsewhere.

So this, then, is where things stood in the early 1960s. The collapse of scientific behaviorism left empirical psychology with no explanatory paradigm other than that of common-sense psychology, which adverts to propositional attitudes. But this common-sense paradigm was suspect because of its historical associations with Cartesian (interactionist) dualism. If propositional attitudes, the theoretical posits of common-sense psychology, were to lay claim to scientific status, then it was going to be necessary to establish their materialistic *bona fides*. The failure of both logical behaviorism and central state identity theory closed off the two well-traveled paths for accomplishing this task. What was needed, it seemed, was a reductive strategy that would provide the needed materialistic vindication of the attitudes, though without type-identifying them with certain physical states (or behavior) of their possessors.

The advent in the early 1960s of so-called functionalist theories of mind offered the possibility of just such a materialistically respectable construal of propositional attitudes. These theories type-individuate mental states in terms of their causal-functional relations to other mental states, sensory stimuli, and behavior. Like talk of valve-lifters and mousetraps, talk of propositional attitudes, it was claimed, was talk of causally efficacious physical states or entities, but it was talk that abstracted away from the physical structures, processes, properties, and the like that underpinned and explained this efficacy. Valve-lifters, for example, were physical devices of unspecified structure and constitution that performed a particular function in combustion engines, namely, opening (and closing) the intake and exhaust valves. Similarly, beliefs, desires, and other propositional attitudes were physical states (presumably of the central nervous system), again of unspecified structure and constitution, which performed the particular psychological functions peculiar to mental states of their types. Functionalist theories promised to avoid the difficulties, while preserving the virtues, of both logical behaviorism and central state identity theory. It preserved claims for the causal efficacy of propositional attitudes, thus avoiding logical behaviorism's inability to reconstruct explanations that adverted to propositional attitudes. At the same time it abstracted away from the details of implementation, thus avoiding central state identity theory's commitment to an implausible type-type identity of propositional attitudes with certain neurophysiological states, events, or properties.

But there were still a couple of problems. First, functionalist theories of mind were fully compatible with Cartesian dualism and thus did not by themselves establish the materialistic *bona fides* of propositional attitudes. Many functionalists also embraced a materialist view that they called 'token physicalism', but these token physicalist convictions provided little by way of vindication, since token physicalism was silent as regards the implementation of these functionally characterized mental states. What was needed was an implementation story, or at very least a compelling reason to suppose such a story could be told. Second, functionalist theories offered a seemingly plausible account of the causal efficacy of propositional attitudes, albeit one that abstracted away from the details of their physical implementation, but it seemed much less plausible as an account of other salient properties of propositional attitudes. If we take literally our common-sense talk about propositional attitudes, then not only are they causally efficacious internal states of an agent, but they are also *semantically evaluable* (as, e.g., in the case of belief, true or false) and furthermore stand in various inferential relations to one another. To these two properties must be added two other seeming properties of propositional attitudes: productivity and systematicity. Propositional attitudes exhibit the full productivity of the linguistic devices by which we attribute them; moreover, the possession of propositional attitudes is systematic in the sense that the capacity for certain propositional attitudes (e.g., the capacity for believing that John loves Mary) is inextricably linked to the capacity for certain other propositional attitudes (the capacity for believing that Mary loves John). On its face, then, functionalism seemed to offer no particular account of any of these four additional properties, so at very least the functionalist account of propositional attitudes needed supplementation.

The Representationalist account of propositional attitudes that eventually emerged during the late 1970s and early 1980s, the major component of what I am calling the Received View, offered an account of these four properties of propositional attitudes. On this account, propositional attitudes were, as functionalists would have it, functionally defined states of their possessors, but they were functionally defined states of a particular kind, viz., representational states, where the salient properties of propositional attitudes were inherited from the properties of the functionally defined representational states with which they were identified. In its explanation of these properties of propositional attitudes, the account took its cue from natural language. Utterances of sentences of a natural language can be (and often are) both semantically evaluable and inferentially interrelated; moreover, they can be (and often are) causally efficacious in getting us to act in various ways (in particular, in ways that depend on the semantic content of these utterances). The use of natural languages by speakers is also both productive and systematic: productive inasmuch as speakers can, leaving aside certain performance limitations, seemingly understand and produce the full range of sentences that a generative grammar specifies as sentences of their language, and systematic inasmuch as the capacity to understand certain sentences seems inextricably linked with the capacity to understand certain other intuitively closely related sentences. The account that emerged was simply this: propositional attitudes are relations to sentence-like mental representations that possess the expressive power of a natural language (cf. Fodor 1975; Field 1978 [1981]). More specifically, they are relations that the possessor of the propositional attitude bears to a sentence-like mental representation that expresses the propositional content of that propositional attitude. Thus, for example, believing that the LA Lakers won the NBA Championship in both 2000 and 2001 is a matter of standing in a particular sort of relation, $R_{believing}$, to a sentence-like mental representation that expresses the proposition that the LA Lakers won the NBA Championship in both 2000 and 2001. Being pleased that they won the Championship in those years is, on this account, a matter of standing in a different sort of relation to that same mental representation, while desiring that they do so again in 2002 is a matter of standing in yet a third sort of relation, $R_{desiring}$, to a different mental representation, one that expresses the proposition that the Lakers win again in 2002.

The mental representations that are one of the relata in the relations that are propositional attitudes are taken by the Received View to be entities (particulars) of a very particular sort: they have both inscriptional (or 'formal') and semantic properties. It is in virtue of their inscriptional, i.e., physical, properties that they are able to play the particular causal-functional roles that they do in the psychological economy of their possessors—roles that are type-individuated by the propositional attitude verb (*believes*, *desires*, etc.). It is in virtue of their semantic properties that they are semantically evaluable and inferentially interrelated. The productivity and systematicity of propositional attitudes do not follow directly from the fact that they are representations. Rather it is by virtue of being representations of a particular sort, viz., sentence-like representations, that they exhibit the productivity and systematicity associated with a natural language. The representations in question are, as proponents of the Received View put it, sentences in an internal 'language of thought'.

The Received View's proposal that propositional attitudes are relations to sentence-like mental representations thus offered a construal of propositional attitudes that seemingly explained what were taken to be their salient properties (viz., causal efficacy, semantic evaluability, inferential relations, productivity, and systematicity), but the proposal did not establish the materialistic *bona fides* of propositional attitudes. For crucially, the postulated mental Representations were simply assumed to have certain semantic properties, which critics would be inclined to regard with no less suspicion than propositional attitudes themselves. It thus remained for proponents of the Received View of propositional attitudes to provide a materialistically respectable 'naturalistic' account of these semantic properties of mental Representations, i.e., a theory of content that made no appeal to intentional or semantic properties. Such an account would also have to explain how the causal properties of propositional attitudes managed to respect their semantic and inferential properties, such that, for example, if someone antecedently believed that if p, then q, and then came to believe that p, then *ceteris paribus*, that person would also come to believe that q.

Attempts to provide the requisite naturalistic account of content have met with arguably little success (for a critical discussion of these efforts, see Cummins 1989); there is, most Representationalists would concede, as yet no plausible naturalistic account of intentional content. Proponents of the Received View have nevertheless taken comfort in the conviction that computational architectures of a familiar sort provide a proof of sorts of the existence of such an account. The idea, quite simply, is that computers with so-called 'classical architectures' just are physical devices whose input/output behavior is mediated by internal representational states that possess both inscriptional (physical) and semantic properties (cf. Fodor 1975; Pylyshyn 1984). The representational states of existing computers, it is conceded, do not possess the representational complexity of propositional attitudes. But at least the existence of genuinely representational states in these unarguably physical devices is not in question, and few, if any, harbor doubts about the materialistic respectability of the semantic properties of these representational states. If, therefore, propositional attitudes could be identified with computational/representational states in a reasonably systematic fashion, then the materialistic *bona fides* of propositional attitudes would be established, or at least placed beyond reasonable practical doubt. So the crucial idea of the Received View, then, is this: having a propositional attitude is a matter of having an 'explicit' representation—what computational theorists call a 'data structure'—that expresses the propositional content of the attitude in question and furthermore plays a particular functional-computational role in the computations that are constitutive of thought. Proponents of the Received View may lack an actual implementation story, but thanks to current computer technology, and more specifically, to the classical architecture that most computers currently implement, these proponents do have something like an existence proof for the needed implementation story, which is apparently enough to satisfy most philosophers worried about the materialistic *bona fides* of propositional attitudes.

2.4. RECAP

The Received View consists of the eight tenets enumerated above, which taken together present (i) reductive metaphysical claims about the nature of propositional attitudes, cognitive capacities, and cognition itself, and (ii) a normative epistemological claim about the proper form of cognitive psychological explanations. What is distinctive and essential to the Received View, and serves to distinguish it from superficially similar views about how cognition is to be understood and explained, is the representational-computational construal of propositional attitudes and their role in cognition presented in tenets (v)–(vii) of the view.

3

Troubles with the Received View

3.1. THE EMPIRICAL STATUS OF THE RECEIVED VIEW

Proponents of the Received View present its claims about the nature of cognitive capacities, propositional attitudes, and cognition as being of a piece with reductive claims in the empirical sciences, specifically as nomologically necessary *empirical* truths. The normative epistemological claim about the proper form of cognitive explanation is said to follow as a consequence of these supposed empirical truths. Proponents are surely right in this. The Received View does make substantive empirical claims about the constitutive structure of cognitive capacities, the Representational/computational basis of cognition, and the nature of the propositional attitudes to which common-sense psychological explanations advert. Each of these claims, furthermore, entails substantive empirical commitments regarding cognitive computational architecture. Even the normative epistemological claim about the proper form of cognitive scientific explanations, which is premised on these empirical claims, is every bit as liable to revision and rejection in the light of empirical developments as the empirical premises themselves.

But if, as seems clear, the claims of the Received View *are* empirical, and thus not amenable to confirmation by a priori argumentation, they are not of a sort that is amenable to direct empirical confirmation in the way that low-level empirical laws and generalizations (such as the Charles-Boyle Law, Zipf's Law, and Gresham's Law) typically are. Rather the claims are abstract, high-level foundational claims whose confirmation by empirical evidence is exceedingly indirect. Proponents argue that the Received View finds strong empirical support in the (admittedly limited) successes of contemporary cognitive science, which, they claim, presupposes the Received View. Proponents argue that the view also finds presumptive support in the putative fact that it is the only explanation on offer of certain salient properties of propositional attitudes and the common-sense psychological explanations that advert to them. The Received View is, as Jerry Fodor often puts it, 'the only game in town' (or as he puts it in his more pessimistic moments, 'the only straw afloat').

In the present chapter, I examine critically these two sorts of argument in support of the Received View's account of the metaphysical nature of propositional attitudes. With respect to the first sort of argument, which I shall dub the 'indirect empirical support argument', I argue that the alleged empirical support is largely non-existent: either the cognitive psychological theories that are claimed to provide indirect empirical support don't actually presume the Received View, or to the extent that they do, there is little or no empirical rationale, given the little that we know about human cognitive computational architecture, for accepting these theories' assumptions about the computational implementation of the propositional attitudes attributed to subjects by these theories. With a few notable exceptions, which are confined almost exclusively to the domains of language and vision, the much-trumpeted successes of cognitive psychology are what Newell (1981) called 'knowledge level' theories, i.e., theories that traffic heavily in propositional attitude talk, but without ever providing the needed computational implementation story necessary to support the reductionist claims of the Received View. And even in those rare cases where an implementation story is provided, the choice of computational architecture is rarely, if ever, empirically motivated. So the fact that these theories impute to the mind a classical computational architecture of the sort entailed by the Received View can hardly provide support for the view.

With respect to the second sort of argument, which I shall dub the 'abductive argument', I argue that the case made by these arguments is actually quite weak. The explanation proposed by the Received View of the seemingly salient properties of propositional attitudes is defective on two counts. First, the proposed explanation fails to offer any explanation whatever of many propositional attitudes that are commonly attributed to subjects by common-sense belief-desire explanations. And, second, even for those propositional attitudes that are supposedly explained, the proposed explanation turns out on close inspection to be implausible on computational grounds, and in some cases radically incomplete, indeed incapable of completion.

The upshot of the problems with these arguments is that the Received View's proposed account of propositional attitudes remains fundamentally unsupported and quite possibly untenable. When viewed from afar, the proposed account of propositional attitudes may *appear* plausible, but when viewed close up, the proposed account can be seen to be more philosophical fantasy than empirical fact. There is little more to this account than a philosophically satisfying picture of what propositional attitudes *might be* in an imaginary world unconstrained by facts about the nature of common-sense belief-desire explanations, about the full range of available computational architectures, and about the constraints imposed by considerations of computational tractability and complexity.

3.2. THINKERS AS REPRESENTATION-USING SYSTEMS

The Received View, specifically tenet (v) of the view, claims that the possessor of a propositional attitude bears a computational/functional relation to an explicit Representation that expresses the contents of that propositional attitude. But what, exactly, does it mean to say this? Minimally, the claim seems to be that the possessor of a propositional attitude has such a Representation, and this Representation plays a characteristic kind of computational/functional role in the cognitive processes of the possessor of the attitude.[1] But to say this is admittedly not to say very much until one spells out in detail the relevant notions of computational/functional role and explicit Representation. Let us consider each in turn.[2]

Presumably, the point of describing the relation, in terms of which propositional attitudes are type-individuated as beliefs, desires, and so on, as

---

[1] Stephen Schiffer has famously offered the following rather picturesque elaboration of this idea. Imagine that the mind is partitioned into a number of functionally defined boxes, each of which is the repository of token Representations. On Schiffer's elaboration, to be, for example, a belief, rather than a desire, is for a tokened Representation of that belief to be found in the 'belief box' rather than the 'desire box', where being located in the one box rather than the other determines the kind of causal role that the tokened Representation can play in cognition.

[2] There are a number of other questions concerning tenet (v) that I shall not address here. For example, how, logically speaking, are we to understand the claim that a subject S has an attitude A to a proposition P if and only if S bears a computational/functional relation R to *an* explicit Representation M that expresses P? Presumably not just any such Representation with the appropriate propositional content will do. For how, then, would the Received View propose to guarantee that these different Representations could all play the same computational/functional role, given that Representations are presumed to have their causal powers in virtue of their formal, and not their semantic, properties? But if the claim is that having an attitude to a proposition P is a matter of bearing a relation to a *particular* Representation with the propositional content P, then how does the Received View propose to specify non-circularly that Representation? Absent such a specification, there seems little reason to presume that there is such a Representation, except on the assumption that the Received View is true.

computational/functional is to make a claim about both the nature of cognitive processes and the kinds of causal role that Representations play in these processes. Cognitive processes, it is claimed, are computational processes that manipulate these Representations in various ways. In particular, cognition is taken to be a species of computationally realized formal inference: thinkers are inference engines, and their behaviors are the conclusions of formal inferences that have Representations as premises (See, e.g., Fodor 1975: 73).

The claim that propositional attitudes are computational-functional relations to Representations thus combines a seemingly conceptual claim about computation, namely, that it is a matter of formal symbol manipulation, with the substantive empirical claim that the symbols manipulated are representations of a particular sort, viz., Representations, i.e., representations whose contents are propositional and moreover are the contents of their possessor's propositional attitudes. The empirical claim will be the primary focus of our discussion here. But the claim that computation is a matter of symbol manipulation also demands examination, since it is not the conceptual truism that proponents often take it to be.

According to the Received View, having an attitude towards a proposition is a matter of bearing a certain computational/functional relation to a mental Representation that expresses that proposition. Clearly it is not enough that the possessor of the attitude simply possess such a Representation, in the way, for example, that a tree possesses by virtue of its annual rings a representation of the climatological history of the tree's immediate environment. The possessor of the attitude must *use* the Representation; moreover it must use it *in the appropriate way*. Specifically, the Representation must figure appropriately in the etiology of behavior and other Representations. The Received View thus construes the possessors of propositional attitudes as *Representation-using systems*, in the sense that they possess certain Representations that they use computationally in the production of behavior and other thoughts, i.e., other Representations. Proponents acknowledge this commitment when they insist that their view presumes the existence of an internal system of Representation, a 'language of thought', that possessors of propositional attitudes *use* in representing the contents of their propositional attitudes (See, e.g., Fodor 1975: ch. 1).

It is often unclear, however, what proponents of the Received View take to be the metaphysical and epistemological status of the claim that possessors of propositional attitudes are Representation-using systems. Proponents sometimes appear to regard the claim as an a priori necessary truth, entailed

$$f_R(s_i) \qquad\qquad \Rightarrow \qquad\qquad f_R(s_f) = F(f_R(s_i))$$

$$\Uparrow f_R \qquad\qquad\qquad\qquad\qquad \Uparrow f_R$$

$$s_i \qquad\qquad\qquad \Rightarrow \qquad\qquad\qquad s_f$$

Figure 3.1. Computation by S, under f_R, of a function F.

by the seemingly conceptually necessary truth that there is, as Fodor (1975: 34) puts it, 'no computation without representation'. For on the standard construal of the notion of computation presented in most textbooks on computation, a construal which Fodor (1975: 75) explicitly endorses, there is indeed no computation without representation. But such representations are not necessarily used by their possessor, or at least they are not necessarily used in the way envisioned by the Received View. For according to this standard construal (See Figure 3.1 above), a physical system S computes a function F just in case in certain specifiable circumstances the system will, in virtue of natural laws that govern the system, always go from one physical state s_i into another physical state s_f such that for every pair of such states, it is possible to specify a representation function f_R such that the value associated with the final state, viz., $f_R(s_f)$, is a function F of the value associated with the initial state, viz., $f_R(s_i)$. In going from s_i to s_f (in the specified circumstances) the system is said to *compute* this function F, since the system's behavior is interpretable under f_R as returning the value of the function F whenever presented with an argument for that function.[3]

On this standard construal of computation, there is necessarily no computation without representation, inasmuch it is only under the interpretation of physical states given by f_R that the physical system computes the function that it does, and under that interpretation, the physical states s_i and s_f *represent*, respectively, the argument and value of the function F that the system computes. Yet computational systems, so described, do not necessarily *use* the representations that, under the interpretation provided by the interpretation function, they instantiate or have. The standard construal provides no obvious interpretation of the notion of using the representations. On the standard construal, for example, the planets compute the Keplerian laws of planetary motion. Certain physical states of these planets represent the values of the variables that are constitutive of these laws, but these representations

---

[3] See Cummins 1989 for an informal elaboration of this model of computation.

are *not* used by the planets to govern their orbits. Indeed, there is no sense in which these states are representations *for* the planets in the way that the Representations hypothesized by the Received View are presumed to be representations *for* the possessor of propositional attitudes, precisely because these representations are not used by the planets in any way whatever.

In order for a system to be a representation-user, it must be possible to distinguish the user from what is used; i.e., it must be possible to distinguish a part of the computational system that uses representations from the representations themselves. But this is precisely the distinction that the standard construal of computation may fail to enforce. The physical states that get interpreted on the standard construal as representations can perfectly well be global states of the system, in which case there is no way to distinguish the user from what is used, and hence no sense in which the system itself is a representation-user. Even in cases where the representations are non-global, localized states of a computational device, there need be no sense in which the device is representation-using. Imagine a beaker filled with liquids of different density, where these different liquids are stratified as a function of their density, in much the way that the different liquors in a layered bar drink are stratified. On the standard construal of computation, this device computes the density of solid objects dropped into it. The density of such an object is represented by the stratum in which it comes to rest. Yet there is no sense in which this representation (the stratum in which the object comes to rest) is *used* by this analogue computer, nor is there any sense in which the representation is a representation *for* the device; it does nothing at all with it.

So the standard construal of computation fails to capture the sense in which certain computational systems might be said to *use* representations in the course of their computations. But what, then, is the sense in which the Received View takes the possessors of propositional attitudes to *use* Representations (and not simply to instantiate them, in the way that the planets instantiate, by virtue of their movements, a representation of Kepler's laws; or merely to have them, in the way, for example, that trees have, by virtue of their annual rings, a representation of the climatological conditions that the tree has experienced)? The evidence that proponents of the Received View cite in support of the claim that there exists a language of thought suggests their answer to this question. Fodor (1975), for example, argues that our best theories of learning treat learning as a species of inductive inference, but this, he claims, is to commit one to the existence of a language or system of representation in which the inductions are carried out, since

(a) an inductive argument is warranted only insofar as the observation statements which constitute its premises confirm the hypothesis which constitutes its conclusion; (b) whether this confirmation relation holds between premises and conclusion depends, at least in part, upon the *form* of the premises and conclusion; and (c) the notion of 'form' is defined only for 'linguistic' objects, viz., for representations.

(Fodor 1975: 42)

Fodor runs a similar line of argument regarding theories of perception: he contends that '(1) perception typically involves hypothesis formation and confirmation, and (2) the sensory data which confirm a given perceptual hypothesis are typically internally represented in a vocabulary in which the hypotheses are themselves couched' (Fodor 1975: 44). If our best theories of learning and perception treat these cognitive processes as inferential, then, as Fodor sees it, we are committed to viewing learning and perception as involving certain explicit Representations over which these inferences are defined, since inferences just are formal operations defined over linguistic Representations. In fact, as I shall argue below, we are not so committed. Our favored proof-theoretic scheme for *representing* inference may require the explicit representation of premises and conclusions, but inference itself does not. But this, of course, is *not* the Received View. For on that view, cognitive agents *are* taken to be Representation-using in the sense that cognition is taken to be a matter of constructing, transforming, and otherwise manipulating certain *explicit* representations, i.e., certain data structures, by means of various hypothesized computational processes. In the case of visual perception, for example, the visual system is said to compute a series of explicit representations, beginning with representations of the proximal stimuli to the retina and ending with a three-dimensional representation of the distal scene responsible for those retinal stimuli (see, e.g., Marr 1982). In the case of language learning, specifically first-language acquisition of syntax, the language faculty is said to compute a series of explicit representations of the grammar of the language to which the learner is exposed, based on explicit representations of the data about that language to which the learner has access. The explicit representation of the language thus acquired is then subsequently accessed and used by the learner in the course of language processing.

So the Received View's claim that thinkers, i.e., possessors of propositional attitudes, are Representation-using systems is just the claim that certain physical structures in the thinker, presumably in the thinker's central nervous system, can be interpreted (under some appropriate representation function f_R) as explicit Representations that the thinker uses. These physical structures are formed, transformed, and otherwise changed by certain physical processes that are themselves interpretable in a principled way as computational processes defined over these Representations.

Representation-using computational systems, so described, are what Newell (1980) termed 'physical symbol systems'. Such systems, Newell points out, constitute a 'broad class of systems capable of having and manipulating symbols, yet realizable in the physical universe' (ibid. 135). A physical symbol system, as Newell defines it,

consists of a *memory* [composed of a set of *symbol structures*, i.e., representations], a set of *operators*, a *control*, an *input*, and an *output*. Its inputs are the objects in certain locations; its outputs are the modification or creation of the objects in certain (usually different) locations. Its external behavior, then, consists of the outputs it produces as a function of its inputs . . . . [Its] internal state consists of the state of its memory and the state of the control; and its internal behavior consists of the variation in this internal state over time.

(Newell 1980: 142)

Such systems, Newell emphasizes, are universal machines: given sufficient (but finite) memory and time, they are capable of computing arbitrary computable functions. Crucially, for our present purposes, these systems have what, following Fodor and Pylyshyn (1988), we might call a 'classical' architecture: they maintain a principled distinction, preserved at the level of physical states and processes, between the system's representations (the symbol structures of memory) and the computational processes (the set of operations), defined over permissible representation-types, that transform, create, and otherwise manipulate the system's representations. The class of physical symbol systems includes not just the LISP-ish type of machine that Newell uses to illustrate his notion of a physical symbol system, but other sorts of universal machines such as Turing machines, which also enforce this principled distinction between representations and processes. The class of physical symbol systems, it should be noted, does not include such computational systems as logic circuits, connectionist networks, or analogue computers, so to the extent that the latter are capable of inference, which clearly some are, computationally realized inference is not the exclusive province of Representation-users.

Some proponents of the Received View, e.g., Pylyshyn (1984), would count as computational devices *only* physical symbol systems, which are representation-using in the sense presumed by the Received View. I see little point to such an unorthodox linguistic prescription, but whatever one's linguistic preferences here, the fundamental point remains that the Received View's presumption that the possessors of propositional attitudes are physical symbol systems represents a substantive *empirical* claim about cognitive computational architecture, one that doesn't follow on any standard construal of computation. The computational architecture of physical symbol systems enforces a principled distinction between representational (symbol) structures, on the one hand, and computational processes and operations defined over these structures, on the other, that other computational architectures might not. If, as a matter of contingent fact, cognitive computational architecture is such a classical architecture, and hence does enforce such a distinction, then this needs to be established empirically, since the tenability of the Received View of propositional attitudes depends on it.

3.3. EXPLICIT REPRESENTATION

The Received View holds that the contents of propositional attitudes are *explicitly* represented. But what precisely is it for such contents to be so represented? Proponents have surprisingly little to say on this crucial matter, but the basic idea seems to be that these representations are explicit in that they are discrete physical structures which are distinct from whatever mental operations may be defined over them. Proponents of the Received View often describe these representations as computational data structures (see, e.g., Fodor 1987: 25), presumably in order to emphasize that they are the physically discrete symbol structures over which the computational operations constitutive of mental processes are defined. As such, these representations could in principle take any number of different forms (e.g., as images, maps, lists, matrices, vectors); however, the Received View presumes that they take a *sentential* form. Thus, for example, believing that it is sunny outside today is said to be a matter of having a sentence token that expresses the content that it is sunny outside today stored in one's 'belief box' (see p. 38 n. 1 above). The intuitive idea here is that the contents of propositional attitudes (what we believe, desire, etc.) are explicitly represented in the mind in much the way that the contents of what we say are explicitly represented by the natural language sentences that express these contents. The mental representations that express the contents of propositional attitudes are taken to be semantically interpreted syntactic structures whose contents are presumed to be readily available to anyone who understands the language ('mentalese' as some call it) in which these representations are couched.

Proponents of the Received View concede that common sense is prepared to attribute to thinkers all sorts of propositional attitudes the contents of which are presumably *not* explicitly represented. Most of us, for example, would claim to believe, and indeed claim to have long believed, though perhaps only tacitly, that herons don't wear galoshes in the wild, that the successor of 24,694,901 is 24,694,902, that we are constantly surrounded by all sorts of things, and so on. Yet it seems implausible to suppose that the contents of these tacit beliefs are explicitly represented, if by this we mean something like being explicitly tokened in us. The point here has nothing to do with whether these tacit beliefs are consciously entertained, though clearly they are not. Proponents of the Received View presume that many explicitly represented beliefs are also not consciously entertained (see, e.g., Harman 1973: 13). The point has rather to do with the fact that because there are so many of these beliefs, indeed uncountably many tacit beliefs about just the successors of natural numbers, it is simply not possible that all tacit beliefs are explicitly represented, at least not in physically embodied minds like ours. And even a very large, but still finite, number of explicitly represented beliefs would spell trouble for the Received View's account of the computational role of these representations in the production of thought and behavior. The clutter would be computationally devastating.

Adopting the Received View clearly demands some adjustment to our common-sense notion of what propositional attitudes we possess, since much of what we would intuitively take ourselves to believe, desire, etc. would not be explicitly represented. Many proponents of the Received View argue that so-called tacit beliefs are not really beliefs at all, but are at best dispositions to form certain beliefs (see, e.g., Field 1978 [1981]: 82–3; Richard 1990: 47–57). We do, they argue, have various (explicitly represented) beliefs about herons, galoshes, and natural numbers, e.g., that herons live mostly in the wild, that galoshes are worn by and only by humans, that every natural number has a successor. And from these beliefs it may indeed follow that herons don't wear galoshes in the wild, that the successor of 24,694,901 is 24,694,902. But these are not things that someone thereby actually believes, any more than one actually believes every existential generalization of one's beliefs, though of course rational thinkers are disposed to embrace such generalizations should the occasion arise, because they are disposed to draw the relevant inferences from their explicitly represented beliefs.

The proposal that tacit beliefs are not really beliefs at all, and hence on the Received View need not be explicitly represented, enables proponents to accommodate an obvious constraint on physically embodied minds, namely, that there is room for only a finite amount of physical stuff within the finite space of any thinker's skull (cf. Field 1978 [1981]: 83–4). If every tacit belief were explicitly represented and thus, as the Received View would have it, individually physically tokened, then there would not be enough space even for our tacit beliefs about the successors of natural numbers. But given that tacit beliefs are not so represented, there is, in principle at least, no space allocation problem.

As convenient as this proposed solution might be for anyone inclined to suppose that propositional attitudes are explicitly represented, it presumes the intelligibility of the notion of explicit representation itself, a notion to which the Received View helps itself but offers no explication. But the presumption here is open to challenge. Kirsch (1990) argues that this notion is not at all perspicuous, especially when applied to some of the non-classical computational architectures currently being investigated by computer scientists. The notion of explicitly represented information, he argues, presumes a particular view of computation, namely, one in which computers are viewed as physical symbol systems, along the lines described in the previous section of this chapter:

> If a computer is seen as a mechanism which applies rules to syntactically structured representations, it is natural to view explicit information as an encoding of information in syntactic structures that are interpretable according to a well-behaved theory of content, such as a truth theory. We can then point to a syntactic structure in the system and say 'that form encodes this content'.
>
> (Kirsch 1990: 340)

But when other kinds of computational mechanisms are considered—e.g., parallel distributed processing (PDP) systems, massive cellular automata, or analogue relaxation systems—it becomes difficult, Kirsch argues, to give a clear sense to the notion of certain information being explicitly represented. It is, he says, 'an open question whether the model of rules operating on explicit representations is a perspicuous model of their style of computation' (ibid. 341). In fact, Kirsch thinks that the notion of explicit representation may not be perspicuous even for the physical symbol systems described by Newell (1980).

Kirsch agrees that we must be able to track the trajectory of information states that computational mechanisms generate; otherwise, we have no reason to think we understand the computations, even any reason to think of the causal processes as computational, rather than simply brute causal. But, he argues, there is no particular reason to suppose that the ability to track such states requires the explicit representation of successive information states: 'We already know that there are many ways information can be implicit in a state, structure or process, and that we are largely ignorant of the full variety of ways that information can be built into architecture, internal dynamics, and environment-system interaction' (Kirsch 1990: 341). But more importantly, Kirsch argues that our intuitions about whether information is explicit (or implicit) are deeply unsettled, if not simply inconsistent, in a way that precludes any clear application of the notion of explicit representation to non-classical architectures. Our intuitions, he argues, are largely shaped by the idea that explicit representations are analogous to the printed words on a page. We attribute to these representations properties that, he claims, we uncritically associate with the printed word: locality (i.e., spatial compactness and separability), movability (syntactic and semantic invariance across contexts), immediate readability, and meaningfulness (definite informational content). But, Kirsch argues, the analogy with printed text fails. The informational states of computational systems, most especially of non-classical systems, but sometimes even of physical symbol systems, don't possess these properties. Indeed, printed words themselves possess them only to a very imperfect and approximate degree. Kirsch concludes that our confused intuitions about explicit representation can only be set aright by realizing that 'Explicitness really concerns how quickly information can be assessed, retrieved, or in some other manner put to use. It has more to do with what is present in a process sense, than with what is present in a structural sense' (Kirsch 1990: 361).[4]

If, as Kirsch claims, explicitness has more to do with process than with structure, then the Received View of propositional attitudes is in trouble. For if the supposed structural differences between genuine propositional attitudes and the merely tacit do not manifest themselves with reasonable

---

[4] Stalnaker (1991 [1999]) shares Kirsch's skepticism regarding the Received View's structural notion of explicit representation. He argues that to the extent that our common-sense notion of belief involves the notion of information that a possessor is able to use in inference and action, then the idea that beliefs are explicitly represented in the structural as opposed to process sense will fail to demarcate correctly what it is a person believes. This is because the relevant distinction between what someone does and does not believe is a distinction between information that is and information that is not easily accessible for use by the possessor of the information. But this distinction, Stalnaker argues, is not captured by the Received View's distinction between information that is and information that is not structurally (i.e., explicitly) represented. The two distinctions, he argues, cross-classify.

reliability in functional or processing differences, then the view offers no non-question-begging way of drawing the proposed distinction between the genuine and the merely tacit to which it appeals. The Received View simply asserts that the contents of genuine attitudes are explicitly represented, and the contents of the merely tacit are not. But what rationale do we have for accepting this assertion if we are not able to distinguish, at least roughly, on independent grounds, genuine attitudes from the merely tacit? Clearly this would not be a problem if most of what common sense took to be propositional attitudes were genuine. The situation would then be analogous to discovering that most of what we call 'water' is H_2O. But that is not the case here, where proponents concede that many of what common sense takes to be our propositional attitudes aren't in fact genuine. The only thing we are left with by way of a rationale for accepting the Received View of propositional attitudes is that for those cases for which the view is true, it would explain their having the intentional properties that they do, though, again, it would offer no non-question-begging specification of those cases, and it would offer no account of the apparent intentionality of the merely tacit cases.

But proponents of the Received View cannot simply embrace Kirsch's suggestion that we reconstrue the notion of explicit representation along process lines. The consequences for their view would be profound. It would effectively undercut the Received View's proposed construal of propositional attitudes, since it would no longer follow that, for any arbitrary propositional attitude true of a thinker, there would necessarily be a syntactically structured representation, i.e., a data structure, possessed by the thinker, that expressed the content of that propositional attitude. And for this reason, the Received View could no longer claim to provide an account of the intentionality of propositional attitudes, inasmuch the view could no longer claim that the intentionality of the attitudes is inherited from the intentionality of the corresponding representations. Nor could it claim to establish the materialistic *bona fides* of propositional attitudes, inasmuch as the Received View would entail no particular constraints whatever on the mapping of propositional attitudes into computational states and processes.

Proponents of the Received View of propositional attitudes might justifiably regard Kirsch's suggested reconstrual as a poisoned pawn, one that they would do well not to take. Kirsch may be correct that the notion of explicit representation upon which the Received View relies is one that has no clear construal within non-classical computational systems, and perhaps even within some classical systems as well. But proponents of the Received View might choose instead to acknowledge their commitment to classical physical symbol systems, perhaps classical symbol systems of a particular sort, conceding that if human computational architecture turns out to be of a different sort, then the Received View is simply false.

This, I think, would be the right move for proponents of the Received View to make here, though it is important to bear in mind the empirical assumptions to which the view is thereby committed. It takes thinkers to be Representation-using systems in the sense of being physical symbol systems. The Representations over which cognitive computational processes are defined are said to be syntactically structured entities that express the propositional contents of the thinker's propositional attitudes. In particular, these Representations are said to have the same contents as the sentences embedded in the sentential complements of the propositional attitude attributions that attribute these propositional attitudes. The language of thought in which these Representations are formulated must therefore have the expressive power of a natural language, since otherwise there would be propositions expressible by these embedded sentences that could not be expressed by these Representations. Now perhaps this is simply the ways things are with the language of thought. But this certainly seems surprising. For why would one suppose that a language of thought would have the expressive power of a natural language? One might rather have supposed, quite reasonably I would think, that the semantics of the language of thought would, like the semantics of various programming languages, take as the denotata of its terms a local set of objects and relations, say, for example, the contents of certain registers, stacks, etc., certain operations, and so on.[5] If such were the case, the language of thought would have no terms that referred to the furniture of a distal world.[6]

There may be a more general argument, having nothing in particular to do with specific empirical theories such as Marr's, for doubting that the language

---

[5] This, incidentally, is precisely the semantics that Newell (1980) assumes for his physical symbol systems.

[6] Egan (1991, 2003) argues that this is precisely the case for the contents of the various representations that Marr (1982) postulates in his theory of early vision. She argues that notwithstanding Marr's informal distal descriptions of these contents, the representations that his theory postulates are not always representations of distal objects and their properties. Chomsky (2000: 159) goes even further, arguing that in the work of both Ullman (1979) and Marr (1982), talk of representation is not to be understood relationally, in terms of 'content' or 'representation of'. For Chomsky, talk of a 'mental representation of *x*' is simply talk of a non-representing cognitive structure of type *x*.

of thought could have the expressive power of a natural language and hence that for any propositional attitude there would exist a Representation couched in the language of thought that would express the propositional content of that attitude. The argument is this: By all accounts, the causal relation between perceptual inputs and behavioral outputs, on the one hand, and any given representation that figures in a subject's cognitive computational processes, on the other, is heavily mediated by other representations (and computational processes defined over them). But if this is so, why suppose that the language of thought for these representations would nonetheless share a domain of discourse with a natural language and hence that these representations have a determinate distal interpretation in terms of this domain? Arguably, perceptual inputs and behavioral outputs must be so interpretable on pain of our not being able to make sense of subjects' interactions with their environment; however, there would seem to be no reason to suppose that the representations that mediate between perceptual inputs and behavioral outputs must be similarly interpretable. Neither engineering constraints, nor evolutionary considerations, nor scientific tractability would seem to require it. Nor does being able to track information flow through the system require it. Of course, if these representations were so interpretable, then cognitive processing would be explanatorily transparent in the sense that computational explanations would not have to traffic in representational contents that were not readily intelligible to the lay public. Explanations would not advert, as Newell envisions it, to the contents of registers, stacks, and the like, and thus be intelligible only to those having a detailed familiarity with human cognitive computational architecture; rather these explanations would advert only to the familiar objects that are the furniture of our common-sense world. Now perhaps, *per mirabile*, this is just the way things are. But if so, this is indeed surprising, because to suppose that the representations that mediate between perceptual inputs and behavioral outputs have determinate distal contents is to suppose that cognition is actually a rather superficial phenomenon, something akin to the traditional picture of thinking as talking silently to oneself—not in the sense that thinking is really a kind of talking, but rather in the sense that the mediation between internal states and external environment is sufficiently limited that it is possible to assign to these representations the sort of distal content that the Received View envisions. The obvious question here is whether proponents of the view can marshal any empirical support whatever for this surprising assumption. I doubt that they can.

3.4. WHY BEHAVIORAL EVIDENCE DOESN'T SUFFICE

Few, if any, proponents of the Received View of propositional attitudes would explicitly endorse the claim that behavioral evidence alone provides strong support for the view.[7] But more than a few proponents come perilously close to implicitly endorsing just this claim when they argue, as Fodor (1987: 17) does, that because cognitive scientific theorizing presumes the view, the successes of such theorizing provides strong empirical support for the view. They come perilously close to endorsing this claim, because the evidence for the theories that are thought to provide empirical support for the Received View of propositional attitudes is overwhelmingly behavioral, in that it has mostly to do with how subjects behave under various environmental conditions. And such experimental evidence as is not behavioral, e.g., reaction time data or perceived complexity data, is typically not of the right sort to support the view inasmuch as it is difficult to draw any firm conclusions from such data about underlying computational processes, and hence computational architecture, in the absence of fairly detailed information about that architecture (resources, primitive operations, etc.), which at this point in time is simply unavailable.[8] The basic problem with trying to mount a purely behavioral argument for the Received View has to do with the fact that the same input/output behavior can be exhibited by a range of different computational devices, some of which don't have the computational architecture presumed by the view. Let me elaborate this point.

Consider how a subject's propositional attitudes might possibly figure in a story about the computational processes that map perceptual inputs into behavioral outputs. Clearly this mapping should be sensitive to changes in the subject's propositional attitudes, since how we react behaviorally to perceptual inputs depends crucially on our beliefs, desires, and other propositional attitudes. One possibility is this: the subject's propositional attitudes (which are themselves causally determined by perceptual input and innate endowment, in conjunction with other propositional attitudes) determine in effect an input/output function f such

---

[7] Some psychologists argue that behavioral evidence *can* provide compelling evidence for the claim, entailed by the view, that cognitive systems like ourselves have a specific kind of computational architecture, specifically the information-processing architecture of what Newell calls a physical symbol system (see p. 43 above). Gallistel (2006: 65), for example, argues that 'behavioral facts imply an information-processing architecture. There is no way to explain the behavioral facts except by assuming [such an architecture].'

[8] For useful discussion, see Pylyshyn 1984: 120–30.

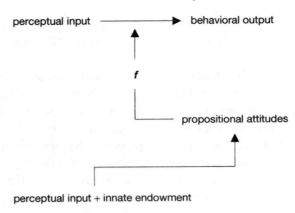

Figure 3.2. How Propositional Attitudes Might Figure In.

that given a particular perceptual input in the domain of this function, these processes return the behavioral output that is the value of the function for that input (See Figure 3.2 above). Change the subject's propositional attitudes, and you probably change the input/output function that the subject implements.

But this is just to say that taken together the subject's propositional attitudes are a *representation* of the function *f* computed by the subject, where this representation controls the computation in basically the way that a representation of the function to be computed by a universal machine, e.g., a universal Turing machine, controls the computations of the machine, causing it to compute the function that it does. If this, broadly speaking, is the picture, then the assumption that behavioral data alone can provide evidence for the Received View is clearly in trouble. For it is an elementary result in the theory of computation that for every device that computes a function by means of a computational procedure that is governed by an explicit encoding of a particular name or representation of that function, there exists another device that computes this same function but without having anything which could be regarded as an encoding of a particular name or representation of that function—a result that is regularly exploited by users of, for example, hardwired LISP machines who want to avoid the computational inefficiencies characteristic of implementing LISP on a universal machine. If this is the picture, there is nothing in the behavior of subjects that provides evidence for the claim that we are representation-users, much less that we are Representation-users, and hence for the Received View of propositional attitudes (which entails the former claim). To establish that we are Representation-users, proponents of the Received View are going to have to provide evidence that bears not simply on the function being computed, but also on the manner in which this function is computed, evidence that, I would argue, is not provided by the sorts of non-behavioral measures presently employed in cognitive scientific theorizing.

Now perhaps proponents of the Received View have a different picture of the role of propositional attitudes in cognitive processing. Perhaps, like Fodor (1975: 73), they think of cognitive processing as a kind of theorem-proving where the Representations, which express the contents of propositional attitudes, figure as premises in a proof whose conclusion is either a behavior or another Representation. Never mind that it is thoroughly unclear on this picture how the fact that a propositional attitude is, for example, a desire or a doubt rather than a belief is supposed to figure in this inferential story. On the account, for example, that Fodor proposes, the inferences are run over Representations of the contents of propositional attitudes and not also over representations of the attitude types, though surely the attitude types themselves must figure in an inference that takes propositional attitudes of different types as premises.[9] But even if this matter could be cleared up, consistent with the Received View's thesis that having a propositional attitude is a matter of standing in a computational relation to a Representation (of the content of the attitude), there would still be no reason to suppose behavioral data could provide any support for the claim that we are Representation-users. The unsupported assumption that cognition is a kind of theorem-proving implemented in a classical architecture is doing all the work here. For all we know, cognitive processes could be implemented by a non-classical connectionist architecture that doesn't traffic in explicit representations of any sort, much less in the explicit Representations postulated by the Received View. It is, after all, an elementary result in the theory of computation that connectionist networks can compute, or at least approximate to any arbitrary degree, any computable function, i.e., any function computable by a universal machine (see Hornik *et al.* 1989). So to establish that thinkers like ourselves

---

[9] Fodor's (1987: 13–14) discussion of cognitive inferential processes, e.g., his discussion of Sherlock Holmes' inference (in 'The Speckled Band') that the Doctor committed the murder with a snake, sidesteps this problem by offering as examples reconstructions of inferential reasoning that takes us from beliefs to beliefs. The relevant cases to consider would be reasoning that involves beliefs and desires as premises and a behavior (or more correctly, a motor command) as conclusion. For in such cases it is completely unclear how the inferences could possibly be run over just the Representations of the premised attitude contents.

are Representation-using systems, minimally it is necessary to establish (i) that we are representation-using systems, i.e., physical symbol systems in Newell's (1980) sense of that expression, and (ii) that the representations used are Representations, i.e., representations of the propositional contents of propositional attitudes. The relevant evidence has to do both with our *computational architecture* (assuming, of course, that we are computational systems) and with the *content and structure* of the representations that are assumed to figure in that architecture. But these are not things that behavioral evidence alone can establish.

It might seem that there is a very quick way around the preceding argument that, for all we know based on behavioral evidence, we might *not* be representation-users at all, much less Representation-users. How, someone might ask, could we be anything but Representation-users? Propositional attitudes, it might be argued, just *are* Representational states, i.e., intentional states that have propositional contents. So on the assumption both that propositional attitudes figure in the etiology of our behavior and that this etiology is computational in nature, it might seem that this alone is enough to establish that we are Representation-users. Attractive as this simple argument might be, it does not establish the conclusion that proponents of the Received View need, namely, that we are Representation-users in the sense of being physical symbol systems in which the representations (over which cognitive computational operations are defined) are Representations. At most it simply reiterates the uncontroversial major premise of the argument, namely, that we are Representation-users in the sense of possessing propositional attitudes, which are themselves Representational states of their possessor. This simple argument establishes nothing as regards the computational implementation of propositional attitudes and hence nothing as regards the computational construal of such states proposed by the Received View. Surely this cannot be the sense of 'Representation-using' that proponents of the Received View have in mind when they claim that we are Representation-using (though see 3.10 below). For if it were, there would be nothing here that would constitute a substantive construal of propositional attitudes, certainly nothing that would go any distance in establishing the materialistic *bona fides* of propositional attitudes. Nor would there be anything here that had any substantive implications for cognitive science. What makes the Received View philosophically, and indeed scientifically, interesting is precisely the fact that it proposes a substantive *inter-theoretic* construal of propositional attitudes that relates intentional, more specifically propositional attitude, descriptions, on the one hand, and computational descriptions, on the other. The view might be mistaken, but at least it is offering an answer to a clearly substantive question about inter-theoretic relations in the domain of cognition. Eliminativists aside, no one doubts that we are Representation-users in the sense of being possessors of propositional attitudes, which are themselves Representational states of their possessors. The Received View undertakes to *explain* this fact, not simply to restate it.

3.5. THE ARGUMENT FROM LINGUISTIC KNOWLEDGE

3.5.1. Psycholinguistics: A Test Case for Claims of Empirical Support

Most proponents of the Received View of propositional attitudes explicitly acknowledge its empirical character and look to empirical cognitive science for its support and eventual confirmation.[10] At best, a priori considerations are thought to be able to lend plausibility to the view by establishing that were it true, then certain salient features of our common-sense conception of propositional attitudes, our linguistic practice in ascribing them, and their role in common-sense psychological explanations would thereby be explained. The obvious question, then, is whether the view enjoys the strong empirical support that proponents claim for it.

Proponents of the Received View of propositional attitudes claim to find empirical support for the view in the successes of computational psychology, most notably in the areas of language and vision. In particular, they find support in this empirical work for the claim, entailed by the view, that we are Representation-using systems. Critics of the view, for their part, have tended to focus on the second of the two requirements for being Representation-using (see p. 54 above), arguing that there is little or no evidence that such representations as figure in computational psychological theories are Representations, i.e., representations of propositional contents. Indeed, some critics argue that there is positive evidence to the contrary. More recently,

---

[10] Fodor (1978 [1981]: 202), for example, says, 'the theory that propositional attitudes are relations to internal representations is a piece of empirical psychology, not an analysis. For there might have been angels, or behaviorism might have been true, and then the internal representation story would have been false.'

critics, especially those of a connectionist bent, have argued that there is little
or no evidence that we are representation-using systems at all, much less
Representation-using systems. Again, some here argue that there is positive
evidence to the contrary.

Psycholinguistics offers an important first test. For years proponents of the
Received View trumpeted the scientific progress in this area as an important
source of empirical support. They claimed that the Received View provided
the foundations of contemporary psycholinguistic theories, and as such the
empirical successes in this domain provided indirect empirical support for
the view. Developments within both computational psycholinguistics and
linguistics itself eventually undercut this claimed support,[11] but the example
remains useful as an illustration of both how empirical theory might be
thought to support the view and how, not surprisingly, such claimed support
is hostage to fine-grained theoretical details.

3.5.2. Speakers as Representation-Using Systems

In the early years of the Received View, proponents argued repeatedly
that psycholinguistic theorizing based on transformational generative syntax
provided strong support for the claim that we are Representation-using
systems. Both linguists and psycholinguists, they pointed out, assumed that
what a speaker(/hearer) *knows* when he knows a language is, among other
things, *a grammar*. Specifically, the speaker knows that $r_1, r_2, \ldots$, where r_i
are the rules, principles, etc. that constitute the grammar of the speaker's
language. Grammars were said by linguists to be mentally represented
and used in the exercise of linguistic abilities such as sentence-processing
and making acceptability judgments. And although there were few specific
proposals as to exactly how the mentally represented grammars were used
in the exercise of linguistic abilities, these grammars were said by linguists
to be used 'computationally'. Chomsky (1980a: 201), for example, claimed
that the system of rules and principles that constitute the grammar 'have,
in some manner, been internally represented by the person who knows a
language and [these rules and principles] enable the speaker, in principle,
to understand an arbitrary sentence and to produce a sentence expressing
his thought'. Linguistic judgments and performance, he argued, 'are guided

---

[11] This claimed support has also been undercut in recent years by Chomsky's growing skepticism
of intentionalist interpretations of linguistic theory, specifically of the 'representations' to which
such theory adverts. See, e.g., Chomsky 2000: 159 ff.

by mental computation involving these internally represented rules and principles' (ibid. 130).

Chomsky's idea here seemed to be this: the grammar is explicitly represented and used in much the way that a universal machine uses an explicit representation of the machine that it is imitating; that is, speakers have an explicit mental representation of the grammar, which they consult in the course of sentence processing, and this mental representation controls their sentence processing.

On a superficial reading, Chomsky certainly sounded like a proponent of the Received View. But if we take seriously his often repeated insistence that a generative grammar is *not* a model for a speaker (Chomsky 1965: 9), that it does *not* prescribe the character or functioning of such a model (ibid.), that the task of linguistics is to describe 'abstract conditions that unknown mechanisms must meet' (Chomsky 1980a: 197), then we should suspect that perhaps the Received View was not Chomsky's view, even in the restricted domain of language.[12] Yet even if the proposed construal of grammars was not Chomsky's, it was unquestionably the construal of a number of linguists and philosophers, all of whom embraced the Received View. The question is whether this particular construal of linguistic knowledge and its use by speakers is one that finds any evidential support within linguistics or psycholinguistics.

3.5.3. Bresnan and Kaplan's Strong Competence Hypothesis

Proponents of the Received View who endorse the still widely accepted view that the grammars proposed by linguists characterize the linguistic knowledge of speakers would presumably agree that to be psychologically 'real' in the sense of providing an accurate characterization of the computational role of linguistic knowledge in language processing, these grammars must satisfy what Bresnan and Kaplan (1982) call the 'strong competence hypothesis':[13]

Suppose that we are given an information-processing model of language use that includes a processor and a component of stored linguistic knowledge K, [where] at a minimum . . . K prescribes certain operations that the processor is to perform on linguistic representations, such as manipulating phrases or assigning grammatical

---

[12] For a discussion of Chomsky's view of these matters, see Matthews 1991b: 192–5.
[13] Cf., e.g., Davies' (1987) so-called 'Mirror Principle', which is quite similar to Bresnan and Kaplan's strong competence hypothesis.

functions . . . . We call the subpart of K that prescribes representational operations the *representational basis* of the processing model. (The representational basis is the 'internal grammar' of the model.) . . . A model satisfies the *strong competence hypothesis* if and only if its representational basis is isomorphic to the competence grammar.

(Bresnan and Kaplan 1982: p. xxxi)

For if a proposed grammar failed to be isomorphic with the representational basis that a speaker in fact uses in the course of language production and understanding, then it would presumably fail to describe correctly the actual role of linguistic knowledge representations in language processing.

Bresnan and Kaplan offer little by way of a justification of their strong competence hypothesis, which is in fact simply a restatement of tenet (v) of the Received View as it applies to linguistic knowledge, on the assumption that such knowledge is specified by a grammar. Indeed, they take it to be 'uncontroversial' that 'stored knowledge structures underlie all forms of verbal behavior' (ibid. p. xix). They suggest that to reject their hypothesis is 'to adopt the theoretical alternative that a different body of knowledge of one's language is required for every type of verbal behavior' (ibid.). But this is incorrect, for their suggestion concerns only the presumed parsimony of speakers' knowledge structures. It does not address the nature of such structures, specifically whether linguistic knowledge is explicitly represented in the form of an internalized grammar. For all that Bresnan and Kaplan have said, a speaker's linguistic knowledge might be parsimoniously represented, but not explicitly represented in the structural manner presumed by the Received View.

Whereas Bresnan and Kaplan simply presume that linguistic knowledge is explicitly represented in a manner consistent with the Received View, and then proceed to argue that as a methodological principle the grammars proposed by linguists as descriptions of that knowledge should be isomorphic to the representational basis of processing models, others have attempted to establish just this presumption. Fodor, Bever, and Garrett (1974), for example, argued that the existence of linguistic universals actually *requires* that an explicit representation of the grammar made available by linguistic theory be part of the language processor:

There are linguistic universals which serve precisely to constrain the form in which information is represented in grammars (i.e., the form of grammatical rules). The question is: If the universals do not also constrain the form in which linguistic information is represented in a sentence-processing system, how is their existence to be explained? Surely, if universals are true of anything, it must be of some psychologically real representation of a language. But what could such a representation be if it is not part of a sentence encoding-decoding system?

(Fodor, Bever, and Garrett 1974: 369–70)

This argument does not provide any empirical evidence for the claim that grammatical rules are explicitly represented and used in language processing. Rather it simply asks: How else are we to explain the existence of linguistic universals? But such 'how else' arguments are hardly compelling if there is any reason to suppose that there might be an alternative explanation. The following concrete example drawn from Marcus (1980) suggests just this, namely, that there may be an alternative explanation of the existence of such universals. Never mind that it concerns a parsing model for a version of Chomsky's so-called Extended Standard Theory (from the late 1970s).[14] The point is simply to respond to Fodor, Bever, and Garrett's 'how else' argument by providing a concrete example of an actual parsing model that implements a putatively universal constraint in a way other than the one they envision.

It is a commonplace within generative linguistic theory that the acceptability of certain sentences, and the unacceptability of other, superficially similar sentences, can be predicted and explained only on the assumption that certain syntactic constituents undergo movement and furthermore that such movement is subject to certain very specific constraints that are universal across all natural languages. The precise characterization of these constraints is a matter of continuing theoretical debate, but generally speaking they involve constraints on how, when, where, and how far these constituents can move. Within Extended Standard Theory, much of the work done within current minimalist theory by general constraints such as the c-command condition on binding, the chain uniformity principle, the economy principle, the greed principle, and the minimal link condition was done by more specific constraints such as the Subjacency Condition, the Specified Subject Condition, Ross's Complex NP Constraint, and the Clausemate Constraint. Within the parser proposed by Marcus (1980) for Extended Standard Theory, these constraints are not, as Fodor, Bever, and Garrett would have it, constraints on the form in which linguistic information is explicitly represented. Nor are these constraints themselves explicitly represented. Rather they are implemented *procedurally*, in the sense that they are entailed by the structure of the parser's interpreter of its internal parsing grammar, specifically by the fact that it maintains two major data structures, a push-down stack of incomplete

---

[14] See pp. 63–5 below for a description of the parsing model proposed by Marcus (1980).

constituents, and a three-cell buffer that the interpreter uses as a workspace, along with certain general *procedural* constraints on operations defined over these data structures. Included among these procedural constraints is the parser's (procedural) implementation of what Marcus calls the 'Determinism Hypothesis', which hypothesizes that sentence processing is deterministic in the sense that it permits no backtracking and no pseudoparallelism. Marcus (1980) introduces his detailed explanation of how his parser implements the constraints of Extended Standard Theory as follows:

> In a series of papers over the last few years, Noam Chomsky has argued for several specific properties of language which he claims are universal to all human languages. These properties . . . are embodied in a set of constraints on language, a set of restrictions on the operation of rules of grammar.
>
> . . . behavior characterized by important subcases of two of these constraints falls out naturally from the structure of the grammar interpreter . . . . many of the properties of the interpreter which crucially cause this behavior are motivated by the Determinism Hypothesis, demonstrating that significant subcases of Chomsky's universals follow naturally from the Determinism Hypothesis and in this sense are explained by it. If Chomsky's claims are true, this demonstration shows that *the mechanisms of the grammar interpreter* [emphasis mine] capture a number of the generalizations which are purportedly universal to all human languages.
>
> (Marcus 1980: 127)

So here, then, is a concrete 'something else' that responds to Fodor, Bever, and Garrett's 'what else' argument for the explicit representation of linguistic universals; and on this response, speakers' knowledge of these linguistic universals is not to be explained in terms of their having and using an explicit Representation of these universals.

3.5.4. The Right View According to Fodor

A more subtle argument for the assumption that linguistic knowledge is explicitly represented rests on a defense of what Fodor (1981), with endearing impartiality, calls the 'Right View', which holds the following:

> (a) Linguistic theories are descriptions of grammars. (b) It is nomologically necessary that learning one's native language involves learning its grammar, so a theory of how grammars are learned is *de facto* a (partial [?]) theory of how languages are learned. (c) It is nomologically necessary that the grammar of a language is internally represented by speaker/hearers of that language; up to dialectical variants, the grammar of a language is what its speakers have in common by virtue of which

they are speaker/hearers of the *same* language. (d) It is nomologically necessary that the intentional representation of the grammar (or, equivalently for these purposes, the internally represented grammar) is causally implemented in communication exchanges between speakers and hearers insofar as these exchanges are mediated by their use of the language that they share; talking and understanding the language normally involve exploiting the internally represented grammar.

(Fodor 1981: 199)

The Right View is a clear expression of the Received View in the domain of language, inasmuch as the internally represented grammar is claimed to be an explicit representation of the speaker's linguistic knowledge, and that internally represented grammar, it is claimed, is used by speakers in the course of language production and perception. As Fodor points out, the view 'construes learning a language as a process that eventuates in the internal representation of a grammar, and it construes the production/perception of speech as causally mediated by the grammar that the speaker/hearer learns' (Fodor 1981: 201).

But appellation notwithstanding, why should we believe the Right View to be the right view? In particular, should we endorse the notion that the speaker's knowledge of language takes the form of an internally represented grammar of any sort, much less of the sort made available by linguistic theory? Fodor's answer, if I understand him correctly, is that the assumption that grammars are internally represented is warranted by a Realist principle to the effect that one should accept the ontology that the best explanation presupposes. Specifically, the appropriate form of argument for the assumption that grammars are internally represented is to show that this assumption, when taken together with independently motivated theories of the character of other interacting variables (such as memory limitations and the like), yields the best explanation of the data about the organism's mental states and processes and/or the behaviors in which such processes eventuate.[15]

While I am inclined to endorse a Realist principle of the sort that Fodor invokes in defense of the Right View, I do not think that it can be used to support the claim that the language processor incorporates an internal representation of the grammar postulated by linguistic theory and presumed to be a representation of the content of the speaker's linguistic knowledge. We do, of course, have linguistic theories that correctly predict many of

---

[15] I am here paraphrasing Fodor's (1979 [1981]: 120–1) account of what would constitute evidence for the claim that the postulates of logic are internally represented.

the linguistic intuitions of speakers. And certainly the best explanation of their predictive success is that speakers have the linguistic *knowledge* that is represented by the grammars attributed to them. But nothing, so far as I can see, suggests that these grammars are internally represented by speakers, if by this one means explicitly represented in the manner described earlier in this chapter. Fodor's Realist principle demands only that we accept the linguistic theory's claim about what speakers know; it does not require that we accept some further claim, seemingly not a part of the theory and certainly not in any way implicated in the predictive successes of the theory, as to how this knowledge is realized in speakers. Given how little we know about the cognitive computational architecture of the brain, we are simply not in a position to say how the linguistic knowledge represented by means of a grammar is realized and used computationally. Indeed, as Stabler (1983) has argued, given what we know about other, better understood computational systems, it seems reasonable to suspect that grammars are *not* explicitly represented at all: the limited plasticity (and lability) of acquired grammatical competence would seem to render explicit representation unnecessary, while the relatively greater computational efficiency of processors whose programs are 'hardwired' rather than explicitly represented would seem to render explicit representation undesirable. But here again, these are speculations whose resolution must await further evidence regarding the computational architecture of the brain. The present point is simply that Realist principles of the sort adduced by Fodor argue for neither the Right View nor the Received View. Of course, these principles *do* dictate that we take the grammar postulated by an explanatorily adequate linguistic theory to have the speaker as a model, but this does not entail that this model incorporates an explicit representation of that grammar. The grammar could be realized in any way whatever, so long as the realization preserved the truth of the claim that the grammar represents the speaker's linguistic knowledge. The realization might turn out to be extremely abstract, by which I mean that there might be no answer to the question 'What specific structures and/or processes of the language processor represent the speaker's knowledge of language?'

To proponents of the Right View (and hence of the Received View in this domain), the suggestion that this question might have no answer may seem tantamount to admitting that there may be nothing for the grammar made available by the true linguistic theory to be true of, except the behavior of the individual to whom the grammar is attributed. Thus, for example, Fodor (1981) writes:

If, then, the notion of internal representation is *not* coherent, the only thing for a linguistic theory to be true of is the linguist's observations (*de facto*, the intuitions of the speaker/-hearer as extrapolated by the formally simplest grammar). Take the notion of internal representation away from linguistic meta-theory and you get positivism by subtraction.

(Fodor 1981: 201)

Yet, contrary to what Fodor claims here, the only options here are *not* just the Right View or positivism (or more specifically, behaviorism). There is the third option mentioned above: the grammar attributed to an individual might be true of an individual, though not in virtue of any explicit representation in the individual of that grammar. Rather than ascribing any particular computational structure to the individual, the attribution of a grammar to an individual attributes to that individual a certain linguistic competence, specifically, the capacity of being able to recover and use the grammatical information marked by the structural descriptions that the speaker's grammar associates with sentences of the speaker's language. The attributed competence, it should be noted, is clearly not behavioral, since there is no presumption that an individual to whom this competence is attributed is able to manifest it behaviorally.

3.5.5. The Computational Realization of Grammars

There are many different ways in which a speaker might realize a grammar (or, equivalently, the grammar be true of that speaker), none of which would have to involve the individual's having an explicit representation of that grammar. Some of these ways might involve the individual's having no 'internal grammar' whatever; others would involve his having such a grammar, but not one isomorphic to the linguist's grammar that the individual realizes.[16] The Marcus (1980) parser, mentioned earlier, is an example of the latter sort.[17] That parser, which implements a version of Chomsky's so-called Extended Standard Theory (EST), incorporates a grammar, i.e., it incorporates a rule system that governs the interpretive processes of the parser; however, the incorporated grammar is *not* a grammar of the sort made available by EST (or any other linguistic theory, for that matter). The incorporated grammar,

---

[16] For an extended discussion of these possibilities, see Berwick and Weinberg 1984.

[17] Berwick (1985) presents a modified Marcus parser which implements a generative grammar that incorporates both X-bar theory and a *Move-α* transformational component.

as Marcus explains, is a set of pattern-action rules similar to the rules of a production system: each rule is made up of a *pattern*, which is matched against some subset of contents of the input buffer and active node stack (the two data structures maintained by the interpreter), and an *action*, which is a sequence of operations on these contents. The pattern-action rules are quite different from the phrase-structure and transformational rules of EST. The most notable difference between the grammar incorporated in the Marcus parser and those made available by EST is that the former's pattern-action rules reflect in direct fashion assumptions about the structure of the parser, namely, that it maintains two data structures (a stack and a buffer), that only certain contents of these structures are accessible, and so on. The grammars of EST, by contrast, do not wear their algorithmic implementation on their sleeves—there is no commitment within the theory as to how the knowledge characterized by the grammar made available by this theory is implemented or used by speakers.

Moreover, and perhaps more importantly, there is no one-to-one pairing of the grammatical rules, and especially the principles, of EST with the pattern-action rules of the Marcus parser's grammar, since the implementation in the parser of these grammatical rules, and especially the principles, is often procedural rather than explicit. The successive steps in the formal derivation of the structural description(s) that an EST grammar for a natural language (e.g., English) associates with an arbitrary sentence of that language is *not* mirrored in the rule-governed computational operations of the parser that maps that same sentence onto its structural description(s). And the reason that these grammatical rules and principles are not directly implemented as the parser's grammar is not fortuitous. There are significant computational impediments to such an implementation, having chiefly to do with considerations of computational complexity (cf. Barton *et al.* 1987), all of which conspire to make the Right View, in all likelihood, computationally intractable and hence psychologically implausible.

Although the Marcus parser does not incorporate (in any usual sense of that word) an EST grammar for English, EST does bear an explanatorily transparent relation to the parsing theory that would have this parser as one of its models. By this I mean that the syntactic generalizations that are captured by means of the theoretical constructs of EST (e.g., rules, principles, and structures) are *explained* in terms of the organization and operation of the mechanisms postulated by the parsing theory. These generalizations are explained in the straightforward sense that one can see, for example, that the generalizations stated in an EST grammar for English would be true of a speaker who incorporated a Marcus parser (or, to put it another way, EST is true of all models of the parsing theory). Moreover, and more importantly, one can see *why* these generalizations would hold for such a speaker. In the version of EST that Marcus's theory satisfies, for example, passive constructions involve the application of a transformation rule ('Move NP') that moves a post-verbal NP into subject position, leaving a phonetically unrealized trace in the post-verbal position that is co-indexed with the moved NP. The Marcus parser builds the same EST-annotated surface structure, not by actually moving an NP from a post-verbal position but rather by creating an appropriately co-indexed trace in the post-verbal position after encountering a verb with passive morphology. If Marcus's theory of parsing were true of speakers, then that theory would provide a detailed explanation of why EST was true of them, too, since EST bears this explanatorily transparent relation to Marcus's theory.

The Right View (i.e., the Received View in this domain), it should be noted, claims that models of the correct parsing theory will bear an explanatorily transparent relation of a very particular sort to the grammar that correctly characterizes the speaker's linguistic knowledge: the parser for the language must include an explicit knowledge structure, i.e., a data structure, isomorphic to the grammar for the language parsed that as a minimum governs the operations that the parser's processor/interpreter performs on linguistic representations. This is a remarkable claim indeed, motivated it seems, not by empirical data or methodological considerations, but rather by general metaphysical speculations about the nature of propositional attitudes. At least Bresnan and Kaplan's strong competence hypothesis was motivated by quite specific methodological considerations: they wanted a methodological principle that would guarantee the pertinence of psycholinguistic experimental results, notably those involving measures of reaction time, to the problem of choosing between competing linguistic theories. The postulated isomorphism, they assumed, would guarantee the pertinence of such results.

Bresnan and Kaplan's methodological proposal was not new. Miller and Chomsky (1963: 481) proposed a similar competence hypothesis, arguing that if such an isomorphism held, then the psychological 'plausibility' of proposed grammars would be strengthened, since 'our performance on tasks requiring an appreciation of the structure of transformed sentences [would be] some function of the nature, number, and complexity of the grammatical transformations involved'. In fact, the task of bringing such psycholinguistic evidence to bear on grammatical theories is *not* so straightforward, even if the hypothesized isomorphism holds. Real time, as measured in reaction time experiments, need not bear any simple relation to 'algorithmic time', as measured by the number of steps executed in the course of a computation. In order to bring psycholinguistic evidence to bear on the evaluation of grammatical theories, Bresnan and Kaplan's strong competence hypothesis would have to be supplemented with a theory of human computational complexity that would relate real time to algorithmic time. Such a theory would minimally specify the computational architecture, the time and resource costs for primitive machine operations, and the implementation of the algorithm on that machine. But a theory of this sort is presently beyond reach: we know very little about the computational architecture that presumably supports language processing. We are not therefore in a position to use experimental evidence regarding language processing, even if the isomorphism postulated by Bresnan and Kaplan's strong competence hypothesis obtains.

Berwick and Weinberg (1984) argue persuasively that it is unlikely that models of a plausible parsing theory of natural language will be, or will incorporate, isomorphic realizations of the grammars of the languages they parse. They offer a number of different reasons why such parsing models are computationally infeasible, but the fundamental difficulty is that while a grammar may provide a recursive, intensional specification of the pairing of sounds and meanings (more correctly, sentences with their structural descriptions) that defines a given language, this specification does not specify a computable function that will take the first member of a given pair as its argument and deliver the second member of that pair as its value, and there is no simple way, indeed often no computationally efficient way at all, that a parser could use such a grammar to control its computational operations so as to map sounds into their associated meanings. Bresnan and Kaplan's strong competence hypothesis thus fails as a methodological principle, not simply for want of an understanding of human computational architecture that would enable us to apply the principle, but also because it seems doubtful that theories within its domain of application are even in principle capable of satisfying it.

It should be clear from the foregoing that there is no compelling reason, empirical, computational, or methodological, for believing that speakers incorporate an explicit representation of the linguistic knowledge that they access and use in the course of language production and understanding. The implementation relation that obtains between grammars and the parsers that implement them, or more generally between competence descriptions and so-called performance models, need not be, and almost certainly is not in fact, of the sort that proponents of the Right View (and hence the Received View) envision. All sorts of different implementation relations could obtain, and yet it still could be the case that the grammar is true of the speaker, i.e., has the speaker as a model. One can only speculate as to why proponents would have imagined that the implementation of the grammar would require its literal incorporation. Leaving aside simple naïveté regarding the implementation possibilities, encouraged perhaps by an a priori commitment to the Received View, two possible rationales suggest themselves. First, they may have taken literally the claim of Chomsky and others that language acquisition is a matter of 'internalizing' a grammar, in which case it would be rather implausible to suppose that this internalized grammar didn't play a role in language perception and production. One certainly would prefer not to be driven to the view of Fodor, Bever, and Garrett (1974: 370 ff.) according to which language acquisition involves the internalization of a grammar of the sort made available by linguistic theory, yet that internalized grammar is not used in language processing, which instead relies on certain heuristic procedures. Second, and this is the more important of the two possible rationales, proponents may have felt, as both Bresnan and Kaplan (1982) and Fodor (1981) clearly do, that any claims for the psychological reality of grammars depended on the truth of the Right View.

The claim that language acquisition involves the internalization of a grammar is of a piece with the claim that a model of language use will incorporate, as a basic component, a grammar for the language in question: both are claims to the effect that a certain description, viz., the description provided by the grammar, is true of the speaker. But neither entails any detailed description of the computational implementation in virtue of which this grammatical description is true of the speaker. Talk of internalizing a grammar, like talk of incorporating the grammar in a model of language processing, is simply a way of characterizing the linguistic competence acquired by a learner and subsequently exercised in language use, *though in a way that abstracts away from any implementation details*. Thus, for example, formal theories of language acquisition will often seek to establish learnability results for specified classes of grammars. Such results typically establish that an arbitrary grammar of the specified class can (or cannot) be acquired under certain specified conditions of access to data regarding the language that this grammar generates. Implementation details are typically irrelevant; hence the theories abstract away from them, treating language acquisition as simply a matter of acquiring a grammar. In circumstances where the implementation details are not irrelevant, for example, in cases where the acquisition account is paired with a parsing model, theorists may continue to talk in abstract terms of language acquisition as the internalization of a grammar; however, the grammar (or more correctly, an explicit representation thereof) will not figure in the story of the computational implementation of the acquisition account, except as a deliberate abstraction that serves to specify the linguistic competence that the computational model has to exhibit, viz., a competence for effecting the pairing of sentences with their structural descriptions specified by the grammar. Berwick's (1985) acquisition model for grammars of the sort made available by so-called Extended Standard Theory is a case in point: it acquires a version of the Marcus parser described above, not an explicit representation of the grammar that this parser implements. In the introductory explanation of his project, Berwick is quite explicit that there are two distinct levels of description of the acquisition process, one of which describes the process as the internalization or acquisition of a grammar (what David Marr, perhaps misleadingly, called 'the theory of the computation'), the other which describes it as the acquisition of the parser (what Marr called 'the theory of the algorithm'). Berwick's project, as he explains, is that of answering in computational terms, i.e., *at the level of algorithm*, how it is that children acquire language, i.e., 'internalize' a grammar. But the answer he provides at that level is not one that involves the internalization of the grammar that children are described, at the level of the theory of the computation, as acquiring. And the grammar that is so described is nowhere explicitly represented in the way proponents of the Received View imagine.

So here, then, is how things seem to stand with respect to the claim that psycholinguistics provides empirical support for the Received View of propositional attitudes. According to this view, if the linguistic knowledge characterized and specified by linguistic theory deserves the name, then it ought to be explicitly represented. But claims to the contrary by proponents of the Received View notwithstanding, there is no evidence that this linguistic knowledge is explicitly represented; certainly some of the better-known computational implementations of grammars made available by linguistic theory fail to incorporate an explicit representation of the grammar that they implement. Nor do there seem to be any principled grounds for thinking that linguistic knowledge must be so represented; indeed, there would seem to be important computational rationales for their not being explicitly represented. Nor does the proper construal of grammars as psychological hypotheses require it. Linguistic theory abstracts away from any architectural claims about the implementation of linguistic knowledge (see Matthews 1991b, 2006).

3.6. THE ARGUMENT FROM CENTRAL PROCESSING: THEORIES OF HUMAN REASONING

3.6.1. Knowledge of Language: Explaining Away the Potential Counterexamples

Faced with the prospect that what was long trumpeted as evidence for the Received View of propositional attitudes might turn out to be a counterexample, if as seems probable speakers' knowledge of grammar is not explicitly represented, some proponents of the view have concluded that what linguists claim to characterize by means of their grammars is not knowledge after all. Such 'knowledge', they argue, is localized in an informationally encapsulated input system, viz., the language faculty, and as such does not qualify as genuine knowledge. Propositional attitudes, they argue (following Stich 1978), are by their very nature inferentially 'promiscuous' in a way that the information encapsulated in input systems could never be. Only such information as is directly accessible to so-called 'central processes' is a plausible candidate for the contents of propositional attitudes. And such contents, these proponents of the Received View assure us, *are* explicitly represented.

A second sort of response, offered by Fodor (1987), concedes that the linguistic knowledge characterized by linguistic theory is indeed genuine knowledge, but denies that such knowledge constitutes a counterexample to the Received View despite not being explicitly represented. Such knowledge, Fodor claims, is of a piece with numerous other examples of non-explicitly represented propositional attitude contents, which, we are told, can be handled as 'derivative' in a way consistent with the Received View. This response, like the previous one, effectively abandons the claim that (psycho)linguistic theory provides empirical support for the Received View, but it does offer a general strategy for deflecting some of the numerous counterexamples that have been adduced against the Received View, namely, by treating these counterexamples as permissible exceptions.

In this section I shall focus on theories of what is presumably a kind of central processing, namely, theories of deductive inferential reasoning, which have recently been claimed to provide strong support for the Received View. In the following section I shall take up Fodor's proposed strategy of treating potential counterexamples to the Received View as a kind of permissible exception.

3.6.2. Central Processes

Central processes, as Fodor (1983) and other proponents of the Received View understand them, are the processes that 'people have in mind when they talk, pretheoretically, of such mental processes as thought and problem-solving' (ibid. 103). Very little is known about these largely unconscious processes, but they are assumed to be non-modular and domain-*in*specific.

To the extent that central processes are non-modular and domain-inspecific, the prospects for cognitive science, Fodor argues, are gloomy:

> The condition for successful science (in physics, by the way, as well as psychology) is that nature should have joints to carve it at: relatively simple subsystems which can be artificially isolated and which behave, in isolation, in something like the way that they behave *in situ*. Modules satisfy this condition; [the systems which incorporate central processes] by definition do not. If, as I have supposed, the central cognitive processes are nonmodular, that is very bad news for cognitive science.
>
> (Fodor 1983: 128)

Fodor believes this gloomy prognosis is borne out by the lack of results. Cognitive science, he claims (Fodor 1983: 38), has in fact made 'approximately no progress' in studying these central processes, and this lack of progress, he believes, is attributable to their non-modularity. We have no idea how, computationally speaking, the global structure of an entire system of belief might be brought to bear on individual occasions of belief fixation: 'if someone—a Dreyfus, for example—were to ask us why we should even suppose that the digital computer is a plausible mechanism for the simulation of global cognitive processes, the answering silence would be deafening' (ibid. 129).

If Fodor is right about the lack of progress in studying central processes, then the bad news for cognitive science is equally bad news for the Received View of propositional attitudes, since on the construal that we are scouting here, the Received View has central processes, specifically processes of thought and problem-solving, as its principal domain. Moreover, if central processes exhibit the isotropy and Quineian holism that Fodor takes to characterize them (ibid. 105 ff.), then the prospects for an empirical vindication of the Received View appear dim.

Not all proponents of the Received View share Fodor's gloomy pessimism. Braine and O'Brien (1998b) and Braine, O'Brien, *et al.* (1998) claim to find empirical support for the Received View in the theories of human reasoning, specifically of deductive reasoning, that have been developed over the last two decades. These researchers argue that for all their differences, theories of deductive reasoning, which are theories of an important aspect of central processing, share one important feature, viz., they all presume the Received View; and as such, their empirical successes provide indirect empirical support for the view.

I don't propose to challenge the underlying assumption here that the empirical successes of theories that presume a foundational view like the Received View would provide strong inductive support for the view. Nor do I propose to challenge the claimed empirical successes of theories of deductive reasoning. But I do want to challenge the assumption that these theories presume the Received View to a degree and in such a way that their successes, such as they are, provide any significant empirical support for the view.

3.6.3. Theories of Deductive Reasoning

Human thought exhibits a variety of different sorts of reasoning: deduction, induction, abduction, inference to the best explanation, analogy, association of ideas, and calculation, to mention only a few. Of these, deduction has, for several decades now, been the most studied. And understandably so, for not only is such reasoning central to many forms of human endeavor, most notably science and mathematics, but also this is the one sort of reasoning for which we have what would seem to be the beginnings of a precise formal characterization of the competence that reasoners exhibit when they reason deductively. The particular form that these characterizations take varies from theory to theory, but virtually in every case the characterization is inspired by one or another formal proof (or resolution) procedure drawn from deductive logic. In the 'mental logic' theories (e.g., Braine 1978; Braine and O'Brien 1998a; Johnson-Laird 1975; Rips 1983, 1994), the competence characterization takes the form of a specification of a set of formal rules of inference that pairs arbitrary sets of premises with their valid conclusions. In other theories (e.g., Cheng and Holyoak 1985, Cosmides 1989, Holyoak and Cheng 1995), the characterization takes the form of a specification of a set of content-specific rules of inference that pairs sets of premises with their content-appropriate conclusions. In the so-called 'mental model' theory

champione by Philip Johnson-Laird (Johnson-Laird 1983; Johnson-Laird
and Byrne 1991, 1993), the competence characterization takes the form of
a specification of a resolution procedure for constructing models consistent
with the premises and then using these models to draw certain conclusions.

The characterizations that these theories propose of the deductive competence exhibited by reasoners is the centerpiece of these theories, not simply
because in the absence of such a characterization one has no characterization
of what the theory is a theory of, but also because these theories are essentially
theories of deductive *competence*. That is to say, these theories are concerned
almost exclusively with the question of what is it that reasoners know and the
molar cognitive capacities that they possess, in virtue of which they are able
to reason deductively, able to recognize valid and invalid conclusions, prone
to certain characteristic errors in deductive reasoning, likely to find certain
sorts of inferences difficult, and so on. To be sure, proponents tend not to
advertise their theories as simply competence theories. Rather they present
their theories as *partial* accounts of the mental processes and mechanisms
that underlie deductive competence. In a manner very reminiscent of both
Bresnan and Kaplan's strong competence hypothesis and Fodor's so-called
Right View in psycholinguistics (cf. pp. 57–63 above), the explanations
offered by these various theories of the deductive competence of reasoners
often literally incorporate within their model of the reasoner the formal logic,
the set of meaning postulates, or the model-theoretic scheme upon which
their characterization of the reasoner's competence is based. Reasoners are
said to *use*, albeit unconsciously, these inference rules, postulates, or models
in a computational reasoning process that takes the reasoner from premises
to conclusion. Proponents of these theories recognize that the logic, meaning
postulates, or models cannot alone be the whole account, since from a given
set of premises there will on any of these accounts be any number of valid
conclusions that are not drawn, and in some cases any number of invalid
conclusions that might be drawn. Nevertheless, the incorporated set of inference rules, model scheme, etc. are said to constitute a major 'component' of
the underlying computational mental mechanism that the reasoner recruits
in the course of deductive reasoning.

Martin Braine's well-known 1978 paper is representative of the claims
made on behalf of these competence theories of deductive reasoning. As
Braine introduces it, the paper is concerned to provide a formal logic for
propositional reasoning, one that will specify the set of inference rules
(what Braine calls 'inference rule schemata') used in such reasoning. Braine's

description of the proposed logic is worth quoting at some length, because although, like Chomsky, he does not regard specification of the logic as tantamount to providing a processing model of propositional reasoning, it is clear that he does assume that such a model will incorporate the logic as a component:

The logic defines only the vocabulary of deductive steps available to the reasoner, it is not a process theory and does not itself generate a proof or a connected chain of reasoning. Thus, in addition to the logic, a complete model requires a comprehension mechanism, a mechanism for selecting from the vocabulary of deductive steps the one that is used at each point in the reasoning, heuristics for planning an argument . . . , and some definition of the amount of short-term memory or 'computing space,' available to the reasoner . . . . However, these other components are, for the most part, characteristic also of other behaviors than deductive reasoning, so there is a sense in which the logic can be said to be the quintessential component. Nevertheless, predictions from a logical model to behavior will always require processing assumptions in addition to the logic.

(Braine 1978: 4)

Braine's supposition that the computational mechanisms defined over the logic, as well as the computational resources exploited by these mechanisms, are also recruited in the production of other behaviors underscores the theoretical double duty that the logic is assumed to serve: it is assumed to characterize both the competence exhibited by subjects in the course of deductive reasoning, i.e., what reasoners know about the pairing of premise sets with conclusions, as well as the distinctive component of the cognitive computational mechanisms that underlie this competence.

Of course, there is a sense in which the competence characterization *does* provide a characterization of the underlying computational cognitive processes, namely, it specifies the pairing of sets of premises and conclusions effected by the reasoner in his deductive reasoning. Such a characterization does not specify the function (or functions) actually computed by a reasoner in the course of deductive reasoning, since any given set of hypothesized inference rules does not pair any given set of premises with a unique conclusion—the mapping is one-many. Rather the characterization specifies a constraint on this function (or functions), viz., that it map a given set of premises into a member of the set of accessible conclusions that the characterization pairs with the given set of premises. The competence characterization does not specify how, i.e., does not specify the mechanisms by which, reasoners go about effecting the pairing in question. It does not even specify the particular conclusion that a reasoner will, in a specific context, pair with a set of premises. The characterization abstracts away from all such details. Of course, it might turn out, *per mirabile* (i.e., despite the computational implausibility of the proposal), that the computational cognitive processes underlying subjects' deductive competence do in fact incorporate an isomorph of the theorist's competence characterization. In such a case, the competence characterization would indeed do the double duty that Braine and others imagine, but certainly there is no a priori reason for supposing this to be the case. The obvious question here is whether there are any empirical reasons either, since in the absence of such reasons, the Received View would enjoy no more support from competence theories of human reasoning than it does from competence theories in (psycho)linguistics.

In assessing the empirical support provided the Received View by current theories of deductive reasoning, I shall focus on mental logic theories as they are arguably the best candidates to provide such support, inasmuch as the postulated rules of the mental logic are taken to operate over mental sentences that express the contents of subjects' propositional attitudes. As Braine, O'Brien, *et al.* (1998) put it, 'A mental-logic theory is a specific elaboration of the "language of thought" hypothesis (Fodor, 1975) in that its representations would be representations in the language of thought and their syntax a proposal about an aspect of the language of thought' (194). Mental logic theorists, moreover, are quite explicit in their assumption that the representations in question here are Representations, i.e., representations of the contents of propositional attitudes. O'Brien (1998), for example, emphasizes that 'Logical reasoning consists of propositional activities. Propositions are proposed, supposed, assumed, considered, claimed, believed, disbelieved, doubted, asserted, denied, inferred, and so forth . . . . Such propositional activities concern intentional states of affairs' (O'Brien 1998: 25–6). But this, I take it, is just to say that logical reasoning is defined over propositional attitudes, or at least over Representations of their contents.

3.6.4. Mental Logic Theories of Deductive Reasoning

Mental logic theories conceive of human reasoning as proof-theoretic in character, i.e., as a matter of inferring conclusions from premises by means of certain inference rules or schemas. These theories construe the proof procedures that apply these rules as purely formal, so that, as Bonatti

(1998: 16) puts it, 'a thinking process can be seen as a set of transformations on symbols according to rules exploiting a high-level concrete property of the symbols—their shape'. Mental logic theories characteristically consist of three components: (i) *a mental logic*, i.e., a set of inference schemas, which provides an inventory of the logical inferences that subjects routinely make; (ii) *a reasoning procedure*, which specifies how subjects employ, or might employ, the schemas in a line of reasoning; and (iii) *a pragmatic component*, which specifies how the mental logic, along with its reasoning procedure, is recruited by subjects in the course of various reasoning and comprehension tasks. Theories can diverge with respect to each of these components, though differences with respect to the postulated set of inference schemas are most salient inasmuch as this component has until now been the primary focus of all mental logic theories. Thus, for example, Rips (1983, 1994) includes within his set of basic inference schemas for mental propositional logic the rule of disjunction introduction, viz., 'p; therefore, p or q', that undergraduate logic students find so counterintuitive, whereas Braine (1978) and Braine and O'Brien (1998c) do not. Braine similarly includes within his postulated set of inference schemas certain schemas not included by Rips in his. The upshot for their respective characterizations of deductive competence is that while both mental logic systems sanction only valid inferences, they differ in the set of inference schemas that they each postulate; consequently, they do not necessarily assign the same proofs to those complex inferences that they both sanction.

The set of basic inference schemas for mental propositional logic, hypothesized by Braine and his collaborators, includes 'core schemas', 'feeder schemas', 'incompatibility schemas', and a number of complex schemas that are employed in indirect-reasoning procedures. Core schemas, which include both introduction and elimination schemas, are applied automatically through a direct-reasoning procedure whenever the appropriate antecedents of the schema are present, whereas feeder schemas, which also include both introduction and elimination schemas, are invoked only when needed to achieve an antecedently specified inference goal.

The reasoning procedure postulated by Rips (1983), by contrast, requires that *all* reasoning proceed towards an antecedently specified inference goal (or subgoal). The postulated set of inference schemas reflects the goal-directed character of the reasoning procedure: there are two classes of schemas, forward and backward. Forward schemas, as the name suggests, extend the premise set in the direction of defined inference goals, while backward schemas construct inference subgoals, which if achieved, will lead to the desired inference goals. This 'outside-in' reasoning procedure, which works alternately forward from the premises and backward from the conclusion, implements a proof procedure common to the AI theorem provers such as PLANNER on which it is based. The basic motivation for adopting such a goal-directed reasoning procedure is processing efficiency: subgoals constrain the procedure's inferences to ones that carry the reasoner towards the desired conclusion. But the psychological plausibility of such a procedure is open to challenge, since in the absence of a conclusion to be validated, Rips' (1983) model will generally draw no inferences from a set of premises. In Rips (1994), the requirement that inferences be goal-directed has been relaxed, with the effect that the revised reasoning procedure is much more similar to that of Braine and his collaborators.

Despite their differences, proposed mental logic theories have much in common. There is substantial agreement both on explanatory goals of a theory of deductive reasoning and on the broad explanatory framework within which such a theory should be articulated. Thus, most theorists would agree that a theory of deductive reasoning should account for the deductive inferences that subjects regularly and routinely make, correctly predicting which inference problems subjects solve correctly and which they solve incorrectly. Many would also agree that such a theory should predict both subjects' response times on simple inference problems and their judgments about relative problem difficulty. This agreement on explanatory goals and framework extends well beyond the central conception of deductive reasoning as proof-theoretic in character. There are striking similarities among proposed mental logic theories, not simply in the details of their universal tripartite structure, but also in the explanatory division of labor that these theories impose on that structure: the explanation of correct inferences rests largely on the postulated set of inference schemas and reasoning procedures, whereas the explanation of incorrect, fallacious inferences rests crucially on the pragmatic component, specifically on various performance failures or environmental effects that allegedly corrupt an otherwise logically perfect system of reasoning. Subjects, for example, will sometimes commit the so-called fallacy of denying the antecedent, but not because they have within their set of inference schemas an invalid schema of the sort: '*if p, then q*, and *not p*; therefore *not q*'. Subjects, it is presumed, are logically competent. In circumstances where subjects are prone to fall victim to this fallacy, subjects are said to have been 'invited', by pragmatic considerations, to construe the asserted conditional 'if p, then q' as the biconditional 'q if and only if p' (as, for example, would usually be the case when someone tells you, 'if you mow my lawn, I'll pay you $15').[18] The pragmatic component thus explains not only how the other two components are recruited in reasoning and comprehension tasks, but also why logically competent subjects are nonetheless prone to certain characteristic pragmatic errors in their logical reasoning.

Proponents of mental logic theories claim that their theories enjoy significant empirical support. The theories, it is claimed, correctly predict a wide range of expressions of subjects' deductive competence in propositional reasoning tasks. Thus, for example, Braine and his collaborators claim that their proposed model correctly predicts (i) which inference problems subjects solve correctly, (ii) response times on simple problems, and (iii) subjects' judgments about relative problem difficulty. The details of the experimental studies reported in Braine, Reiser, and Rumain (1998) and Braine, O'Brien, *et al.* (1998) are not important here, but basically they claim to have established experimentally two things: first, that the set of inference schemas postulated by their model correctly inventories the kind of valid inferences made by subjects, and second that a problem complexity measure defined on this set of inference schemas, viz., one that uses the sum of the difficulty weights of the inferential steps needed to solve a problem coupled with a measure of the difficulty attributable to problem length alone, correctly predicts both response latency and reported relative difficulty. Thus, Braine, Reiser, and Rumain (1998) conclude,

Correlations ranged up to. 95, for the joint prediction of rated difficulty from the weighted-sum index combined with problem length. There were high correlations with both errors and rated difficulty that were independent of problem length. These relationships make a case that in solving these problems, subjects do in fact go through the mental steps that the theory claims that they do, and thus that the schemas of [the model] are a psychological reality.

(Braine, Reiser, and Rumain 1998: 121)

Braine and his collaborators (in Braine, O'Brien, *et al.* 1998) claim that their model also correctly predicts (iv) subjects' reported intermediate inferences in the course of a complex deduction (both the conclusions of these intermediate inferences and their order) as well as multiple conclusions in the case of problems in which only premises were given.

---

[18] See O'Brien 1998: 31–2 for a discussion of 'invited' inference.

The claims made by Braine and his collaborators in support of their model, it should be noticed, focus almost exclusively on *successful* exercises of deductive competence. Relatively little is said about the model's predictions regarding inference problems on which subjects are prone to error. This is not surprising. Mental logic theories, as Braine, Reiser, and Rumain (1998: 93–4) explain, allow basically three sorts of reasoning errors: *comprehension errors*, which involve a misconstrual of the premises or conclusion of an argument; *heuristic inadequacy errors*, which occur when a subject's reasoning program fails to find a line of reasoning that solves a problem; and *processing errors*, which comprise lapses of attention, errors of execution in the application of schemas, and so on. The burden of predicting and explaining comprehension and heuristic inadequacy errors falls largely on the so-called pragmatic component of the model, but this component remains largely unspecified. The burden of predicting and explaining processing errors falls largely on the model's account of the reasoning process, what O'Brien calls the reasoning program, but this component, like the pragmatic component, also remains so underspecified as not to be able to generate the sorts of predictions and explanations that any satisfactory account would demand. As O'Brien (1998: 30) notes, 'relative to the schemas, little empirical work has been done on the reasoning program, but the need for further investigation of how the inference schemas are implemented becomes apparent a fortiori with the realization that lack of sophistication [on the part of subjects] in using the reasoning program is a principal source of reasoning errors'.

3.6.5. Do Mental Logic Theories Provide Any Support for the Received View?

Mental logic theories are, as Braine, O'Brien, *et al.* (1998: 194) claim, a specific elaboration of central elements of the Received View within the domain of human deductive reasoning. In particular, these theories presuppose and elaborate the notion that thinking is a proof-theoretic activity in which mental sentences (of a language of thought), which represent the contents of a subject's propositional attitudes, are manipulated and transformed in accordance with certain formal rules of inference. As such, mental logic theories will confer upon the Received View, within their specific domain, whatever empirical support they themselves enjoy. At least they will confer empirical support upon the Received View to the extent that this support bears on features of these theories that elaborate the Received View.

So to determine the support that these theories provide to the Received View, we would have to determine (i) whether these theories enjoy the empirical support claimed for them, and (ii) the extent to which this support, such as it is, bears on the specific aspects of these theories that elaborate the Received View. I shall not challenge the experimental findings that mental logic theorists present in support of their theories. Rather I shall simply accept these findings and then ask whether these findings, thus accepted, provide the empirical support claimed for these theories, and by extension for the Received View. The empirical support, I argue, is considerably more modest than proponents claim.

Braine, Reiser, and Rumain (1998) and Braine, O'Brien, *et al.* (1998), it will be recalled, claim that their proposed mental logic model of propositional deductive reasoning correctly predicts (i) which inference problems subjects solve correctly, (ii) subjects' response times on these problems, (iii) their judgments about relative problem difficulty, and (iv) their reports of intermediate inferences made in the course of complex deductions (both the conclusions of these intermediate inferences and their order) as well as their reports of multiple conclusions in the case of problems in which only premises were given. Braine, Reiser, and Rumain (1998: 121) conclude from the fact that their proposed model correctly predicts these data that in solving inference problems, subjects actually go through the 'mental steps' that their mental logic theory postulates, and hence that the inference schemas postulated by their theory are 'psychologically real'.

But of the four sorts of prediction that Braine and his collaborators claim to have confirmed, only the last three could possibly provide any support whatever for this conclusion. The fact that their model predicts the pairing of premise sets and conclusions effected by subjects in the course of deductive reasoning says nothing about how subjects actually go about effecting this pairing. Specifically, it says nothing about what function (or functions) reasoners compute in effecting this pairing, much less how reasoners go about computing whatever function (or functions) they do. And because the functions that are computed can, consistent with the competence characterization, be computed in any number of ways, and by means of any number of different computational architectures, any support for the conclusion that Braine and his collaborators would draw regarding the computational processes that underlie deductive competence, and hence for the Received View, will have to come from the last three sorts of prediction that they claim to have confirmed.

There is no reason to suppose that Braine and his collaborators would disagree with my construal of the import of their claimed confirmation of predictions of the first sort. But this is not to say that the confirmation of such predictions is of no theoretical significance. Developing a specification of the pairing of premise sets with conclusions that reasoners effect in the course of deductive reasoning is of crucial importance to the development of a computational processing account of deductive reasoning, since in the absence of such a specification, theorists are hardly in a position even to speculate about the function(s) computed by reasoners in the course of deductive reasoning, much less about the computational mechanisms that reasoners might employ to compute the functions that they do. Nor is the task of providing the needed specification a trivial task, any more than is the analogous task in linguistics of constructing an empirically adequate grammar for one or another natural language. Not surprisingly, there continues to be substantial disagreement over the proper specification of subjects' deductive competence, with proponents of different theories such as Braine and his collaborators expending considerable effort comparing and evaluating different specifications-in-intension of subjects' deductive competence.

But if the confirmation of predictions of the first sort do not provide empirical support for the conclusion that (i) subjects go through the mental steps that their model claims and hence (ii) the postulated inference schemas are psychologically real, it is not clear that confirmation of the three other sorts of prediction, most especially of subjects' response times to problems and subjects' reports of relative problem difficulty, does any better. For what remains crucially unclear is just how, independently of specific assumptions about computational cognitive architecture, empirical data about response time and relative problem difficulty could possibly be brought to bear on questions of the psychological reality of the postulated inferences schemas. Arguably it cannot.[19]

The predictions of relative problem difficulty and response time reported by Braine, Reiser, and Rumain (1998) for their model are based on a problem complexity measure (PCM, for short) defined in terms of (i) problem length, measured by the total number of words in the premises and the conclusion, and (ii) the sum of the difficulty weights of the specific inference schemas that subjects are hypothesized to use at each step in the reasoning process that they go through in the course of solving a particular reasoning problem:

---

[19] See Berwick and Weinberg 1984 for a discussion of similar questions in the domain of language processing.

(PCM) Problem Complexity = .4176 + .0728(number of words)
         + Σ(difficulty weights of the schemas used)

The difficulty weight for each individual schema is determined by having subjects rank, on a scale from 1 to 5, the difficulty of simple inference problems that involve only that schema. Predictions of the relative difficulty of complex inference problems are constructed using PCM. In effect, they are predictions that relative problem difficulty will compose for complex inference problems in the additive manner specified by PCM. The predictions of relative response time are predictions to the effect that subjects' response to complex inference problems will similarly exhibit a relative latency that composes in the additive manner specified by PCM.

The reported correlations between predicted and observed relative problem difficulty are very high, especially when problem length is factored out. The reported correlations for relative response time are not quite as dramatic, but they are nonetheless impressive when one considers that the latencies involved are often on the order of seconds, an order of magnitude for which psychometric latency measures are typically quite unreliable. The obvious question here is whether there is any reason to credit these reported correlations as confirmatory of the theory, when that theory is understood as a theory of the computational cognitive processes that constitute a reasoner's inferential competence. The fundamental issue, which, as far as I can determine, is never addressed directly by Braine and his collaborators, is whether PCM is entailed, or even motivated, by their theory of mental logic. It is hard to see how it could be, at least not in the absence of quite specific assumptions about cognitive computational architecture. But if it is not, then the reported correlations provide no direct empirical support for the theory and hence no indirect empirical support for the Received View. The point here is simply this: there is no reason to take confirmation of PCM to provide empirical support for the model unless the model predicts that relative problem difficulty and relative response time will compose in a manner specified by PCM.

There seem as well to be serious difficulties with the processing story itself. Braine, Reiser, and Rumain (1998: 125) assume that subjects employ a direct reasoning routine in solving complex inference problems whose relative difficulty and response latency are predicted by PCM. This routine matches the premises of the problem (plus the antecedent of the conclusion, when the conclusion takes the form of an *if–then* statement) with the antecedents of the postulated inferences schemas and applies any of the schemas that fit. If the conclusion is not reached, the routine is repeated on the newly created problem that consists of the original premises plus the new proposition produced by applying the schema.[20] Crucially, Braine, Reiser, and Rumain (1998: 125) assume that in solving problems by means of this postulated direct reasoning routine, subjects 'find the shortest solutions . . . without getting lost in blind alleys'. This assumption is crucial to the claimed empirical support for the theory, because without it there would be no rationale whatever for adopting the proposed additive measure of problem complexity, which assumes that problem complexity is a function of the sum of the difficulty weights of the inference schemas that would figure in this shortest solution. But how, one must wonder, does PCM succeed in predicting relative problem difficulty or response latency, given that it does *not* include any measure of the difficulty or time required to find this shortest solution?

One can concoct a number of possible answers to this question, but none, it would seem, succeeds in salvaging Braine, Reiser, and Rumain's (1998: 121) conclusion that their experimental findings 'make a case that in solving these problems, subjects do in fact go through the mental steps that the theory claims that they do, and thus that the schemas of [the model] are a psychological reality'. One possible answer, for example, is that the difficulty or time required to find the shortest solution is constant across all problems and thus is not reflected in a measure of relative difficulty or response time. But if this is the case, the obvious next question would be why, then, would the number of reasoning steps along the shortest solution be predictive? After all, if subjects find the shortest solution (and hence, a fortiori, find the solution!) in constant time, why should there be the relative differences across problems that PCM predicts and the theory claims to explain? Surely it is implausible to suppose that subjects, having found the solution in the course of finding the shortest solution, proceed to compute the shortest solution yet a second time and in such a way as to confirm the predictions of PCM. Now maybe, contrary to what we were just assuming, there are in fact differences in difficulty or time required to find the shortest solution (and hence, a fortiori the solution), and these differences are precisely what the proposed PCM predicts. Surely it is no less plausible to suppose that a complexity measure defined over the reasoning steps that supposedly constitute the shortest path would predict the relative difficulty and response time required to find that

---

[20] In the event that the repeated application of this direct reasoning routine fails to produce the desired conclusion, certain indirect reasoning routines are available. Problems whose solution requires such indirect reasoning routines were not included in the reported experiments.

shortest path. But even if, *per mirabile*, it did, and this is the important point here, there would still be no reason whatever to suppose that the postulated reasoning steps are psychologically real in the sense of specifying steps in a procedure that subjects execute.

The conclusion that I am arguing for here is not that PCM rests upon an implausible account of deductive reasoning processes, although arguably this is the case; rather it is that in the absence of a detailed explanation of how the complexity measure is entailed or motivated by the proposed mental logic theory, the claimed predictive successes of the measure provide no support whatever either for the proposed theory or for the Received View. Braine and his collaborators are unable to provide the needed theoretical motivation for PCM because their account of deductive reasoning processes is woefully underspecified. They have, so far as I know, no account of how subjects might go about finding the shortest solution to an inference problem or how, finding such a solution, that solution is utilized by subjects in a way that would lend the complexity measure diagnostic powers. Nothing short of a fairly detailed computational model of these reasoning processes, one grounded in empirically justified assumptions regarding computational architectures and resources recruited in the course of deductive reasoning, would provide the needed theoretical motivation. But such a model is presently beyond our grasp, precisely because we know virtually nothing about available architectures and resources, e.g., about available primitive computational operations, about the time and resource costs for such operations. Without such knowledge, mental logic theorists can offer only ungrounded speculations about the theoretical import of their findings regarding relative problem difficulty and response time.

There is more than a little '*déjà vu* all over again' in the claims of mental logic theorists to find experimental support for their claim that subjects, in their deductive reasoning, go through a series of steps wherein they employ the postulated inference schemas and hence that these schemas are psychologically real. In the 1960s, many psycholinguists embraced the so-called Derivational Theory of Complexity (DTC) according to which the rules of then proposed transformational grammars figured in sentence processing and thus were psychologically real.[21] The similarities between the claims made on behalf of the DTC and those made on behalf of mental logic theory are striking. Like Braine and his collaborators, psycholinguists who defended the DTC were proposing a processing interpretation of a competence theory, specifically a

---

[21] For discussion and criticism of the DTC and its claimed experimental support, see Fodor, Bever, and Garrett 1974 and Berwick and Weinberg 1984.

theory of linguistic competence. They claimed to find empirical support for the DTC in experiments of a sort very similar to the ones that are claimed by Braine and his collaborators to provide support for the psychological reality of the postulated inference schemas. These claims were challenged, and eventually discredited, on a number of different grounds, including the one that I have raised against mental logic theory's claim to provide empirical support for the Received View: namely, the DTC offered no sufficiently well-specified, empirically grounded computational model of sentence processing that might establish the relevance of the experimental findings to the DTC's proposed processing interpretation of grammars. Like PCM, the DTC's proposed measure of derivative complexity remained theoretically unmotivated, so that empirical support for the measure could provide no support for the proposed processing interpretation of grammars.

Mental logic theories are going to require considerable elaboration, specifically as regards their accounts of reasoning processes, if these are to generate empirical predictions of the sort envisioned by Braine and his collaborators. Only then will these theories be in a position to provide any empirical support for the Received View. But at present this much seems clear: whatever their merits as theories of human deductive competence, theories of the sort scouted here currently provide no obvious empirical support for the Received View.

3.6.6. A Concluding Remark

In surveying these three different sorts of empirical argument for the Received View, viz., the argument from behavior, the argument from linguistic knowledge, and the argument from theories of deductive reasoning, I don't claim to have established that the Received View, particularly the Received View of propositional attitudes, enjoys no empirical support. Three examples hardly exhaust the empirical literature. But I do think I've said enough to suggest that the claimed support for the Received View might be considerably exaggerated. At the very least, one should be struck by how little detailed empirical argument proponents of the Received View have offered in support of their claim that the view enjoys strong empirical support.

3.7. EXPLAINING AWAY APPARENT COUNTEREXAMPLES: FODOR'S WAY

Fodor, we noted earlier, is prepared to grant that the linguistic 'knowledge' attributed to speakers by linguistic theory could be genuine knowledge even if it were not explicitly represented by speakers; but he denies that such knowledge would constitute a counterexample to the Received View. Such knowledge, he argues, is of a piece with numerous other examples of propositional attitudes whose contents are not explicitly represented, all of which can be handled in a manner consistent with the Received View. This response, if successful, offers a way of deflecting some of the numerous counterexamples that have been adduced against the Received View by treating them as permissible exceptions.

Fodor (1987) insists that the Received View of propositional attitudes, what he calls the 'Representational Theory of Mind' (hereafter, the RTM), enjoys empirical support from cognitive science, but he concedes (ibid. 20) that the view needs a bit of 'polishing' if it is to survive certain well-known objections. The polishing that he proposes involves reformulating the view in a way that effectively restricts it to *occurrent* propositional attitudes. As Fodor presents it, the RTM consists of two claims, the first of which is precisely tenet (v) of the Received View, the second of which is a version of tenet (vi):

Claim 1 (the nature of propositional attitudes):
For any organism O, and any attitude A towards the proposition P, there is a ('computational'/'functional') relation R and a mental representation MP such that MP means that P, and O has A [to P] iff O bears R to MP.

Claim 2 (the nature of mental processes):
Mental processes are causal sequences of tokenings of mental representations.[22]

(Fodor 1987: 17)

Fodor describes Claim 1 as requiring both that 'for each tokening of a propositional attitude, there is a tokening of a corresponding computational relation between an organism and a mental representation, and that for each tokening of that relation, there is a tokening of a corresponding propositional attitude' (ibid. 20), where by 'tokening' here he seems to mean simply the having of (and, in the case of mental representations, also being able to use) whatever is tokened. Fodor concedes that the equivalence fails in both directions: there are cases of attitude tokenings without corresponding relation tokenings, and there are cases of relation tokenings without corresponding attitude tokenings. Cases of the second sort present little difficulty for the

---

[22] Thus, according to this second claim, a train of thought is 'a causal sequence of tokenings of mental representations which express the propositions that are the objects of the thoughts' (Fodor 1987: 17).

Received View, since, as Fodor points out, there is no reason to suppose that the common-sense psychological inventory of propositional attitudes is exhaustive. Faced with a case of this sort, proponents of the Received View can simply coin a corresponding attitude (cf., for example, Chomsky's 'cognize', the propositional attitude that native speakers are said to bear to the grammatical rules of their language). Cases of the first sort, however, do present a challenge. As an example of such a case, Fodor cites Dennett's (1977 [1981]: 107) example of a chess-playing program that we might describe as 'thinking that it should get its Queen out early'. In the program that Dennett describes, there are many levels of explicit representation, but at none of these levels is there anything explicitly tokened that is even roughly synonymous with the English sentence 'I must get my Queen out early'.

Cognitive science is replete with examples similar to Dennett's. Consider, for example, Shimon Ullman's (1979) computational theory of the human visual system's ability to recover the three-dimensional structure of rigid objects from two-dimensional retinal projections of their motion through space. Ullman (1979: 146) explains the visual system's ability to recover structure from motion in terms of a constraint on that system's interpretation of two-dimensional motion that he dubs the 'rigidity assumption'. The visual system, he says, is able to recover structure from motion, because it *assumes* that 'any set of elements undergoing a two-dimensional transformation which has a unique interpretation as a rigid body moving in space should be interpreted as such a body in motion' (ibid.). Yet this assumption, which figures crucially in Ullman's informal, propositional attitude explanation of the recovery of structure from motion, is nowhere explicitly represented in Ullman's computational model. Rather, as Ullman explains, the visual system is counted as assuming what he claims it assumes, inasmuch as (i) the output of the postulated structure-from-motion algorithm is veridical only if the objects viewed are in fact rigid under translation, and (ii) the visual system accepts as veridical any and all outputs of the algorithm. Cases such as this are ubiquitous, because in virtually every computational model of one or another cognitive process or human capacity, some of the propositional attitudes that researchers would plausibly attribute to its possessor as part of an informal explanation of that subject's behavior will not be explicitly represented anywhere in the model. Sometimes the attributed attitude will be implemented procedurally, often because computational considerations (e.g., efficiency, resource availability, theoretical preference for known algorithms) militate against the explicit representation of the contents of these attitudes.

Such is the case, for example, in the Marcus parser's implementation of certain universal constraints that linguists hypothesize speakers know innately (see pp. 59–60 above). In other cases, such as Ullman's rigidity assumption, the attributed attitude will not be implemented at all, inasmuch as the attributed attitude represents a real-world constraint that computational cognitive processes have evolved to exploit (in Ullman's case, the fact that most objects in the our world are rigid under translation). In these cases a cognitive system (or individual) counts as having the propositional attitude simply in virtue of having a functional design whose successful operation depends on the system's environment being a particular way.

Dennett takes his proposed counterexample to show that claim (1) of the RTM (p. 85 above) is false, since a subject can have a propositional attitude, viz., think it should get its Queen out early, without having any explicit Representation of the content of that attitude to which this subject could be said to bear a computational relation. Fodor, by contrast, takes Dennett's example to show, not that the RTM is false, but that it needs to be reformulated to apply only to certain 'core cases', specifically to propositional attitudes that are episodes in mental processes:

According to claim 2, mental processes are causal sequences of transformations of mental representations. It follows that tokens of attitudes *must* correspond to tokenings of mental representations when they—the attitude tokenings—are episodes in mental processes. If the intentional objects of such attitudes are *not* explicitly represented, then RTM is simply false. I repeat for emphasis: if the occurrence of a thought is an episode in a mental process, then RTM is committed to the explicit representation of its content. The motto is therefore No Intentional Causation without Explicit Representation.

Notice that this way of choosing core cases squares us with the alleged counterexamples.... Roughly: According to RTM, programs—corresponding to the 'laws of thought'—*may* be explicitly represented; but 'data structures'—corresponding to the contents of thoughts—*have to be.*

(Fodor 1987: 24–5)

From this it follows, quite plausibly, that '*none* of the principles in accordance with which a computational system operates needs be explicitly represented by a formula tokened in the device; there is no guarantee that the program of the machine will be explicitly represented in the machine whose program it is' (ibid. 22–3). So it is not a counterexample that it is true to say of Dennett's chess program that it thinks that it should always get its Queen out early, since this thought is not an 'episode' in the mental processes of the machine; rather it is one of the 'laws of thought'—part of the program—that governs the program's chess play. But, Fodor insists, 'the representations of the board—of actual or possible states of play—over which the machine's computations are defined *must* be [explicitly represented], precisely *because* the machine's computations are defined over them' (ibid. 25). These computations over successive representations of the board, says Fodor, 'constitute the machine's "mental processes", so either they are causal sequences of explicit representations, or the representational theory of chess playing is simply false of the machine' (ibid.).

Fodor's proposed polishing of the RTM effectively concedes Dennett's basic point, which is that a subject can have a propositional attitude without having what the unpolished RTM and the Received View require, namely, an explicit representation of the propositional content of that attitude. Fodor attempts to parry Dennett's objection and salvage the RTM by distinguishing between 'core cases' of attitude tokenings whose contents must be explicitly represented and 'derivative cases' of attitude tokenings whose contents do not have to be so represented, because they are not 'episodes' of thought. But there is an obvious difficulty with this proposed way around Dennett's counterexample. Fodor's defense of the RTM and the Received View is purchased only at the price of having to concede that the view provides no account whatever of what he calls 'derivative' cases of propositional attitude attribution, despite the fact that such cases are *ubiquitous* in propositional attitude explanations of behavior. This is no small price to pay. Dennett's chess program, for example, is said to play chess in the way that it does *because* it thinks that it must get its Queen out early; yet because that thought is not explicitly represented within the program, the Received View provides no account of the explanatory role of that particular thought attribution in a propositional attitude explanation of the program's chess play. And similarly, too, for Ullman's rigidity assumption: Ullman describes the visual system as being able to effect the recovery of structure from motion *because* it assumes rigidity. But the Received View provides no account of the explanatory role of that assumption in Ullman's propositional attitude explanation of the recovery of structure from motion. The explicit representation of the contents of propositional attitudes was supposed to explain both the causal and intentional properties of propositional attitudes, but with this proposed polishing of the view, we are left with a very large number of propositional attitudes, the so-called 'derivative' cases, for whose causal and intentional properties we are offered no explanation whatever. If the goal of the

Received View of propositional attitudes is, as Fodor claims, to establish the materialistic *bona fides* of propositional attitudes, and hence of propositional attitude explanations, the proposed polishing of the view must be judged a failure, since the *bona fides* of these derivative cases has not been established.

It is important to be clear that we are offered no account of the sense in which these 'derivative' cases are derivative. Talk of 'core' and 'derivative' cases suggests that the latter are somehow *derivable* from the former, perhaps in the way that some proponents of the Received View assume that so-called 'tacit beliefs' are derivable from a set of explicitly represented 'core' beliefs (see pp. 45–6 above). But the issue here has nothing to do with the closure of belief sets under various operations. One cannot derive Dennett's chess program's thought that it should get its Queen out early from its episodic beliefs during chess play about board configurations. We can, to be sure, infer this thought from the observed play of the chess program, but such behavior arises out of beliefs *both* about how to play the game *and* about current board configurations, not out of beliefs about board configurations alone. The chess program, and the principles upon which it operates, contribute something that the 'data structures' over which the program operates cannot. So whatever the sense in which the 'derivative' cases are derivative, it is not that they are derived from the core cases and thus can be said to have their causal and intentional properties derivatively from core cases.

So to recap the foregoing: there are clear examples in which it is plausible to attribute to the possessors of certain cognitive capacities specific propositional attitudes (e.g., knowing a grammar for a language, assuming that objects are rigid under translation), but in which, judging from computational theories of these capacities, the contents of these attitudes are *not* explicitly represented as the Received View requires. Proponents of the Received View can reformulate the view in such a way that it applies only to those propositional attitudes the contents of which might be held by computational theories to be explicitly represented, but the price of such a reformulation is to lack any account of the causal and intentional properties of those attitudes which are no longer subsumed by the reformulated view. At very least then, the account is incomplete for it fails to explain in the case of these excluded attitudes precisely what the account was supposed to explain, namely, their causal and intentional properties. The account also fails for these attitudes to establish their materialistic *bona fides*. Once one realizes that these excluded attitudes apparently have the same causal and intentional properties as those attitudes subsumed by the reformulated account, then one must wonder whether whatever explanation is eventually given for the properties of these excluded attitudes might not equally well explain these same properties in the attitudes that are currently subsumed by the reformulated account. Put another way, the lack of generality, given its unprincipled character, might be taken as both a symptom that the account is false and an impetus for looking for a general account of the causal and intentional properties of both core and derivative cases.

3.8. THE ABDUCTIVE ARGUMENT FOR THE RECEIVED VIEW: THE STRIKING PARALLELISM

In addition to the argument criticized above, to the effect that the Received View enjoys indirect but nevertheless strong empirical support from cognitive science, there is a second argument, which I have dubbed the 'abductive argument'. This argument holds that if propositional attitudes were the sorts of relations to explicit Representations that the Received View claims they are, that would explain their having the salient properties that they do, most notably, their being causally efficacious, semantically evaluable, inferentially involved, productive, and systematic; hence, this is a reason for thinking that the view is true. The form of non-demonstrative reasoning instanced here seems unobjectionable; certainly such reasoning is widespread both in science and everyday life. Yet one might very well challenge the truth of the conditional upon which the conclusion is premised. It is not obvious that the Received View would, if true, *explain* in any robust sense of that term the salient properties of propositional attitudes. The imagined explanation fails to offer any explanation whatever of the fact that so-called 'derivative' cases, no less than core cases, exhibit all of these salient properties.

Consider Fodor's (1987) claim that one of the best reasons for endorsing his polished version of the RTM (and hence the Received View) is that it is able to explain the 'striking parallelism' between causal relations among propositional attitudes, on the one hand, and the semantic relations that hold among their contents, on the other. Common-sense propositional attitude psychology, Fodor claims, presumes that thought is a causal process in which one semantically evaluable mental state gives rise to another. In such a psychology, he argues, it is not just that causal powers are attributed to states that are taken to be semantically evaluable, 'it's also that causal relations among propositional attitudes somehow typically contrive to respect their relations of content, and belief/desire explanations often turn on this' (Fodor 1987: 12). All this leads Fodor to ask, 'what sort of mechanism could have states that are both semantically and causally connected, and such that the causal connections respect the semantic ones?' (ibid. 14). The answer, Fodor argues, is a mechanism of the sort postulated by the Received View, viz., one in which the mental Representations postulated by the Received View interact causally in a way, dictated by their syntactic structures, that preserves the appropriate semantic relations between the contents of these representations. The mind, he argues (ibid. 18–20), is a 'syntax-driven machine' whose operations are proof-theoretic in character and thus satisfy both syntactic and semantic descriptions: under their syntactic description mental operations instantiate certain causal relations, while under their semantic description they instantiate certain inferential relations.

Fodor claims to find support for the Received View in the supposed fact that if the mind were a mechanism of the postulated sort, then that would explain both the 'striking parallelism' between the causal relations among propositional attitudes, on the one hand, and the semantic relations that hold among their propositional contents, on the other, as well as the salient properties of propositional attitudes. But arguably, the claimed support is illusory. Proof-theoretic devices of the sort presumed by the Received View certainly exhibit a parallelism between syntactic relations and semantic relations, but they do not provide a model that explains the psychological parallelism that Fodor finds so striking. The reason, very simply, is that this parallelism is exhibited *both* by propositional attitudes that satisfy the Received View (Fodor's core cases) *and* by those that don't (his derivative cases), and yet only the parallelism of the former can possibly be explained on the view's proof-theoretic model. The propositional contents of the latter are said *not* to be explicitly represented and hence could not be subsumed under the hypothesized proof-theoretic explanation. The parallelism of derivative cases might be explainable in terms of the parallelism of core cases, were the former derivable from the latter (perhaps in the way that so-called tacit beliefs are said to be derivable from explicitly represented beliefs). But they aren't, and so they can't be so explained. At very least Fodor's explanation of the 'striking parallelism' cannot be general; we know that the parallelism exhibited in derivative cases demands a different explanation. But once we concede this, the abductive argument is effectively undercut, or at least substantially weakened, since for all proponents of the Received View know, the parallelism that Fodor finds so striking is to be explained for *all* cases in

the way that it is to be explained in derivative cases, whatever that turns out
to be.

3.9. THE PERSISTENCE OF THE RECEIVED VIEW

If, as I have argued, the Received View enjoys neither the indirect empirical
support nor the abductive support claimed for it, then why do proponents
nevertheless find the view so compelling? Why, in other words, is the view
so persistent? In part it has to do with the fact that the view gives voice to a
deeply entrenched relational conception of the attitudes, a matter to which
I shall return in the next chapter. But it also has to do with the underlying
motivation of the Received View, namely, establishing the materialistic *bona
fides* of both propositional attitudes and the common-sense psychological
explanations that advert to them. The claim of the Received View to
have vindicated common-sense propositional attitude explanations depends
crucially on the *transparency* of the proposed computational construal of
propositional attitudes. For if the computational realization of propositional
attitudes is not reasonably transparent in the sense that one can readily
understand what, computationally speaking, propositional attitudes are, and
how they figure computationally in the production of behavior and other
propositional attitudes, then one can hardly claim to have vindicated the
common-sense explanations that advert to propositional attitudes.

Absent an account like the Received View, the desired vindication may
be elusive. Consider, once again, Dennett's description of the chess program
that, as the program's designer puts it, thinks that it should get its Queen out
early:

> But for all the many levels of explicit representation to be found in that program,
> nowhere is anything roughly synonymous with 'I should get my Queen out early'
> explicitly tokened. The level of analysis to which the designer's remark belongs
> describes features of the program that are, in an entirely innocent way, emergent
> properties of the computational processes that have 'engineering reality.' I see no
> reason to believe that the relation between belief-talk and psychological-process talk
> will be any more direct.

> (Dennett 1977 [1981]: 107)

The prospect that Dennett describes will seem bleak to anyone who believes
that common-sense psychological explanation requires scientific vindication.
For what such a person would presumably demand by way of a vindication

is an account of the computational realization of the attributed propositional attitudes that would lay to rest *reasonable* doubts about their materialistic respectability. That is to say, the required account would establish beyond reasonable doubt that the attributed attitudes were physical states (events, properties, or whatever) of the system to which they were attributed. But the prospect that Dennett describes would preclude just such an account: propositional attitudes turn out to be 'emergent' properties of their computational realization, which is to say that the implementation would be so *diffuse* as to preclude any vindication of common-sense psychological explanation; there would simply be no answer to the question of which computational structures and processes realize a given propositional attitude.

The Received View proposes with its tenet (v) a *computationally localist* realization of propositional attitudes. Thus, to the question, 'How are propositional attitudes realized computationally?' the Received View proposes a single, general answer, namely, that the propositional content of the attitude is explicitly represented by some specifiable data structure, while the attitude itself is realized by some specifiable computational process defined over that data structure. Thus, for example, what makes it true that I believe that it is sunny outside today is that there is a data structure that represents this putative state of affairs, and this data structure plays the particular causal functional role in my computationally characterized mental processes that beliefs in fact play.

The Received View thus seeks to preclude the possibility that Dennett's example suggests, namely, that the computational realization of propositional attitudes might turn out to be so lacking in transparency as to preclude the sought-for vindication. In so doing, it ends up committing itself to a very strong, but empirically unsupported claim about the computational realization of propositional attitudes. Propositional attitudes are mapped into computational states and processes in a very specific way: the attitudes themselves are mapped onto certain computational processes, the propositional contents of these attitudes onto certain data structures over which these processes are defined. More precisely, there is a *homomorphism* between propositional attitudes and computational states and processes that preserves, at the level of the computational algorithm, the type distinction drawn at the intentional level between attitudes and their contents. The Received View does not require that tokens of a given type of attitude or content be mapped to tokens of a single type of computational relation or data structure, respectively; it is compatible with the Received View that tokens of the first sort be mapped to tokens of *different* types of computational relations, tokens of the second sort be mapped to tokens of *different* types of data structure. Thus, although two subjects who share a given propositional attitude will both implement that propositional attitude in the same general way, viz., in both subjects the content of the propositional attitude is implemented as a data structure, and the attitude itself by a computational relation defined over that data structure, these subjects may implement the attitude and its content by means of different computational relations and different data structures. Thus the Received View is not a kind of computational type-type identity theory. Nevertheless, the postulated computational realization of the attitudes can only be effected within a computational architecture in which one can draw the required principled distinction between data structures, on the one hand, and the computational processes defined over these structures, on the other. This precludes the possibility that propositional attitudes might be implemented in non-classical architectures which fail to preserve such a principled distinction. The Received View thus makes a significant empirical claim regarding human cognitive computational architectures, one that no doubt explains the particular vehemence of the attacks mounted by proponents of the Received View against connectionist claims to be able to explain cognition.[23]

3.10. A WEAKER, NON-REDUCTIVE CONSTRUAL OF PROPOSITIONAL ATTITUDES

There is a weaker, non-reductive construal of propositional attitudes which, I find, is often the fallback position to which proponents of the Received

---

[23] Proponents of the Received View, who dub themselves 'classicists' because they embrace the classical physical system symbol model of computational architecture presupposed by the Received View, argue that, as Fodor and Pylyshyn (1988: 33) put it, 'the mind cannot be, in its general structure, a Connectionist network'. Connectionist architectures are alleged to suffer from a variety of disqualifying defects, but the basic complaint is that they lack the representational resources necessary to sustain the Received View's claims about the nature of cognitive capacities, intentional states (viz., propositional attitudes), and cognition. In particular, they are said to lack a crucial explanatory resource found only in classical architectures, namely, representational states that possess a recursive constituent structure. And because connectionist architectures lack this resource, they allegedly cannot explain certain salient properties of human cognition, in particular its pervasive 'systematicity', i.e., the property of having systematically related cognitive capacities such as the capacities for thinking, for example, both the thought that John loves Mary and the systematically related thought that Mary loves John. At most, and at best, connectionist architectures can offer 'an implementation architecture for a "classical" (language of thought) model' (Fodor and Pylyshyn 1988: 184). For a critical discussion of these claims, see Matthews 1997.

View retreat when they are pressed regarding the unsupported cognitive computational architectural commitments of their view. On this construal, which I shall dub simply the 'weak construal', having a propositional attitude is still, as the tenet (v) would have it, a matter of having a representational state over which certain computational processes are defined. But tenet (v)'s claim about the character of the mapping of propositional attitudes into computational states and processes is abandoned, replaced simply by the idea that propositional attitudes are to be thought of in computational/representational terms. There is no longer any claim about the explicit representation of the contents of propositional attitudes, no longer any claim to the effect that the common-sense distinction between attitude type and attitude content is preserved at the computational level in terms of a distinction between computational processes and explicit representations. It is some measure of this weaker construal that it is one that anyone who believes both that propositional attitudes are causally efficacious and that cognitive processes are computational should endorse, even someone who like Dennett imagines that propositional attitudes might turn out to be innocently emergent from their underlying computational implementation. For to believe both these things without also endorsing the weak construal would be tantamount to embracing the causal overdetermination of the effects of propositional attitudes.

This weak construal manages to save something of the general flavor of the Received View, but it does so only at the price of having to assume what that view had intended to establish, namely, the materialistic *bona fides* of propositional attitudes. For the construal simply assumes without argument the existence of a mapping of propositional attitudes into computational states. There is an explanatory price to be paid, too. The weak construal can provide no explanation of what common-sense psychology *seemingly* takes to be the salient properties of propositional attitudes, viz., causal efficacy, semantic evaluability, and inferential involvement.[24] The construal can offer no explanation of these properties because it remains completely noncommittal as to the computational implementation of propositional attitudes and their relations, which explains how this construal is able to avoid the computational architectural commitments and hence the troubles that afflict tenet (v). The weak construal makes no reductive claim about

---

[24] I say 'seemingly' here, because I believe it to be an open question whether common-sense psychology takes propositional attitudes to have the properties that proponents of the Received View assume that it does.

what propositional attitudes are, how they manage to interact causally among themselves (and with perception and action), or how their possessors manage generally to think and behave in ways that accord with certain rules of inference and principles of rationality and various empirically discovered laws of perception and behavior. What is right about the weak construal, even though it doesn't do the explanatory work that the proponents of the Received View desire, is that it recognizes, as the stronger construal does not, that propositional attitude explanations carry *no* architectural commitments whatever beyond the very general constraint that whatever internal states and processes there are, computational or not, they must be capable of producing the gross molar input/output behavior that such explanations purport to explain.

4

Are Propositional Attitudes Relations?

4.1. THE RECEIVED VIEW'S RELATIONAL CONCEPTION OF THE ATTITUDES

The burden of the previous chapter has been to argue that the Received View of propositional attitudes does not enjoy the empirical support claimed for it. In fact, given what we do know about human cognitive architecture (which, it must be conceded, is at this point really very little), it would be quite surprising, indeed something of a miracle, if the view turned out to be correct. What are the chances, after all, that evolution would have conspired to endow us with just the cognitive computational architecture that the view presumes, namely, the 'classical' architecture that is incorporated in much of our current computer technology? Yet even if proponents became convinced that the Received View was not empirically supported, they would probably not be moved. Their conviction that the Received View is true is not grounded in the belief that there is empirical support for the view; on the contrary, their belief that there is such support is grounded in their conviction that the view *must* be true. If contemporary cognitive science fails to provide empirical support, then so much the worse for contemporary cognitive science. There are other reasons, these proponents would insist, for thinking that the Received View is true. Most fundamentally, it provides what they take to be an antecedently plausible explanation of many of the salient properties of propositional attitudes (e.g., their causal efficacy, semantic evaluability, inferential involvement, opacity, productivity, and systematicity). In the absence of any alternative explanation of these properties, the lack of empirical support from contemporary cognitive science, they would argue, is hardly devastating.

But not only does the Received View of propositional attitudes not enjoy the claimed empirical support; it also does not, I argued in the previous chapter, enjoy the abductive explanatory support that might justify continued allegiance to the view in the absence of the claimed empirical support. Where not empirically implausible, or simply untenable, the explanations that the Received View proposes of the salient properties of propositional attitudes and their role in cognition are so imprecise and so lacking in relevant detail as to provide no abductive support for the view. The proposed explanations are little more than imaginative speculations on how these various properties *might* be explained in the absence of relevant empirical constraints. And yet proponents remain unswayed in their conviction that the Received View must be true.

The reason, I think, why proponents remain unswayed is this: fundamental to the view is the foundational assumption that propositional attitudes are *relations*, specifically relations between the possessor of the attitude and a causally efficacious, semantically evaluable particular that is the 'object' of the attitude, i.e., the belief, the desire, the hope, etc. Proponents believe that this foundational assumption, which I shall dub the 'relational conception' of propositional attitudes, is unquestionably true. Thus, Fodor (1978: 178), for example, holds it to be an adequacy condition on any account of propositional attitudes that they be construed as such relations. Proponents of the Received View are convinced of the truth of the relational conception, even in the absence of empirical and abductive support for the Received View, because they presume that the relational character of the attitudes can simply be read off the sentences by which we canonically attribute propositional attitudes.[1] Thus, there is, they believe, an inconvertible argument for the relational conception, and this, they further believe, is tantamount to having something approaching an equally incontrovertible argument for the Received View itself, since there are persuasive arguments for why the Received View is the most plausible relational construal of the attitudes on offer. So not surprisingly, the Received View has for its proponents the status of something approaching a necessary truth: protestations to the contrary notwithstanding, and notwithstanding the claimed empirical status of the Received View, proponents are confident that the view *cannot* be false.

Proponents of the Received View are not alone in embracing what I am call-ing the relational conception of the attitudes. It is the dominant view. There is, to be sure, considerable disagreement as to the nature of the semantically

---

[1] Consider, e.g., Fodor: 'Propositional attitudes should be analysed as relations. In particular, the verb in a sentence like "John believes it's raining" expresses a relation between John and something else, and a token of that sentence is true if John stands in the belief relation to that thing' (1978 [1981]: 178). Or Stephen Schiffer: 'Believing is the relation expressed by "believes" in a sentence of the form "x believes that S" ' (1992: 491).

evaluable particulars that are the 'objects' of propositional attitudes, e.g., whether they are complex Fregean senses, Russellian propositions, intensional isomorphisms, sentences of a natural language, mental representations, or perhaps things considerably more exotic. But the relational conception itself is rarely in dispute. Relationalists, as they might be called, simply take it as given that propositional attitude attributions of the form *x believes (desires, etc.) that S* assert that the referent of *x* stands in a particular relation, viz., the relation of belief (desire, etc.), to an entity that is the referent of the sentence's sentential complement clause (the '*that*-clause'), where that entity is the 'object' of the attitude, i.e., what *x* believes (desires, etc.).[2] Such defenses of the relational conception as one does find rarely focus, as presumably they should, on the metaphysics of propositional attitudes or the psychology of their possessors; instead, they focus almost exclusively on the logical form of the sentences by which we attribute propositional attitudes, apparently on the assumption that the relational conception of the attitudes finds support there. Relationalists presume that the relational nature of propositional attitudes can simply be read off the apparently relational logical form of propositional attitude attributions.

In this chapter, I want to challenge this presumption. My interest here is not to argue against the relational conception itself, but only against the presumption that the relational conception finds support in the apparently relational logical form of the sentences by which we attribute propositional attitudes. My discussion will focus on belief (and the sentences by which we attribute belief); however, I assume that my conclusions can be readily generalized to all other propositional attitudes.

4.2. THE RELATIONAL LOGICAL FORM OF BELIEF SENTENCES

Relationalists, I said, take it as given that the sentences by which we attribute propositional attitudes have a relational logical form. There are, they argue, no plausible alternatives to treating propositional attitude verbs as relational

---

[2] One could think that propositional attitudes are relations, without being a relationalist in the binary sense described here. Russell (1913), for example, thought that propositional attitudes were relations among the possessor of a propositional attitude and constituents of the proposition that expresses the content of the attitude: 'It seems obvious, as a matter of inspection, that belief is a multiple relation, not a dual relation, so that belief does not involve a single object called a "proposition"' (153).

predicates. As Fodor (1978: 179) puts it, 'the only known alternative to the view that verbs of propositional attitude express relations is that they are (semantically) "fused" with their objects, and that view would seem to be hopeless'.

So-called fusion theories propose to treat the propositional attitude verb as semantically fused with its sentential complement clause (*that S*) in much the way that the constituents of the predicates in idiomatic expressions such as *John bought the farm* are semantically fused, so that the logical form of such expressions would be *Fx* rather than *Fxy*. As Quine (1960: 216) presents the view, 'the verb *believe* here ceases to be a term and becomes part of an operator *believes that*, or *believes [ ]*, which, applied to a sentence, produces a composite absolute general term whereof the sentence is counted an immediate constituent'. It is, fusion theorists claim, an orthographic accident that the sentences by which we report propositional attitudes seem to have a relational logical form, since what they predicate of their possessors, it is claimed, are monadic, not relational, properties.

As a way of defending a non-relational conception of the attitudes that takes propositional attitudes as causally efficacious monadic properties of their possessors, fusion theories are, as Fodor says, hopeless. Quine (1960: 215) concedes that to adopt a fusion view we must, as he puts it, find it in us to be 'indifferent' to the truth values of sentences such as 'Paul believes something that Elmer does not', something that strikes him as a small price to pay in order to be rid of intentional objects. But there are other costs as well. Fusion theories commit us to the view that propositional attitude predicates are syntactically complex but semantically simple expressions, which leaves us with the obvious question: How, then, do we manage to understand propositional attitude attributions that we have never before heard? Our use of these predicates is clearly productive, and yet the fusion theory has no story about how this could be possible. Also problematic is the fact that propositional attitude predicates do not behave like a fused idiom in which all of the constituents are syncategorematic. First, there are seemingly valid inferences such as (1) that apparently quantify over the so-called object of the attitude:

(1) Jones believes that the monkey bit the lab technician.
     Hence, there is something that Jones believes.

Second, there are seemingly valid inferences such as (2) that apparently involve existential generalization of certain constituents of propositional attitude predicates:

(2) Jones believes that the monkey bit the lab technician.
    Hence, Jones believes that something bit someone.

Third, constituents of propositional attitude predicates can stand in anaphoric relations, as in (3):

(3) Jones believes that the monkey bit the lab technician, and
    it did in fact do so.

Now maybe these difficulties can be finessed with a bit of ingenuity, but even if they can, there will still be other problems. There will be a fourth problem of explaining why these predicates often permit free substitution of co-referring and synonymous expressions without change of truth value. Fused idiomatic expressions typically do not permit such substitutions without significant change in both meaning and truth conditions. ('Buying a piece of land upon which crops or animals are raised' is not synonymous with 'buying the farm' in the idiomatic sense of the latter expression.) It is not at all clear how this explanation might go. Fifth, the fusion view effectively abandons the idea that, for example, belief predicates pick out a class of properties distinct from those picked out by other propositional attitude predicates. Thus, for example, there is no reason on the fusion view to think that the property picked out by the predicate *believes-that-p* has anything more in common with the property picked out by *believes-that-q* than it does with the property picked out by the predicate *desires-that-r*. Finally, the fusion view leaves it quite mysterious why natural language should have evolved such a bizarre way of designating these supposedly monadic properties. In the case of idioms, there is generally an explanation of how the idiom could have come to mean what it does. 'Buying the farm', for example, makes perfect sense as an idiomatic expression for dying, in a linguistic community such as ours with an agrarian past where the customary practice is to bury the dead in a purchased cemetery plot. It's not clear how the fusionists would explain the emergence of fused attitude predicates.

It should be noted that for all their differences, fusionists share with relationalists one crucial assumption, namely, that the metaphysical nature of propositional attitudes themselves is revealed in the logical form of propositional attitude reports. Committed as they are to a non-relational account of propositional attitudes according to which propositional attitudes are causally efficacious monadic properties of their possessors, they feel compelled to argue that the logical form of the sentences by which we report propositional attitudes is likewise monadic. One of the burdens of this chapter is to challenge this assumption, since on any plausible construal of the notion of logical form, the logical form of these sentences is *probably* relational in just the sense that relationalists take it to be: These sentences assert a relation between (i) the possessor of the attitude, (ii) the referent of the *that*-clause, and perhaps, as some proposals would have it, (iii) some third thing, e.g., a mode of presentation.[3] Virtually all recently proposed formal semantics for the sentences by which we report propositional attitudes take propositional attitude verbs (*believes, desires,* etc.) to be relational predicates that express a relation of this sort.[4] And yet, I want to argue, this fact provides no reason for supposing that propositional attitudes themselves are relations.

4.3. PROBLEMS WITH THE RELATIONAL CONCEPTION OF BELIEF

Relationalists, I have said, assume that the relational nature of propositional attitudes can simply be read off the sentences by which we attribute propositional attitudes. For them, the relational logical form of such sentences reveals the relational form of the attributed attitudes. The assumption is not taken to be apodictic, but it is certainly thought to be presumptive. But even a cursory examination of the problems that plague the relational conception of belief should disabuse anyone of the notion that this assumption has any presumptive status. These problems have been carefully catalogued elsewhere (e.g., Richard 1990; Schiffer 1987, 1992), so I shall limit myself to a few brief reminders, which are intended to set the stage for a criticism of the relationalist presumption that one can read the relational logical form of belief sentences back onto the attributed belief states themselves.

There is general agreement that an account of belief should meet the following adequacy conditions: it should (i) provide an account of what belief is, i.e., what the having of a belief comes to, that explains or at least respects the individuation conditions on belief; (ii) explain the salient apparent properties of beliefs, viz., their semantic evaluability, their causal role in the production

---

[3] I say 'probably', because there are a number of difficulties facing such accounts that have not as yet been adequately addressed. See Prior 1971, Ascher 1993, Bach 1997, King 2002, and Moltmann 2003.

[4] Moltmann (2003), by contrast, follows Russell, arguing that while attitude verbs are indeed relational predicates, 'propositional attitudes are in fact not relations between agents and propositions and . . . the semantic role of the *that*-clause complement of the attitude verb is not that of providing an argument of an attitudinal relation' (77).

of behavior, their inferential relations to other propositional attitudes, and their apparent productivity and systematicity; and (iii) offer a solution to, or at least explain, the various puzzles about belief that have driven philosophical theorizing, e.g., failures of substitution, failures of existential generalization, Kripke puzzles. Finally, the account should do all this consistent with (iv) a plausible metaphysics, (v) a plausible semantics (and perhaps pragmatics) not just for belief sentences, but also for the natural language of which they are a fragment, and (vi) a plausible cognitive psychology for the believer.

These adequacy conditions, it should be noted, leave open the question of what constitutes an appropriate division of explanatory labor between the semantics of belief sentences, the metaphysics of belief, and the psychology of believers. This is not something that can be determined a priori. In particular, it cannot be assumed that the metaphysics and psychology can simply be read off the semantics. It might turn out, as indeed I think it does, that the former are not at all transparent in the latter.

Relational accounts of belief tend to fail these adequacy conditions in predictable ways, in ways that depend crucially on what the account in question takes to be the nature of the relatum to which the believer is related by the belief relation. Traditional propositionalist accounts, whether Fregean and Russellian in spirit, construe the object of belief as a proposition (i.e., as a language-independent, abstract entity that has its truth conditions essentially). Both sorts of propositionalist account have difficulty capturing both the truth conditions on belief attributions and the individuation conditions on belief, as well as providing a solution to the standard puzzles about belief, consistent with the demand that such an account be compatible with an independently plausible semantics.[5] Fregean accounts, for example, which take propositions to be complex senses, do a reasonably good job of explaining how there could be failures of substitution; however, they accomplish this only at the price of being committed to an arguably implausible semantics for belief sentences that is difficult to accommodate within a general truth-theoretic semantics for natural language. In particular, they have difficulty preserving 'semantic innocence', the desideratum, roughly, that linguistic expressions should have the same semantic value (make the same semantic contribution) irrespective of the linguistic context in which they appear. On Fregean accounts, for example, terms change their reference in intentional contexts. There are, to be sure, ways around this problem (see, e.g., Pietroski 1996),

---

[5] For a detailed discussion of these problems, see Richard 1990.

but they are invariably purchased at the price of some other desideratum, e.g., compositionality. Russellian (so-called direct reference) accounts, by contrast, fare much better on the semantics side, providing a semantics for belief sentences that can be more easily accommodated within a broader semantic theory; however, they achieve this only at the price of getting right neither the individuation conditions on beliefs nor the truth conditions on beliefs sentences, and hence not being able to offer plausible solutions to the various puzzles about belief. Thus, for example, these accounts find themselves forced to deny the seemingly firm intuition that (4) and (5) can differ in truth value:[6]

(4) Lois Lane believes Clark Kent is a reporter at the *Daily Planet*.
(5) Lois Lane believes Superman is a reporter at the *Daily Planet*.

Traditional propositionalist accounts also have difficulty accounting for the context-sensitivity of the truth conditions of belief attributions, e.g., how it is that a sentence such as (5) might be false in certain contexts, but true in others. In recent years, many propositionalists have embraced so-called hidden-indexical theories,[7] which among other explanatory virtues offer an explanation of this context-sensitivity. These theories are so-called because while like traditional propositional accounts they take belief attributions to express a relation to a proposition that is the object of belief, they claim that belief attributions also contain a hidden, indexical reference to a particular mode of presentation of the proposition believed. The reference to this mode of presentation is *hidden* in that it is not carried explicitly by any word or expression in the belief sentence; it is *indexical* in that the particular mode of presentation type referred to is contextually determined. In effect, hidden-indexical theories discover that the attitude verb *believes* has a third, syntactically unarticulated argument place that refers to a contextually determined mode of presentation. These theories thus ascribe to belief sentences of the form *x believes that S* the logical form given by (6):

(6) $(E\mu)(M\mu \ \& \ B^3(x, p, \mu))$

where x is the individual to whom the belief is attributed, p the proposition believed, μ the mode of presentation of type M, and B^3 the three-place *believes* relation that x bears under μ to the p expressed by *S*.

---

[6] Nothing turns on the fact that these are fictional characters. The same point could be made using real people, e.g., Frances Ethel Gumm, better known as Judy Garland.
[7] See, e.g., Schiffer 1987, Crimmins and Perry 1989, and Crimmins 1992.

Hidden-indexical theories arguably have the respective virtues, without the attendant vices, of both the traditional Russellian and Fregean accounts. The postulated hidden, indexical reference to a mode of presentation offers a ready explanation of failures of substitution that Russellians find so problematic: for example, (4) and (5) can differ in truth value, because Lois Lane believes the Russellian proposition <Superman/Clark Kent, being a reporter at the *Daily Planet*> under the mode of presentation of Superman/Clark Kent being a bespectacled geek reporter and not a be-caped superman. At the same time, these theories preserve unchanged the semantic values of the terms that appear within the sentential complement clause of the verb (the '*that*-clause'), thereby enabling them to explain the inferential and anaphoric relations that give the traditional Fregean accounts such trouble. The theories also offer an explanation of the context-sensitivity of truth conditions: the same belief sentence can be true when uttered in some contexts, and false in others, because the referent of the unarticulated mode of presentation argument can change with context. In effect, these theories explain the context-sensitivity of belief attributions by building into the Russellian account a hidden context-sensitive Fregean component.

Schiffer (1992) has pointed out a number of serious, possibly irremediable problems with hidden-indexical theories, which have mostly to do with the semantics that these theories propose for belief sentences. But when taken as a theory of belief, hidden-indexical theories share with other propositionalist accounts an even more serious failing: it is difficult to see how the mere standing in a relation to an abstract entity, even under a mode of presentation, could possibly be causally efficacious, which beliefs surely are. Believing that there are still two beers left in the fridge may prompt me to ask you to stay for another beer, but what gets my lips and tongue moving to issue this invitation is not some relation that I bear to an abstract entity, specifically a proposition, but some physical goings on in my head that are capable of causing these physical events.[8] Perhaps not surprisingly, relationalists concerned with the problem of explaining the causal role of belief have been more inclined to embrace a sententialist account, which takes the object of belief to be a sentence-like entity that has its truth conditions contingently. Such theories seem to offer an account of the causal efficacy of belief, assuming that the sentential relata in question turn out to be sentence tokens rather than types. But here, too,

---

[8] I'm assuming, without argument here, that relations to abstract particulars are never causally efficacious. Having a lottery ticket with the winning number can bring all sorts of goodies, but it is not the fact of being related to a number that brings about such good fortune.

there are potential problems concerning the causal efficacy of belief. Some sententialists, e.g., Carnap (1947) and Davidson (1968), propose to construe belief as a relation to a sentence in a public language. Thus, for example, the belief sentence *Galileo believed that the earth moves* is said to express a relation between Galileo and the English sentence *the earth moves*. But what, one must ask, is the nature of this relation that Galileo bears to a sentence of a language he presumably didn't speak, and how can this relation, whatever it is, have been causally efficacious in causing him, for example, to say, 'Eppur si muove'? And even if he did speak English, how would that have helped, unless perhaps he actually tokened *in thought* an instance of the sentence-type *the earth moves*? Failing an answer to this question, going sententialist would seem to offer no particular advantage over the propositionalist versions of the relationalist conception. For in the event that the believer does not token in thought an instance of the sentence-type, it seems hard to envision how the mere standing in a relation to such other tokens of this sentence-type as the believer might be related to could possibly provide the basis of a plausible account of the causal efficacy of belief. Causal efficacy in the production of behavior, it would seem, requires some internal state or entity of which the sentence embedded in the *that*-clause is at best a *representative*.[9]

There are still other problems with sententialist accounts. For example, beliefs would seem to have their truth values essentially and in most cases independently of language: my belief that it's sunny today would seem to be true, if in fact it is, irrespective of whatever words happen to express that belief, indeed irrespective of whether there are any public languages at all. But on sententialist accounts this is not the case. Sententialist accounts also seem not to get the individuation conditions on belief right; at least it is unclear how sententialist accounts propose to explain the fact both that tokens of different sentence-types can express the same belief and that different tokens of the same sentence-type can, in the appropriate contexts, express different beliefs.

For these and other reasons, many sententialists have come to favor accounts that construe belief as a relation not to a sentence in a public language, but to a sentence in a language of thought, i.e., to a quasi-linguistic mental representation, that is taken to be the object of belief. Such accounts are attractive because they also offer a seemingly plausible account of the causal efficacy of belief in the production of behavior: the mental representations that are the objects of belief play a causal role in the etiology of behavior by virtue

---

[9] This point will loom large in the measurement-theoretic account I present in the second part of the book.

of their formal-syntactic properties (in just the way that the representation-al states of computers play a causal role in the outputs of those devices). These accounts also offer a seemingly plausible explanation of the semantic evaluability of beliefs: they inherit their semantic properties from the mental representations that are their objects.

But here, too, there are characteristic problems. First, there is the problem of accounting for the apparent validity of inferences such as (7):

(7) Galileo believed that the earth moves.
   It is true that the earth moves.
   Hence, Galileo believed something true.

On pain of equivocation, the referents of the *that*-clauses in the two premises must be the same; yet surely what the second premise asserts to be true is not a mental representation (or even a mentally represented proposition) and indeed is not in any way dependent even on the existence of mental representations. Second, there is the difficult problem of making a compelling case for the existence of the postulated language of thought. Minimally, the task here is twofold. On the one hand, it needs to be shown that it is possible to provide a semantics for such a language. On the other hand, it needs to be shown either that the language of thought could be innate, or, if not innate, that it could be acquired. Proponents have for a number of years now been laboring on both these tasks, though arguably with limited success. But even if these tasks were to be accomplished, there would remain yet a third problem, viz., that of specifying the relation that pairs the *that*-clause in the belief sentence with the mental sentence that it supposedly specifies and which supposedly expresses the content of the belief. The *that*-clause cannot, as some have assumed, be functioning simply as a singular term that has the mental sentence as its referent, because one would then be unable to capture the context-sensitivity of the individuation conditions on belief.

Richard's (1990) quasi-Russellian account addresses the third of these problems. This account preserves the relational conception of belief as a rela-tion between the believer and a semantically evaluable entity that is the object of belief, in this case a semantically interpreted sentence, what Richard calls a 'Russellian annotated matrix' (RAM),[10] in the believer's representational

---

[10] A RAM is an ordered pair consisting of a sentence and the Russellian proposition expressed by an utterance of that sentence in the context of utterance. On the case of a mentalese RAM, it consists of simply the mentalese sentence paired with the Russellian proposition that is its distal interpretation.

system. It also preserves the assumption, common to traditional relational accounts, that the belief report's *that*-clause is a singular term. But it abandons the central assumption of such accounts that the *that*-clause in the sentence used to attribute the belief refers to the object of belief. Rather, on Richard's account, the *that*-clause refers to a *representation* of that object; specifically, it refers to a public-language RAM that *represents* the believer's mentalese RAM. The context-dependency that the hidden-indexical theory built into the implicit, contextually determined reference to a mode of presentation is now located in the representation relation that relates these two RAMs. Thus, for Richard, sentences of the form *x believes that S* have the logical form given by (8):

(8) $(E\rho)(P\rho \ \& \ B^3(x, \mathfrak{R}, \rho))$

where x is an individual, $\mathfrak{R}$ the RAM determined in a context c by the sentence's *that*-clause, ρ a context-sensitive representation function of type P, and B^3 the *believes* relation that x bears to $\mathfrak{R}$ under ρ. On Richard's account, the truth conditions for sentences of the form *x believes that S* are given by (9):

(9) *x believes that S* is true in context c if and only if under the representation function ρ, $\mathfrak{R}$ represents a mental representation, a sentence in the language of thought, included in x's set of belief representations.

The logical form of belief sentences that Richard proposes, like that proposed by hidden-indexical theories, is said to explain the context-sensitive truth conditions of belief attributions, their inferential and anaphoric relations, and the usual semantic puzzles such as failures of substitution.

Richard's account successfully skirts a number of the problems that typically afflict relational accounts, but certain problems remain. First, the account seems vulnerable to all the objections raised in the previous chapter against the Received View, since the account is just a version of that view, albeit one that focuses primarily on providing a semantics for propositional attitude attributions capable of handling successfully a number of the semantic and inferential difficulties that propositional attitude attributions present. Second, the account shares with other language-of-thought versions of the Received View the presumption that the sentences in the language of thought can explain, but are not subject to, the usual failures of substitution that characterize intentional contexts. This would seem to require that these sentences, which are the objects of belief, are considerably richer, grammatically speaking, than Richard might have imagined. For suppose, as Larson and Ludlow

(1993) argue, it is possible that someone believes that John F. Kennedy went to /hahvahd/ but not that he went to /harverd/, that someone believes that [old [men and women]] are at risk of infection, but not that [[old men] and women] are at risk.[11] Minimally, the mentalese RAMs, i.e., the distally interpreted mentalese sentences in the language of thought, that Richard's account takes to be the objects of belief will have to be annotated phonologically and syntactically in such fashion as to provide an object sufficiently rich as to be able to capture the complex individuation conditions on belief. Moreover, given the supposedly universal character of the language of thought, the annotated structure of these sentences will presumably have to be able to capture subtle distinctions in attributed belief expressible in any natural language whatever. Perhaps this is not impossible, but it certainly imposes a *significant* empirical burden on the notion of a language of thought. Finally, and perhaps most importantly for our present purposes, Richard's account ascribes to belief sentences a logical form, given by (8) above, that is seemingly at odds with any plausible truth-conditional semantics for such sentences. Simply put, the verb *believes* seems to be a two-place, *not* a three-place, predicate. Richard is driven to treating *believes* as a three-place predicate by his strategy for explaining the context-sensitivity of belief attributions. On his account, the context-sensitivity of belief attributions is explained in terms of the context-sensitive representation function ρ that maps the RAM specified by the *that*-clause of a belief sentence to a sentence in the believer's language of thought. The account treats the representation function ρ as an argument of the verb. This seems not only to get the polyadicity of the verb wrong, but it also seems to locate the context-sensitivity in the wrong place—on the verb rather than on the *that*-clause. Intuitively, context seems to determine what the *that*-clause specifies. The problem facing Richard is that once he takes a belief sentence's *that*-clause to specify a RAM, a RAM that supposedly represents a sentence in the subject's language of thought, he does not have any obvious way of capturing the context-sensitivity of the representation relation in the logical form of the belief sentence, except by taking it to be an argument of the verb. But an obvious question is why take (9) as expressing the truth conditions of belief sentences, rather than simply (10)?

(10) *x believes that S* is true in context c if and only if the RAM $\Re$ specified by the sentence's *that*-clause is in c the representative of one of x's beliefs.

---

[11] The slash brackets represent phonetic forms, the square brackets syntactic constituents.

After all, the truth conditions for sentences that attribute a numerical physical magnitude to an object, e.g., *x has a mass of 14 kilograms*, would not mention the representation relation in virtue of which the attributed magnitude is mapped to the positive real number 14 that is its representative on the kilogram scale. Thus, the T-sentence for the sentence just mentioned would presumably be simply this: *x has a mass of 14 kilograms* is true if and only if x has a mass whose real number representative on the kilogram scale is 14. The same would presumably be true of the truth conditions for belief sentences, on the sort of account that Richard proposes.

4.4. SEMANTIC VS. PSYCHOLOGICAL 'OBJECTS' OF BELIEF

The relational accounts typically get into trouble because they attempt to identify the referent of the belief sentence's *that*-clause with the belief itself, i.e., with the particular to which the believer supposedly stands in a psychological relation. On the one hand, it is difficult to find suitable objects of a sort that can both account for the usual semantic puzzles and at the same time be objects to which the believer can plausibly be said to bear a psychological relation; on the other hand, it is difficult to account for the context-sensitivity of belief reports (e.g., the fact that in one context it can be true to say of someone who knows Cicero only as 'Cicero' that this person believes that Tully denounced Catiline, but in another context false to say this). Some recent relational accounts (e.g., Crimmins and Perry 1989; Richard 1990; Crimmins 1992) attempt to avoid these difficulties by distinguishing what are in effect two different sorts of objects of belief, a semantic object and a psychological object. Richard, for example, distinguishes in his account two sorts of RAMs: the natural language RAM that is the referent of the *that*-clause, what he calls the 'semantic object' of belief, and the mentalese RAM to which the believer is said to be psychologically related, the so-called 'psychological object' of belief. Together, the semantic and psychological objects do all the explanatory work done by the 'object of belief' in traditional propositionalist accounts, but there is a division of labor: the semantic object does the semantic work, the psychological object the psychological work. Thus, on Richard's account, the *that*-clause of the belief sentence does not refer to the mentalese RAM, the sentential representation, to which the believer is said to be psychologically related; rather it refers, as I noted, to a complex semantic object that is a representative of that mental representation. The context-sensitivity of the representation relation allows Richard to explain both how in the same context different *that*-clauses can pick out one and the same psychological object and how in different contexts the same *that*-clause can pick out different psychological objects. More importantly for our present discussion, the distinction enables Richard to attribute distinct properties to these two different sorts of objects. Thus, for example, he can attribute to the psychological object of belief the property of being causally efficacious in the production of the believer's behavior without attributing this same property to the semantic object of belief. Similarly, he can attribute to the semantic object certain properties dictated by the semantics for belief sentences without thereby having to attribute these properties to the psychological object. By thus distinguishing the two things to which these different sorts of properties are attributed, he is able to avoid the fundamental implausibility of there being any single sort of object with both sorts of properties, capable of fulfilling both sorts of explanatory roles. Arguably relationalists have not until recently seen any need to distinguish, as Richard does, between semantic and psychological objects of the attitudes, because their accounts of both the semantics of attitude attribution and the psychology of the attitudes themselves were not sufficiently developed to force the distinction. As long as the accounts were fairly primitive, it seemed plausible to think that a single object, one to which the possessor of a propositional attitude was related, could do all the explanatory work.

In presenting their 'interpreted logical form' (ILF) semantics for belief sentences, Larson and Segal (1995) introduce a similar distinction in their informal discussion of how belief sentences relate to the belief states that these sentences attribute. But before examining the role that this distinction plays in their account, let me say a bit about the ILF semantics that they propose for the sentences by which we attribute propositional attitudes to individuals.

Following Larson and Ludlow (1993), Larson and Segal propose T-sentences of the following form for belief sentences of the form *x believes that S*:

(11) Val (t, [$_S$ *x believes that S*], σ) iff x believes* $[\![S]\!]$

where (11) is to be read, 'the sentence *x believes that S* receives the semantic value "true" relative to some sequence of assignments σ if and only if x believes* the interpreted logical form $[\![S]\!]$ of *S*', where *believes** is an unexplicated technical term, a two-place predicate, in the metalanguage.[12] ILFs, as Larson and Segal (1995: 438) explain, are syntactic phrase-markers whose terminal and non-terminal nodes are annotated with semantic values.[13] Thus, the basic idea of their ILF semantics for belief sentences is that propositional attitude verbs such as *believes* expresses relations between individuals and these complex structured entities.

The details of, and rationale for, Larson and Segal's ILF semantics are not important here. Suffice it to say that the postulation of ILFs as the relatum to which the possessor of a propositional attitude is said by the attitude attribution to be related is intended to provide a formal object that is sufficiently complex, in the appropriate ways, as to predict and explain both failures of substitution into, and inferential properties of, propositional attitude sentences. In this respect, Larson and Segal's ILF account shares with accounts such as Richard's the strategy of finding a semantic object, i.e., a RAM, ILF, etc., of suitable complexity to enable the account to accomplish its explanatory and predictive goals. On Larson and Segal's proposed semantics, propositional attitudes verbs are two-place predicates, taking as arguments a noun phrase that refers to the possessor of the attitude and a sentential complement clause that refers to an ILF. On their account, the logical form of belief sentences of the form *x believes that S* would be given by (12):

(12) B^*xy

where B^* is the relation specified by the metalanguage verb *believes**, x is the believer, and y the ILF expressed by the sentence's *that*-clause. The focal question here is this: What follows from (12) as regards the relational conception of belief?

Larson and Segal, as I mentioned above, draw a distinction similar to Richard's between the semantic and psychological objects of the attitudes. More precisely, they point out (1995: 444) that while their account of the semantics of belief sentences takes what they call the 'semantic object' of *believe* in (13) to be the ILF of the sentence embedded in the *that*-clause, viz., the ILF of the English sentence *Carthage must be destroyed*, as given in

---

[12] Larson and Segal don't actually mark, as I do here, the metalanguage term *believes** as distinct from the object language *believes*, though surely it is such, since the latter verb does not takes NP-constructions of the postulated sort as arguments.

[13] As Ludlow (2000: 32) explains it, 'ILFs, in effect, conjoin a semantic value with its linguistic mode of presentation'. ILFs are thus like Richard's RAMs, except that they also exhibit the syntactic structure of the sentence.

the T-sentence (14) for (13), it is implausible to suppose that Cato, himself, ever stood in a doxastic relation to that semantic object.

(13) Cato believed that Carthage must be destroyed.
(14) Val (t, *Cato believed that Carthage must be destroyed, σ*) iff

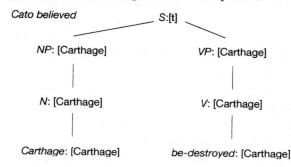

There is, Larson and Segal insist, nothing problematic in all this, because, as they put it, ILFs are simply linguistic objects that 'give expression' to attitudes. They are objects 'one can use to express what Cato said and believed' (444): 'to believe an ILF is to have a belief expressed by it' (445). Put another way, ILFs are, like the natural language RAMs in Richard's account, simply ways of representing what Cato believed. They are not the beliefs themselves.

Now it is consistent with Larson and Segal's claims about ILFs that Cato's believing that Carthage must be destroyed might be a matter of his standing in a psychological relation to an ILF (perhaps to the ILF of the Latin sentence *Carthago delenda est*). But it seems implausible to suppose that having a belief is a matter of standing in a relation to an ILF,[14] and certainly nothing that Larson and Segal say suggests that they suppose that it is. They note that 'the psychology module will have its own way of representing propositional attitudes. These representations may well not involve ILFs' (455).[15]

---

[14] Fiengo and May (1996) point out that a person who truly believes that Cicero is not Tully cannot possibly have epistemic access to the objectual annotations of the ILF of the sentence that expresses that belief, viz., *Cicero is not Tully*, since if he did, he would presumably know that *Cicero* and *Tully* were co-referential, and hence could not believe the contrary.

[15] Larson and Segal do say that 'ILFs are represented within the semantics module of the language faculty' (1995: 455), but presumably what they have in mind here is that the ILF in question here, viz., in (14), is represented in the language faculty of the speaker making the belief attribution, not in the language faculty of Cato himself, unless the case at hand is one of Cato saying of himself, 'Cato believed that Carthage must be destroyed' (which is unlikely, given that he presumably didn't speak modern English). Ludlow (2000: 34) presumably has the same point in mind when he says,

So here is where things stand. According to Larson and Segal, a belief sentence such as (13) is true just in case the believer stands in the *believes** relation to the ILF of the sentence embedded in the sentence's *that*-clause, but nothing in their account of the semantics of belief sentences entails that a believer stands in this relation to that ILF only if that believer stands in a psychological relation to a representation of that ILF, or of any other ILF for that matter. Indeed, for all their semantics tells us, a believer's believing something might not be a matter of standing in any relation at all. It is compatible with their semantics that the relational conception of belief might simply be false. But what, then, is the relation between ILFs, which are the 'semantical objects' of belief, and beliefs themselves? Larson and Segal, I said, speak of ILFs as 'expressing' what is believed, but how is this to be understood? And how does this bear on the relationalist presumption that the relational nature of belief can be read off the relational nature of the sentences by which we attribute beliefs?

Relationalists, we have seen, claim to find support for their relational conception in the existence of valid arguments, such as (1) and (2), which seemingly quantify over beliefs or belief contents, what Richard calls the psychological objects of belief. But if we embrace, as both Richard and Larson and Segal do, a theory of belief and belief attribution that distinguishes between the semantic and psychological objects of belief, this claimed support is effectively undercut. It is the logical form of belief sentences that determines their inferential properties. And within the context of a theory of belief and belief attribution that distinguishes between semantic and psychological objects of belief, it is the *semantic*, not the psychological, object of belief that figures in the logical form of the belief sentence and hence also in arguments such as (1) and (2). This is hardly surprising, since the basic rationale for drawing this distinction is to enable a theory that avails itself of such a distinction to postulate an object to which the believer is semantically related that is suitable to capture the semantic and inferential properties of belief ascriptions, but without thereby having also to ascribe to the believer a psychological, specifically doxastic, relation to this object.

Of course, distinguishing between semantic and psychological objects of belief comes with a price which relationalists who draw this distinction have yet to pay: one then has to explain how the former manages to

'ILFs aren't intended to describe episodes in the creature's language of thought, but rather are intended to provide information for the benefit of a hearer who wants to construct a theory of the creature's mental life.'

track the latter, and how native speakers are able to exploit the fact that the former tracks the latter to obtain information about the believer. For otherwise one has no account of how true belief ascriptions manage to be informative.

Of the recent proposals that distinguish between semantic and psychological objects of belief, Richard offers the most explicit account of the tracking relation. On his account, the semantic object specified by the belief sentence's *that*-clause is mapped to the psychological object, a belief representation in the believer's belief representation set, by the context-sensitive representation function ρ, mentioned in (8) and (9) above. Richard does not offer much by way of an explicit characterization of this mapping function; nor does he offer any characterization of the contexts that are presumed to be one of the arguments of this function. Rather what he offers are a number of illustrations of the context-sensitivity of our interpretation of belief sentences, which suggest that minimally the mapping function preserves the Russellian proposition expressed by the *that*-clause.

Larson and Segal are even less explicit on this matter. For them, the relation between the semantic and psychological objects of belief is, as we noted, one of *expression*: the ILF 'expresses' what the believer believes. Larson and Segal intend their expression relation to be a generalization of Davidson's (1968) *samesaying* relation, but like Davidson before them, they offer no characterization of this relation by virtue of which the semantic object succeeds in tracking the psychological object. More significantly still, neither Richard nor Larson and Segal offer any account of how speakers might exploit the tracking relation in understanding just what claim is being made about the psychological state of the believer. It remains a mystery how being told that a believer stands in a certain relation to a semantic object of some sort, viz., the relation given by the logical form of a belief sentence, provides any information about the believer's psychological state.

4.5. READING BACK LOGICAL FORM: THE PROBLEM FOR RELATIONALISTS

So here is where things stand. Relationalists assume that we can read the logical form of belief sentences back onto the believers that belief attributions using these sentences are about, specifically onto the believer's belief state, so that if the logical form of belief sentences is relational, then so, too, is the belief state. If this assumption were well-founded, then relationalists would have good grounds for their relational conception of belief, since the logical form of belief sentences is probably relational, specifically, a binary relation between a believer and an entity of the sort that we've been calling the semantic object of belief. But there is reason to challenge the reading-back assumption that underpins this argument for the relational conception of belief, since the semantic object of belief cannot plausibly be identified with the putative psychological object of belief to which, according to the relational conception, the believer is doxastically related. At best, the semantic object *tracks* the psychological object. Yet relationalists have no explicit characterization of this putative tracking relation; nor do they have any account of how native speakers might exploit such a relation in gaining information about a person's belief states from true belief attributions about that person. But in the absence of a characterization of the tracking relation, the relationalist's claim to find support in the logical form of belief sentences for the relational conception of belief is in trouble, since in the absence of such a characterization, the relationalist has no justification for reading the logical form back onto the belief state, no reason to assume that the belief states are relational.

There is, of course, going to have to be some mapping of both the relation and the relata specified in the logical form of belief sentences onto believers and their belief states, since otherwise the reports using these sentences would carry no information about these states. But nothing requires that the psychological image of the logical form be a single sort of relation relating a believer to a single sort of object. Consistent with the requirement that belief attributions carry information about the belief states of believers, the logical form of belief sentences could have as its image any number of different relations, each with a different relatum to which the believer was related, or it could as well have as its image the possession by the believer of one or more monadic properties.

Predicates that are used to attribute physical magnitudes to objects illustrate just this last possibility, viz., of a predicate with a relational logical form being used to attribute a monadic property. Consider the following sentences:

(15) Jones weighs 150 lbs.
(16) Jones has a temperature of 98.6°F.

On any plausible semantics, the logical form of both (15) and (16) is a binary relation, relating Jones to a number on a scale. Yet Jones's weighing what he does or having the temperature that he does is *not* a matter of his standing in a substantive relation to the relata that figure in the logical forms of these reports. Having a certain weight and temperature are *monadic* properties of their possessor.[16] The binary relations that figure in the logical forms of these sentences simply provide a way of specifying these properties, by relating their possessor to certain abstract entities, viz., numbers on a scale, that are, in a sense to be made precise in the next chapter, the measurement-theoretic *representatives* of these properties. Arguably, something similar could be true for belief sentences, since in their case the relatum to which the believer is said by the belief sentence to be related is not, if the accounts just surveyed are correct, the psychological object of belief, i.e., not something to which the believer is psychologically related; rather it is an object that presumably tracks, and hence is a *representative* of, a particular psychological state of the believer.

4.6. THE PSYCHOLOGICAL IMPORT OF LOGICAL FORM: A MEASUREMENT-THEORETIC WAY OF THINKING ABOUT THE ISSUE

Suppose that belief sentences do function in the way suggested, viz., they predicate a belief state to a person by relating that person to an abstract object that is the representative of the belief state in roughly the way that numbers on a scale are the measurement-theoretic representatives of certain physical magnitudes. Then the task for someone who wants to move from the logical form of the belief sentence to the metaphysics of belief or the psychology of believers is to discern the mapping between these abstract objects and the belief states of which they are the representatives. The task, in other words, is to construct a 'measurement theory' for belief states. In a manner similar to measurement theory for physical magnitudes such as length, mass, and temperature, such a 'measurement theory' would presumably specify the structure of the belief states (properties, etc.) that find an image in the linguistic representatives of these states. It might also specify certain invariance transformations defined over these representatives, which preserve the empirical content of belief reports. Of course, there

---

[16] Strictly speaking, of course, Jones' having a certain weight is a relational property, but it is not the relation captured by the logical form of (15). Rather it is a relation between Jones, specifically his mass (which is one of his intrinsic monadic properties), and the gravitational force to which he (his mass) is subject.

would be significant differences between a 'measurement theory' for belief states and the measurement theory for physical magnitudes. Most notably, the representatives for belief states are not positive real numbers, and the structure of relations that they exhibit are not the sorts of arithmetic relations defined over such numbers which permit the numerical quantification of physical magnitudes. Rather the domain of belief state representatives will constitute something like a space rather than a scale, where the salient relations defined on this representation space will presumably be inferential, and the mapping of belief states onto their linguistic representatives will exhibit a context-sensitivity that the mapping of physical magnitudes into the positive reals does not.[17]

Constructing such a 'measurement theory' for belief states would not be a simple task, any more than was the development of a measurement theory for physical magnitudes. Most of us are tolerably reliable, at least in most normal circumstances, in 'measuring' and reporting the belief states of fellow humans (which is hardly surprising given our evolved social character), but this reliability as 'measuring' instruments does not appear to presume any explicit understanding of the mapping relation by virtue of which we achieve this reliability. In this respect, we are not different from many other measuring instruments, both natural and artificial, that while reliable have little or no understanding of the principles that explain their reliability. Our grasp of this relation, like our grasp of the linguistic principles that underlie our linguistic competence, is largely tacit. But presumably our competence in 'measuring' and reporting the propositional attitudes of others (and even ourselves) should be no less amenable to empirical investigation than other cognitive competences.

The point that I wish to emphasize here is that in the absence of a worked out 'measurement theory' for belief states which specifies the mapping of belief states onto their linguistic representatives, we have no way of interpreting the import of the logical form of belief sentences for the metaphysics of belief and the psychology of believers. Our situation is akin to trying to interpret a map of an unfamiliar territory in the absence of an interpretive key. The logical form of belief sentences, like the map, is not self-interpreting.

---

[17] My use here of scare quotes when speaking of a 'measurement theory' for belief states and other propositional attitudes, or of 'measuring' propositional attitudes, is intended to call attention to these differences, though I shall abandon the quotes once the analogy to standard measurement theory for physical magnitudes has been sufficiently developed to make clear the precise sense in which the proposed 'measurement-theoretic' account does and does not deserve the name.

Faced with the difficulty, indeed the impossibility, of reading back the logical form of belief sentences onto the belief states of believers, and in the absence of independent arguments for the relational conception, some relationalists may be tempted to become Fregeans of a sort, treating belief as simply a relation to the abstract entity that, according to the 'measurement-theoretic' conception of belief states being envisioned here, is the representative of certain psychological states of the believer. Such a move would preserve the relational conception of belief. It would also allow relationalists to continue to predicate of the belief semantic properties such as semantic evaluability and inferential relations that would on both the measurement-theoretic account and the dual-object accounts scouted above turn out to be possessed by the semantic object that measures the belief but not necessarily possessed by the belief itself. But there would, of course, be a price to be paid. On this neo-Fregean conception, relationalists would be forced to abandon what they have tried heroically to preserve, namely, the causal efficacy of belief. Common sense would turn out to be mistaken. Strictly speaking, propositional attitudes would play no role in the production of behavior; rather it would be their images, under the mapping of propositional attitudes onto the states of individuals that we describe mistakenly as the 'possessors' of propositional attitudes, that would be causally efficacious. Relationalists convinced of the philosophical import of logical form might consider this revision to common sense a small price to pay.

Relationalists not tempted by this neo-Fregean gambit may try to take some comfort in the thought that the foregoing arguments against a simple reading back of the logical form of the attitudes do not show the relational conception to be untenable. At most the arguments show that the relational conception finds no support in the presumably relational logical form of propositional attitude attributions. The relational conception, they might conclude, is still in the running, at least until such time as non-relationalists put a reasonably well-developed alternative on the table. In my view, such a conclusion seriously underestimates the challenge posed by the foregoing arguments against reading back, especially to relational accounts of the sort proposed by the Received View, which take the objects of the attitudes to be mental representations. For the basic point made by those arguments, and supported by contemporary relational accounts, such as those scouted above, which find themselves forced to distinguish between semantical and psychological objects of the attitudes, is the difficulty, if not the impossibility, of discovering a single particular that could be a plausible candidate for the object of an attitude to which the possessor of the attitude could be suitably related. The problem for relationalists is not simply that the case for the relational conception has yet to be made, but also, and more importantly, that the prospect that a case can be made appears exceedingly dim.

PART II

A MEASUREMENT-THEORETIC ACCOUNT OF PROPOSITIONAL ATTITUDES AND THEIR ATTRIBUTION

5

Foundations of a Measurement-Theoretic Account of the Attitudes

5.1. THE BASIC IDEA

The sentences by which we canonically attribute propositional attitudes appear to have a relational logical form: the main clause verb of sentences of the form *x believes (desires, etc.) that S* expresses a dyadic relation between the possessor of the attitude and some as yet unspecified particular that is the referent of the *that*-clause. Yet for reasons developed in the preceding chapter, it is an open question whether, as the Received View would have it, propositional attitudes are themselves relations, specifically, relations between the possessor of the attitude and some particular that is the referent of the *that*-clause. One possibility raised in the preceding chapter is that propositional attitude predicates are like the numerical measure predicates used to attribute physical magnitudes: they are relational in form, and hence express relations, but the relations that they express are *not* substantive relations that are in any way constitutive of possessor's possession of the propositional attitudes attributed by these predicates. Perhaps to say that a subject has a certain propositional attitude is no more to say that the subject stands in a substantive psychological relation to the particular that is the referent of the *that*-clause than to say that an object has a temperature of 30°C is to say that the object stands in a substantive physical relation to the number 30. Rather, it might be to attribute to that subject a certain psychological state or property which is specified by means of an abstract representative of that state or property, in much the way that we specify the temperature of an object by means of a real number representative of that temperature on a numerical scale. The referents of *that*-clauses, like numbers, might simply be abstract entities used to *represent* measurement-theoretically the propositional attitudes of those to whom these attitudes are attributed. They might not be, in any sense, the psychological 'objects' of these states.

A number of contemporary philosophers have been attracted to the idea that propositional attitude predicates might be a kind of 'measure predicate', i.e., might function very much like the numerical predicates by which we attribute physical magnitudes, though none has attempted to develop the idea in any detail.[1] Churchland (1979) is attracted to the idea because it offers a way of avoiding what he regards as a metaphysically vexing commitment in psychology to propositions. As he puts it,

> The idea that believing that p is a matter of standing in some appropriate relation to an abstract entity (the proposition that p) seems to me to have nothing more to recommend it than would the parallel suggestion that weighing 5 kg is at bottom a matter of standing in some suitable relation to an abstract entity (the number 5). For contexts of this latter kind, at least, the relational construal is highly procrustean.
>
> (Churchland 1979: 105)

Field (1981), for his part, sees in the idea not simply a way of avoiding any commitment in psychology to propositions, but also the possibility of a Representationalist solution to Brentano's problem of the intentionality of propositional attitudes:

> The theory of measurement. . . explains why real numbers can be used to 'measure' mass (better: to serve as a scale for mass). It does this in the following way. First, certain properties and relations among massive objects are cited—properties and relations that are specifiable without reference to numbers. Then a representation theorem is proved: such a theorem says that if any system of objects has the properties and relations cited, then there is a mapping of that system into the real numbers which 'preserves structure.' Consequently, assigning real numbers to the objects is a convenient way of discussing the intrinsic mass-relations that those objects have, but those intrinsic relations don't themselves require the existence of real numbers. . . .
>
> Can we solve Brentano's problem. . . in an analogous way? To do so we would have to postulate a system of entities inside the believer which was related via a structure-preserving mapping to the system of propositions. The 'structure' that such a mapping would have to preserve would be the kind of structure important to propositions; viz., logical structure. So the system of entities inside the believer would have to have logical structure, and this I think means that the system of entities inside the believer can be viewed as a system of sentences, an internal system of representation.
>
> (Field 1981: 114)

---

[1] See Churchland 1979: 105, Field 1981: 113–14, Stalnaker 1984: 8–11, Dennett 1987: 123–5, Davidson 1989, Matthews 1990, 1994, and Beckermann 1996. Suppes and Zinnes (1963: 7) were perhaps the first to suggest the possibility of a measurement-theoretic account of 'attitude statements'. Swoyer (1987: 281–3) offers a sketch of how the idea might be developed.

Field's proposal may solve Brentano's problem, conceived narrowly in the way that Brentano apparently did, viz., as the problem of how (intentional) mental states such as propositional attitudes can possibly be about things, have truth or fulfillment conditions, etc. They have such content, Field proposes, in virtue of the fact that the physically tokened sentential mental representations with which propositional attitudes are identified have it. But Field's solution is purchased at the price of having now to explain how these mental representations manage to have the representational contents that they do, which of course explains why proponents of the Received View such as Fodor have been so exercised over the years to provide a naturalistic account of representational content. What Field's proposal does offer is a way of dispensing with the idea that the intentionality of propositional attitudes is to be explained in terms of their being relations to semantically evaluable abstracta such as propositions.

Stalnaker (1984: 5) presents the 'measurement analogy' as a way of blunting the intuitive force of what he terms the 'linguistic picture' of propositional attitudes, a view which he describes as undertaking to explain thought by analogy with speech, construing propositional attitudes as relations to semantically contentful linguistic entities of some sort. The measurement analogy, he thinks, enables us to see that our canonical way of attributing propositional attitudes, by relating the possessor of an attitude to a proposition, might simply be a way of picking out the relevant causal properties of those inner states that are the attitudes: 'the analogy suggests that to define a relation between a person or a physical object and a proposition is to define a class of properties with a structure that makes it possible to pick one of the properties out of the class by specifying a proposition' (ibid. 11). The measurement analogy thus makes conceptual room for the 'pragmatic picture' of the attitudes which Stalnaker favors, according to which propositional attitudes 'should be understood primarily in terms of the role that they play in the characterization and explanation of action' (ibid. 4). On this pragmatic picture, propositional attitudes are conceived as functionally defined states of rational agents that explain why they act as they do, and as such, 'this picture suggests that the primary objects of attitude are not propositions but the alternative possible outcomes of agents' actions, or more generally, alternative possible states of the world' (ibid.). Stalnaker argues that

Just as the empirical relations that fix the reference of physical magnitude terms determines [sic] which features of numbers are physically significant and which are not, so the empirical relations which a functional theory uses to explain propositional attitude concepts will determine which features of abstract propositions are significant, and so what conception of proposition is appropriate.

(Stalnaker 1984: 11)

In his development of the 'measurement analogy', Stalnaker is particularly concerned to challenge Field's suggestion that it provides support for the linguistic picture. In particular, he rejects Field's suggestion that, as Stalnaker describes it, 'a solution to the problem of intentionality which parallels the explanation of physical magnitudes provided by measurement theory would support his thesis that mental representation requires a system of internal linguistic representation' (ibid. 10).

For his own part, Stalnaker apparently does *not* think of the measurement analogy as offering a solution to the problem of intentionality. For having presented his pragmatic picture, according to which beliefs and desires are, as he puts it, 'correlative dispositional states of a potentially rational agent' (ibid. 15), he continues to speak of beliefs, desires, and other propositional attitudes as representational states with determinate contents. He doesn't consider the possibility, suggested by the measurement analogy, that perhaps propositional attitudes no more have intentionality than do the physical magnitudes have numerosity, so that there really is no 'problem of intentionality' for the attitudes.[2] Rather he concludes that 'the content of belief and desire cancels out on the pragmatic analysis. Even if that analysis does give us an account of the structure of explanations of rational action, by itself it gives us no account at all of how beliefs and desires can represent the world' (ibid. 18). Thus, for Stalnaker, as for proponents of the Received View, the project of providing a (presumably naturalistic) theory of representational content of propositional attitudes remains. At most Stalnaker can take himself to have shown that these contentful states which stand in need of a theory of content need not be linguistic, which raises the obvious question of just what sort of theory of content would be appropriate for these non-linguistic dispositional states that he takes to be the attitudes.

Dennett (1987) and Davidson (1989) see in the measurement idea, not simply a way of avoiding a vexing commitment in psychology to abstract objects, but also a way of avoiding altogether a relational account of propositional attitudes. Both see in the idea the possibility of a *non*-relational, *non*-Representationalist account of the attitudes. Dennett points out (1987: 125n.) that while we attribute a particular mass to an object by relating that object to

---

[2] For a useful discussion of this issue, see Beckermann 1996.

a particular real number, we don't suppose that the object's having the mass that it does is a matter of its being related to some particular. Having the mass that it does is an intrinsic (monadic) property of the object. Perhaps, Dennett suggests, the same is true for propositional attitudes: we attribute them to an individual by relating that individual to a particular, but propositional attitudes are not themselves relations that their possessors bear to particulars.

Davidson, for his part, insists that it does not follow from the fact that we specify what a thinker thinks by relating him to a certain object that the thinker bears any psychological relation to that object. Indeed, he says, 'We are free to divorce the semantic need for content-specifying objects from the idea that there must be *any objects at all* [emphasis mine] with which someone who has an attitude is in psychic touch' (Davidson 1989: 9). According to Davidson, the analogy then between measuring weight and attributing states of belief is this:

> Just as in measuring weight we need a collection of entities which have a structure in which we can reflect the relations between weighty objects, so in attributing states of belief (and other propositional attitudes) we need a collection of entities related in ways that will allow us to keep track of the relevant properties of the various psychological states.
>
> . . . we do not need to suppose there are such entities as beliefs. Nor do we have to invent objects to serve as the 'objects of beliefs' or what is before the mind, or in the brain. For the entities we mention to help specify a state of mind do not have to play any *psychological* or epistemological role at all, just as numbers play no physical role.
>
> (Davidson 1989: 11)

So while all these five philosophers are clearly attracted to the idea that propositional attitude predicates might be a kind of 'measure predicate', there is no consensus on the import of this idea for an account of propositional attitudes. And of those who find in the idea support for a non-relational, non-Representational account of the attitudes, there is little or no development of the claim that the idea does provide support for such an account, much less that such an account is at all empirically plausible.

I am attracted to the idea that propositional attitude predicates might be a kind of measure predicate for basically the same reasons as Davidson. Propositional attitude predicates have an apparently dyadic relational logical form, yet I see little reason to suppose that propositional attitudes are themselves relations to particulars of any sort. Indeed, I think both that propositional attitude predicates *are* a kind of measure predicate, and that these predicates are used to attribute certain non-relational (monadic) properties to those to whom they are applied. I am also inclined to doubt that propositional attitudes are representational states in anything like the way proponents of the Received View imagine, so that there is not, so far as I can see, a problem of intentionality for these states that would require a theory of representational content, any more than there is a problem of numerosity for the physical magnitudes that requires a theory of numerical content for them. My intent in the remaining chapters of this book is to provide a plausibility argument for these claims. I begin in this chapter with an informal, admittedly very cursory introduction to the numerical measurement theory upon which the 'measurement-theoretic' account of the attitudes I develop will be modeled. Given the sophistication and richness of numerical measurement, I can only focus on those aspects and concepts that are directly relevant to a measurement-theoretic account of the attitudes.

5.2. THE HISTORICAL DEVELOPMENT
OF MEASUREMENT THEORY

Numerical measurement is the systematic assignment of numbers to objects in order to represent certain of their properties, specifically those properties, which we call 'magnitudes', that are capable of instantiation in different quantities. Such assignments are possible, because the magnitudes to be measured satisfy certain well-defined empirical conditions, which are the possibility conditions of a measurement practice for the magnitudes in question. Numerical measurement, of course, is an ancient practice—civilized peoples the world over have for millennia been measuring time, duration, length, area, volume, weight, density, hardness, etc.; however, measurement theory, the theoretical investigation of the mathematical and empirical conditions that make numerical measurement possible, is little more than a century old. It traces its origins to Helmholtz (1887), Hölder (1901), and later Campbell (1928), who first investigated the numerical measurement of fundamental 'extensive' physical magnitudes (i.e., magnitudes such as mass and length, where, roughly speaking, the things being measured can be ordered with respect to the quantity of the magnitude being measured that they possess and furthermore there is an addition-like operation on these things).[3] Hölder proved that on the assumption that such magnitudes share

---

[3] For a very useful historical introduction to measurement theory, see Díez 1997.

certain well-defined properties, there is a constructive procedure for assigning positive real numbers to objects as a function of their possession of specific quantities of these magnitudes. In particular, he proved that if an empirical system of objects satisfies certain formally specifiable conditions or axioms, then there is a constructive procedure for assigning positive real numbers to those objects that *preserves*, in a sense made explicit below, the quantitative relations of magnitude among these objects, such that the assigned numbers reflect the relative quantities of the magnitude in question possessed by the objects. Specifically, consider any relational structure $\mathcal{X} = <X, \succcurlyeq, \circ>$, where X is a set of objects, $\succcurlyeq$ a binary ordering relation on X, whose interpretation is '. . . is greater than or equal to. . . in magnitude', and $\circ$ a binary 'concatenation' operation on X, whose interpretation is '. . . physically concatenates or combines with. . . to form. . .'. Hölder proved that if $\mathcal{X}$ satisfies certain specific conditions or axioms,[4] then there exists a uniform procedure for constructing a numerical assignment ϕ on X such that for each x, y in X, $x \succcurlyeq y$ iff $\phi(x) \geq \phi(y)$, and $\phi(x \circ y) = \phi(x) + \phi(y)$, where $\geq$ is the usual ordering relation 'greater than or equal to, and $+$ is the addition operation on the positive reals. Satisfaction of these conditions or axioms effectively guarantees that ϕ is a homomorphism[5] of the represented empirical relational structure $\mathcal{X} = <X, \succcurlyeq, \circ>$ into a representing relational structure $\mathcal{N} = <Re^+, \geq, +>$ comprising the positive real numbers and the ordering relation and the addition operation defined on them.

The empirical procedure for constructing such a numerical assignment ϕ, i.e., a scale, is straightforward. One chooses an arbitrary element u of X as the unit of measurement (e.g., the Standard meter bar, a liter of water) and assigns to that element some arbitrary number, say the number 1 (in which case, $\phi(u) = 1$). Given the required properties of the numerical assignment ϕ mentioned above, the choice of unit fixes for every other element x in

---

[4] These include *solvability* (if an object is smaller than another, there is a third one that concatenated with the first is equivalent to the second), *positivity* (the concatenation of any two objects is greater than either of these objects), and *archimedianity* (if one object is smaller than another, then there is some finite n such that the concatenation of that object with itself n times will exceed the second object).

[5] The relevant notion of homomorphism employed here, and in measurement theory more generally, is examined in the next section. It is defined as follows: Let $\mathcal{X} = <X, R_1, \ldots, R_n>$ and $\mathcal{Y} = <Y, S_1, \ldots, S_n>$ be relational structures, where X is a non-empty set of objects and R_i are relations or operations on X, and Y is a second non-empty set of objects and S_i are relations or operations on Y. Then ϕ is said to be a *homomorphism of $\mathcal{X}$ into $\mathcal{Y}$* if and only if (i) ϕ is a function from X into Y, (ii) for each i and n, R_i is an n-ary relation if and only if S_i is an n-ary relation, and (iii) for each i, if R_i is an n-ary relation and $x_1, \ldots, x_n$ are in X, then $R_i(x_1, \ldots, x_n)$ iff $S_i(\phi(x_1), \ldots, \phi(x_n))$.

X the value of $\phi(x)$ to within an arbitrarily small error. These values are determined by certain fairly elementary empirical procedures. In the case of mass, for example, one can use a single-arm pan balance to establish either that two objects have the same mass or that one has a greater mass than the other. By successively concatenating objects of unit mass, one can construct a scale for arbitrary whole multiples of unit mass. This scale can (subject to certain practical limitations on weighing operations) be arbitrarily refined by using the pan balance to identify objects of mass 1/n (in effect by finding n objects of identical mass that together have unit mass) and then successively concatenating one or more of these objects both with themselves and with the objects of whole multiples of unit mass to construct a more fine-grained scale.

The early work of Helmholtz, Hölder, and Campbell was further developed and extended by Stevens (1946). Prior work in measurement theory had focused almost exclusively on what has come to be called the 'representation problem', the problem of specifying the conditions (axioms) that an empirical system must satisfy in order for there to exist an homomorphism, or more stringently an isomorphism,[6] into the positive real numbers that allows a numerical assignment to physical magnitudes. Stevens' work on scale types (nominal, ordinal, interval, proportional, etc.) brought to measurement theory an acute appreciation of a second important problem, what has come to be called the 'uniqueness problem', which concerns the relative uniqueness of acceptable numerical assignments. Stevens proposed to define scale types by their transformation groups, what he called their 'admissible transformations'. Thus, for example, he defined as interval scales those for which the admissible transformations $f(x)$ are positive linear transformations, i.e., transformations of the algebraic form $f(x) = ax + b$. Stevens offered no argument for the claim that for a specific scale type only certain transformations are admissible, but he clearly thought that it is only under admissible transformations of a particular scale type that the empirical content of what is represented numerically by means of such scales is preserved, with the consequence that numerical assignments are unique only up to admissible transformations of scale, and different scales that are related by such transformations do not differ in the empirical facts concerning magnitudes they can represent.

A seminal paper by Suppes (1951) defined the path that much subsequent work in measurement theory has taken. In this paper Suppes attempted to integrate previous work on the representation and uniqueness problems. He

---

[6] ϕ is said to be an *isomorphism of* $\mathcal{X}$ *into* $\mathcal{Y}$, if and only if ϕ is an homomorphism of $\mathcal{X}$ into $\mathcal{Y}$, and ϕ is one-to-one.

undertook, first, to specify minimal conditions (axioms) for the existence of a homomorphism representation in the reals of objects possessing extensive magnitudes and, second, to specify the relation that such homomorphism representations bear to one another. The first undertaking resulted in what Suppes and Zinnes (1963) would later dub a 'representation theorem', i.e., a proof of the existence of such a homomorphism representation in the reals; the second undertaking resulted in what they would dub a 'uniqueness theorem', i.e., a characterization of the class of possible homomorphisms, where this characterization takes the form of a numerical function that maps possible homomorphisms into other such homomorphisms, thus effectively specifying the relative uniqueness of the numerical assignment specified by any member of this class. Together these two theorems answered the question, not satisfactorily answered by Stevens, of what counts as an admissible transformation of a scale type: a transformation is admissible if and only if it maps homomorphisms into homomorphisms.

Suppes' work was important not simply because it provided the first reasonably satisfactory analysis of the empirical conditions that make the numerical measurement of extensive magnitudes possible, but more importantly because it provided an analytical approach that could easily be extended to the study of the numerical measurement of non-extensive magnitudes such as temperature. Much of the subsequent work in measurement theory, especially during the 1950s and early 1960s, was directed to just this end.[7] Especially important for our present interests is the generality of Suppes' analytical model. Arguably this model could be extended not only, as it subsequently was, to the measurement of non-extensive magnitudes, but also to cases of representation in which the properties of objects that get represented are *not* magnitudes and the domain in which they get represented is *not* the positive reals, including not only various analytic geometries, but also perhaps, as Suppes and Zinnes (1963) suggested, the linguistic representation of propositional attitudes.[8] Díez (1997) describes Suppes' analytical model as follows:

[7] See Krantz *et al.* 1971, Roberts 1979, Narens 1985, and Suppes *et al.* 1989, to mention only the most prominent contributions to this recent work.

[8] Some strongly disapprove of including such representations under the rubric of measurement, precisely because they don't involve the numerical representation of magnitudes. Thus, Díez (1997) complains about Suppes *et al.*'s (1989) inclusion of various analytical geometries in the second volume of their definitive *Foundations of Measurement*. Perhaps such representational structures are, as Díez insists, better regarded as part of a more general theory of morphism representation, i.e., representation based upon a formal morphism relation between represented and representing relational structures, of which measurement theory is only a specific subtheory. But arguably nothing of substance hangs on this terminological issue. There are natural, and indeed illuminating,

Let A be a set of objects to which certain numbers are to be assigned representing the 'quantity' of a particular magnitude that they have. The facts related to the magnitude are expressed by certain empirical relations $R_1, \ldots, R_n$ (some of them can be operations) between the objects. Because the objects possess the magnitude 'in a more or less degree' some of these relations will be of (some type of) order. The domain and the relations make up an empirical system $E = <A, R_1, \ldots, R_n>$ which expresses the essential nature of the property as a magnitude. Measurement assigns numbers to the objects, usually real numbers if the whole wealth of mathematics is to be applied. Empirical relations (and operations) $R_1, \ldots, R_n$ are represented by 'natural' numerical relations $S_1, \ldots, S_n$ which along with a set N of numbers . . . constitute a mathematical system $M = <N, S_1, \ldots, S_n>$. The statement that numerical relations S_i represent empirical relations R_i means that M expresses with numbers what E expresses without them, i.e., that E is homomorphic to M. An analysis of how measurement is possible consists, then, in studying how such a homomorphism is possible, i.e., investigating the conditions which E has to satisfy for there to be a homomorphism into M, and establishing the corresponding representation and uniqueness theorems.

(Díez 1997: 241–2)

The extension of Suppes' analytical model to propositional attitudes would undertake to prove representation and uniqueness theorems for our natural language representations of propositional attitudes. The representation theorem would characterize the conditions that the empirical relational structure of propositional attitudes would have to satisfy in order for that structure to find a homomorphic representation in the representing relational structure defined by the natural language sentences by which we represent the attitudes. This would ensure that the essential properties of propositional attitudes have a faithful image in their natural language representations. The uniqueness theorem would characterize the relative uniqueness of the mappings that provide such a representation, specifying admissible transformations of the representing structure that preserve its empirical content.[9]

---

extensions of numerical measurement theory, and it may be useful to describe these extensions as kinds of 'measurement' if only to underscore their important affinities to numerical measurement.

[9] The mapping of the empirical structure of the attitudes into their natural language representations might turn out not to have the formal simplicity of the mappings of the extensive magnitudes into their numerical representations. It is possible, as we shall see, to abandon the requirement that the empirical structure of the attitudes have a homomorphic image in their natural language representations, and yet this empirical structure nonetheless be faithfully represented by the relational structure of their natural language representations.

5.3. HOMOMORPHISMS AND OTHER STRUCTURAL RELATIONS

The import of measurement theory lies primarily in the explanation and justification that it provides of established measurement practices, thereby enabling us to understand more clearly the empirical content of our measurement claims. Numerical measurement theory explains both how the real numbers can be used to represent empirical magnitudes and also the extent to which different numerical assignments to objects possessing these magnitudes are equivalent in empirical content. It accomplishes this by providing solutions to both the representation problem and the uniqueness problem, both of which are typically defined in terms of the set of possible homomorphisms of the represented empirical structure into different representing numerical structures.[10]

A solution to the representation problem proves a representation theorem; specifically, it typically proves that for a given empirical relational structure $\mathcal{X} = <X, R_1, \ldots, R_n>$, where X is a non-empty set of objects and R_i are relations or operations on X, and a given representing relational structure $\mathcal{Y} = <Y, S_1, \ldots, S_n>$, where Y is a non-empty set of objects, real numbers in the case of numerical measurement, and S_i are relations or operations on Y, there exists a homomorphism ϕ of $\mathcal{X}$ into $\mathcal{Y}$. In effect, a representation theorem establishes that there exists an assignment of members of Y to the members of X, specified by the mapping ϕ of X into Y, that provides an accurate way of representing the empirical properties and relations R_i of the members of X. It accomplishes this by proving that ϕ *respects*, in the sense explained below, those empirical properties and relations.

Recall the definition of a homomorphism of $\mathcal{X}$ into $\mathcal{Y}$, given above and reproduced here for convenience:

Let $\mathcal{X} = <X, R_1, \ldots, R_n>$ and $\mathcal{Y} = <Y, S_1, \ldots, S_n>$ be relational structures, where X is a non-empty set of objects and R_i are relations or operations on X, and Y is a second non-empty set of objects and S_i are relations or operations on Y. Then ϕ is said to be a *homomorphism of $\mathcal{X}$ into $\mathcal{Y}$* if and only if (i) ϕ is a function from X into Y, (ii) for each i and n, R_i is an n-ary relation if and

---

[10] For a standard exposition of these two problems, see Suppes and Zinnes 1963, Krantz *et al.* 1971, Narens 1985, or Díez 1997.

only if S_i is an n-ary relation, and (iii) for each i, if R_i is an n-ary relation and $x_1, \ldots, x_n$ are in X, then $R_i(x_1, \ldots, x_n)$ iff $S_i(\phi(x_1), \ldots, \phi(x_n))$.

This definition, which is standard within contemporary measurement theory, is stronger than the usual definition favored by set theorists, which would have the conditional 'if $R_i(x_1, \ldots, x_n)$, then $S_i(\phi(x_1), \ldots, \phi(x_n))$' in place of the biconditional in (iii). This stronger definition, like the weaker one, requires that ϕ *preserve* in the representational structure $\mathcal{Y}$ all empirical relations R_i, in the sense that each n-ary relation R_i among objects $x_1, \ldots, x_n$ in X is represented by some surrogative n-ary relation S_i among surrogate objects $\phi(x_1), \ldots, \phi(x_n)$ in Y. But the strengthened definition also requires that ϕ *counter-preserve* in $\mathcal{Y}$ all empirical relations R_i, in the sense that there is no n-ary relation S_i among objects $\phi(x_1), \ldots, \phi(x_n)$ in Y that is not the surrogate of some n-ary relation R_i among objects $x_1, \ldots, x_n$ in X. A mapping ϕ that both preserves and counter-preserves all empirical relations R_i is said to *respect* these relations.[11] It respects these relations in that by preserving and counter-preserving them, it insures that the representation in $\mathcal{Y}$ of these relations represents *all* and *only* the true facts about them.

Because a homomorphism ϕ of $\mathcal{X}$ into $\mathcal{Y}$ respects the relations R_i on X, a system of representation based on ϕ satisfies an absolutely crucial practical desideratum, namely that it can support what Swoyer (1991) has dubbed 'surrogative reasoning' about the represented domain. In such reasoning, we reason indirectly about relations R_i among objects in the represented empirical domain X by reasoning directly about the surrogative relations S_i among objects in the representational domain Y. Thus, we can reason surrogatively about mass relations among physical objects by reasoning about relations among numerical representatives of their masses, concluding, for example, from the fact that one object has a mass represented by the number 2 on the kg scale (i.e., has a mass of 2 kg), that a second object has a mass represented by the number 3 on that scale, and that a third object has a mass represented by the number 5 on that scale, and in conjunction with such arithmetic truths as $2 + 3 = 5$ and $2 < 3 < 5$, that the third object has a greater mass than either of the other two, that the third has the same mass as the combined mass of the first two objects, and so on. The fact that ϕ respects the relations R_i guarantees that these empirical relations will be represented

---

[11] The terminology here is Swoyer's (1991). Mundy (1986) dubs homomorphisms that both preserve and counter-preserve the relations on the empirical domain 'faithful homomorphisms' in order to distinguish them from homomorphisms that, as set theorists would understand them, merely preserve such relations.

in the homomorphic representation and furthermore that truth-preserving inferences defined over the surrogative relations S_i will entail true conclusions about the relations R_i for which they are surrogates. Arguably, the *entire* point and purpose of homomorphic representation is to enable such surrogative reasoning. That we typically overlook the surrogative character of such reasoning testifies to the seamless nature of the representation of $\mathcal{X}$ in $\mathcal{Y}$ that underpins it: we think of the magnitudes *themselves* as intrinsically numerical, and not simply as sets of *non*-numerical properties that are structured in a manner that permits their numerical representation. We think of the magnitudes as intrinsically numerical precisely because their homomorphic representation in the real numbers offers the only practicable way of thinking and reasoning reliably about the magnitudes. How else, for example, are we to worry about our weights, the effects of our diets, except in numerical terms!

There is little reason to demand, as some might suppose, that such a homomorphism ϕ of $\mathcal{X}$ into $\mathcal{Y}$ must in fact be an isomorphism, since the former suffices to guarantee that the empirical relations R_i of $\mathcal{X}$ are respected, in the sense defined, and this is the most that the surrogative uses of numerical representation requires. Indeed, taking ϕ to be an isomorphism would require taking the domain of $\mathcal{X}$ to be equivalence classes of objects, rather than objects themselves, since typically more than one object can stand in the same relations R_i to other objects: many objects have the same mass, length, or temperature, something that is precluded by the assumption that the mapping relation is one of isomorphism (between structures of individual objects). But, and this is the crucial point here, representation morphisms *weaker* than even a homomorphism will sometimes suffice. Sometimes representation users like ourselves can get by with something less than complete and faithful representations. Failure to preserve in the representational domain all the relevant properties and relations defined over objects of the empirical domain may be tolerable, provided that those objects do have the properties and relations that they are represented as having. For in such event, surrogative reasoning about those specific objects is not vitiated, although generalized reasoning about the entire domain clearly is. Failures of counter-preservation, by contrast, as Swoyer (1991: 473) points out, typically do vitiate surrogative reasoning in a way that failures of preservation typically do not,[12] since in the former case, but not in the latter, representations about the relations among represented objects

---

[12] See Swoyer (1991: 473) for a discussion of cases where failures of preservation vitiate surrogative reasoning. For example, in cases where the mapping function runs in the opposite direction, i.e., *from* the representation *to* what it represents, as arguably it does in the case

can be wrong, and hence surrogative reasoning using those representations can lead to false conclusions about those objects. But even here we can often tolerate limited failures, provided the conclusions based on surrogative reasoning using such representations are regarded as only presumptive.

Consideration of cases in which mapping relations weaker than a homomorphism nevertheless suffice for sound surrogative reasoning leads Swoyer (1991: 474) to a definition of what he calls 'Δ/Ψ-morphism', which accommodates homomorphic representation as a special case of this more general sort of representation relation. The basic idea is to define two possibly disjoint subsets, Δ and Ψ, of the full set of relations R_i of $\mathcal{X}$, at least one of which is non-empty. Then ϕ is a Δ/Ψ-morphism of $\mathcal{X}$ into $\mathcal{Y}$ if and only if it preserves all of the relations in Δ, and counter-preserves all of the relations in Ψ. He then identifies the 'structural representations' of $\mathcal{X}$ in $\mathcal{Y}$, what I have been calling morphism representations of $\mathcal{X}$ in $\mathcal{Y}$, with those Δ/Ψ-morphisms of $\mathcal{X}$ into $\mathcal{Y}$ in which either Ψ or Δ is non-empty depending on the direction of the mapping function between X and Y. This requirement on Ψ or Δ insures that the image of one or the other set under ϕ contains the relations S_i in $\mathcal{Y}$ that are of representational significance and hence make sound surrogative reasoning possible. The details of Swoyer's proposal are not important here; the crucial point is that if, as is surely the case, the practical purpose of morphism representation is to support surrogative reasoning, then morphisms weaker than homomorphisms will sometimes suffice. As Swoyer puts it, 'Just which bits of surrogative reasoning are possible in a given situation will depend on which relations (primitive and defined) are preserved and counter-preserved, and this, in turn, will depend on features of the particular mapping' (Swoyer 1991: 475).

Δ/Ψ-morphisms weaken in one direction or the other the biconditional that figures in (iii) of the definition of a homomorphism of $\mathcal{X}$ into $\mathcal{Y}$ (see pp. 133–4 above), thereby abandoning the desideratum, satisfied by homomorphisms, of respecting the empirical relations R_i of represented structure. Representations based on these weaker morphisms don't provide a complete and faithful representation of all such relations. Yet there is another kind of morphism representation, not depending on homomorphism, that does provide a complete and faithful representation of the relational structure that it represents. Consider the very familiar interpretation of the rational

---

of linguistic representation, surrogative reasoning will deliver only true conclusions about the represented domain only if relations are preserved in the mapping.

numbers in the integers, where each rational number expressed by the fraction m/n is mapped to an ordered pair of integers $<m, n>$. Addition and multiplication of rationals can be expressed in terms of addition and multiplication operations defined over these integers, but neither of the former operations have a single representing relation defined over the pair of integers to which the rational is mapped (at least no non-Goodmanesque, natural relation which anyone would recognize as such). Rather, as every school kid knows, each of these operations is represented by specific sequences of operations of addition and multiplication over *members* of the pair. So the mapping that pairs each rational number expressed by the fraction m/n with the pair of integers $<m, n>$ is *not* a homomorphism, even in the weaker sense of that term favored by set theorists (see p. 134 above). Hodges (1993: 212 f.) describes the mapping as an instance of what he calls an (n-dimensional) *interpretation* of one relational structure in another, in this case a two-dimensional interpretation of the rational numbers in the integers. The basic idea here is that in an (n-dimensional) interpretation of a structure *A* in a structure *B* (such as the above two-dimensional interpretation of the rationals in the integers), there are two maps, one a surjective map of the n-dimensional objects of the interpreting structure onto the objects of the interpreted structure that assigns to every object in *A* a n-dimensional object in *B*, and the other a syntactic map, i.e., a translation manual, that pairs every atomic sentence statement in the language L used to describe relations among (and operations on) objects in *A* with a complex sentence in the language K used to describe relations among (and operations on) the n distinct components of the n-dimensional objects in *B*. Together these two maps guarantee that an atomic statement in language L about relations among (and operations on) the objects in *A* is true if and only if a complex statement in language K about relations among (and operations on) the n distinct components of the n-dimensional objects in *B* is true (e.g., that a certain rational number m_i/n_i is the sum of two rational numbers m_j/n_j and m_k/n_k if and only if $n_i \cdot (m_j \cdot n_k + m_k \cdot n_j) = m_i \cdot n_j \cdot n_k$). The upshot is that such an interpretation can provide a complete and faithful representation of the empirical relations defined over the objects in the empirical domain that provably supports sound surrogative reasoning, though without the interpreting structure being a homomorphic image of the empirical structure that it interprets. The more general point here is that any number of different representation relations may suffice for the surrogative purposes to which representations are put—it depends on the specific purposes, on the relational structure being represented, and on the available representation resources. We need not think solely in terms of homomorphisms, and certainly not solely in terms of isomorphisms.

5.4. REPRESENTATION, ABSTRACTION, IDEALIZATION, AND REPRESENTATIONAL ARTIFACTS

Representation, as it is construed within measurement theory, is a relation between two formal relational structures: one structure *represents* the other just in case the former is a 'morphic' (i.e., structural) *image*, typically a homomorphic image, of the latter. Objects in the domain of the chosen representing structure (e.g., numbers in the case of numerical structures) do not, strictly speaking, represent entities in the domain of the represented empirical structure; they represent them only in the sense of being their *representatives* within a given representing structure. An entity in the one domain is a representative of an entity in the other by virtue of, and only by virtue of, the fact that the one structure represents the other. It is, for example, only within the context of a particular representing structure, e.g., the Fahrenheit scale, that the number 80 represents, in the sense of being the representative of, an object's having the particular temperature that it does. Change the scale, e.g., to the Centigrade or the Kelvin scale, and that same number will be the representative of a different temperature.

Representations are useful as representations precisely because they do not undertake to represent the represented empirical domain in all its detail and complexity. As a consequence, representation always involves significant abstraction and idealization. Of the uncountably many empirical relations that obtain among objects in the represented structure's empirical domain, only a small number will constitute that structure's relation set, and hence be preserved, counter-preserved, or respected, by the representation relation. Moreover, those relations that do constitute the relation set will typically be idealizations in one respect or another of the actual empirical relations. Thus, for example, on simpler first-order measurement theories for extensive magnitudes, these magnitudes are assumed to be closed under the concatenation or summation operation, even though it is implausible to suppose that there actually exists any such operation on objects of great magnitude. If the concatenation or summation operation is restricted to objects below a certain size, as some first-order measurement theories for extensive magnitudes do, these theories still assume that for any two objects of magnitudes m_1 and m_2 satisfying the restriction, there exists some third object of magnitude $m_1 \circ m_2$. This, too, is an idealizing empirical assumption, in this case about the plentitude and diversity in size of objects smaller than a certain size that comprise the empirical domain of the theory.

Given the significant role of abstraction and idealization, one might reasonably conceive of the represented and representing structures as themselves *models* of a class of empirical phenomena and a class of representations, respectively, and of measurement theory itself as a theory of the morphism relations between such models which explains how the members of the one class manage to represent the members of the other. The measurement theory explains this possibility by characterizing the morphism relation between these model structures that makes faithful representation possible. Conceiving of the relation between representations and represented phenomena as thus mediated by morphically related relational structures provides a useful antidote to the presumption that constructing a measurement-theoretic account of some established measurement practice, e.g., the numerical measurement of extensive physical magnitudes, is simply a matter of proving the requisite representation and uniqueness theorems for a pair of antecedently given relational structures. Crucially, the measurement theorist must first specify appropriate structural models for both the representations and the represented phenomena, and this involves making the facilitating abstractions and idealizations necessary to construct these models. It was, for example, the genius of both Helmholtz and Hölder in their pioneering development of a numerical measurement theory for extensive magnitudes to discern the relevant empirical relations among physical objects and their counterpart mathematical relations on the real numbers that makes such measurement possible. If one fails to recognize this crucial first step, one may fail to appreciate that not only is the mapping between representing and represented structures non-unique up to admissible transformations of scale (as specified by the uniqueness theorem), but also that the choice of representing structure will itself be non-unique. Thus, for example, the empirical structure of extensive magnitudes could as well be represented in the *multiplicative* reals, where the empirical concatenation operation has as its numerical counterpart multiplication (rather than addition) on the reals (see Díez 1997: 242–3, and Krantz *et al.* 1971: 13, 99–101, 152). Also, and perhaps more importantly for the present interests, there is the added possibility that in overlooking this crucial first step in the construction of a measurement theory for some established measurement practice, one may overlook the possibility of significant theoretical error and misunderstanding introduced by an incorrect specification of these relational structures, since to specify these structures is effectively to specify the relevant relations that can be preserved, counter-preserved, or respected (or possibly interpreted, in the sense of Hodges) in the representation.

Specifying the relational structures that are the models of the representing and represented domains is typically quite difficult, since in the absence of a worked-out measurement-theoretic account of the relation between these two domains, it is often quite difficult to distinguish *artifactual* features of a representation from features that are the image of features of the represented domain. The proof of a uniqueness theorem provides a criterion for drawing the relevant distinction between artifactual and empirically meaningful features: the latter are just those features that are preserved under admissible transformations of scale, i.e., that are preserved under all automorphisms of acceptable mapping relations. But once again, being able to prove a uniqueness theorem presumes that much of the heavy lifting has already been done in constructing structural models of both representation and represented domains.

5.5. A SECOND-ORDER INTENSIONAL VERSION OF MEASUREMENT THEORY

In its standard presentations, numerical measurement theory is a first-order, extensional theory that affects an assignment of numbers to *objects* (or sets of objects), not to the quantitative properties, i.e., the magnitudes, possessed by these objects. What gets measured, strictly speaking, is not these properties, e.g., the property of having a certain mass or length, but rather the objects themselves, albeit in a way that reflects, by means of their relations-in-extension to other objects, their possession of these quantitative properties. It is this assignment of numbers to objects rather than to magnitudes that permits measurement theory to be formulated within a first-order framework, something that empiricists, and more especially nominalists, would no doubt count as a virtue, since the theory traffics only in objects and set relations thereof. But the assignment can as well be made directly to magnitudes, provided one is willing to abandon one's nominalistic scruples and countenance a second-order framework that quantifies over magnitudes. Mundy (1987) and also Swoyer (1987) sketch just such an alternative. The resulting theory, which Mundy dubs a 'theory of quantity' in order to mark his rejection of the nominalist, indeed operationalist, connotations of the expression 'theory of measurement', employs a second-order logical syntax that permits quantifiers and second-order predicates that range over first-order magnitudes. The semantics of this language is logically elementary (i.e., it utilizes only the truth-functional connectives of the propositional logic and the existential and universal quantifiers of standard first-order predicate logic), so that the logic is both complete and recursively axiomatizable.

Mundy claims that the second-order theory is superior to the first-order theory in two important respects. First, it better captures our common-sense intuitions, e.g., that measurements measure certain quantitative properties of objects, that measurement attributions attribute quantitative properties that could be shared by other objects. As an illustration of a counterintuitive consequence of the first-order theory, consider, for example, the assertion that Jones weighs the same now as he did then. On its face, this assertion seems to be about a single property, a particular weight, that Jones possessed at two different times, but on the standard first-order theory it would have to be about the set relations that Jones bears to other weighty objects at the two different times. Second, and perhaps more importantly, first-order theories, as we saw in the previous section, depend essentially upon at least one strong existence axiom asserting the *existence of concatenations*, e.g., the existence, for any two objects x and y, of an object $z = x \bigcirc y$ whose magnitude is the concatenation of the magnitudes of x and y. Measurement theorists readily concede that this axiom is unrealistic because of practical limitations on concatenation procedures, but the problem, Mundy (1987: 32) argues, is more serious than these theorists allow. For even within the bounds of practical limitations on concatenation, whatever they happen to be, the clearly empirical assumption that for any two objects whose concatenation does not exceed that bound there *actually exists* an object equal to that concatenation seems quite implausible, or at very least not empirically supported. Moreover, why should measurement theory depend on such a contingency? As Mundy puts it, 'surely the whole structure of physical quantities and quantitative laws would not collapse if through some cosmic accident all of the actual examples of objects precisely two meters long were to be destroyed while the standard meter itself remained intact' (ibid.). There are, to be sure, ways around this problem. One could, for example, adopt a possibilist interpretation of the quantifiers, construing the existence axiom as asserting the existence of a merely possible object equal to the concatenation of any two other objects. Or one could construe the concatenation of two objects to be their Goodmanian concatenation. But these ways around the problem come only at a high price. The possibilist interpretation requires the explicit introduction of modal apparatus, since quantifier expressions are otherwise ambiguous. But the introduction of such apparatus largely undercuts the empirical rationale for a first-order theory, since we have no obvious way of determining the truth or falsehood of the axiom. And the Goodmanian construal of concatenations makes a shambles of the idea that the measurement theory should provide a justification of actual measurement practice (cf. Swoyer 1987: 254–7, and Mundy 1987: 32–4).

Swoyer (1987), for his part, emphasizes the consilience of a second-order theory with both a realism with respect to measurement and a realism with respect to the measured properties themselves, each of which he takes to be empirically well supported. Swoyer understands by the first sort of realism, the view that measurement gives us information about objective features of empirical phenomena, and that it does so by virtue of the fact that these features satisfy certain specifiable conditions that make measurement possible. He understands by the second sort of realism, the view that properties and relations are, as he puts it, 'genuine entities in their own right' (Swoyer 1987: 240). Swoyer's argument for a realism with respect to measurement rests on the seemingly insurmountable difficulties that anti-realist views of measurement encounter in trying to account for actual measurement practice and its role in scientific inquiry. His argument for realism with respect to the measured properties rests on their explanatory value: scientific theory in general, and scientific measurement in particular, he argues, needs something that plays just the explanatory role that properties and relations appear to play, and this fact, he thinks, is good grounds for being realist about such properties and relations, and in particular about the magnitudes that are the object of measurement. These magnitudes, Swoyer argues further, are, as the second-order formulation of measurement theory would have it, intrinsic features of objects, not set relations that hold among individual objects.

A property-theoretic formulation of numerical measurement theory for physical magnitudes assigns numbers to quantities of these magnitudes, rather than to the objects that possess these magnitudes. The mathematical relations defined over these numerical assignments, e.g., the ordering relation $\leq$ and the addition operation $+$ in the case of the extensive magnitudes, are the images of certain second-order relations (and operations) defined over these quantitative properties. Adopting such a property-theoretic formulation requires replacing the extensional relational structures that model the represented empirical phenomena in the standard first-order measurement theory with intensional relational structures that both permit quantification over these quantitative properties and also countenance the possibility that different properties might share the same extension (i.e., properties are not to be construed set-theoretically). One could resort here to an intensional relational structure with a rich type-hierarchy, but a second-order intensional relational structure will seemingly suffice, where this structure has the form of an ordered quadruple of the form $\mathcal{X}' = <I, {}^{f}R_i, {}^{s}R_i, {}^{\vee}>$, where I is a set of objects, ${}^{f}R_i$ a set of first-order relations (including one-place relations, or properties), ${}^{s}R_i$ a set of second-order relations, and ${}^{\vee}$ a unary function (on ${}^{f}R_i$ and ${}^{s}R_i$) that assigns an extension in I to each member of ${}^{f}R_i$ and an extension in ${}^{f}R_i$ to each member of ${}^{s}R_i$. A morphism of $\mathcal{X}'$ into a numerical relational structure $\mathcal{Y}$, as defined in an earlier section, will be a *trans-type* mapping of first-order relations (properties, in the case of extensive magnitudes) into objects (real numbers), where the second-order relations of $\mathcal{X}'$ (ordering and concatenation, in the case of extensive magnitudes) have as their image certain first-order relations of $\mathcal{Y}$.

The point of mentioning the availability of a second-order formulation of measurement theory is not to endorse that particular formulation, though in fact I find it attractive for just the sorts of reasons given by Mundy (1987) and Swoyer (1987) and will therefore presume it without further argument in the discussion that follows. Rather I want simply to point out that the assignment of numbers to objects rather than to magnitudes is not intrinsic to the theory of numerical measurement, and as a consequence there would seem to be no a priori reason to require that a measurement-theoretic account of propositional attitudes treat them as relations-in-extension between the possessors of attitudes rather than, as a second-order formulation would have it, relational properties (possibly monadic properties) of their possessors. The basic point remains unaffected by the choice of framework: our talk about magnitudes is relational, i.e., couched in terms of relations to numbers, but no one supposes that an object's, or a magnitude's, standing in a relation to a number is in any way intrinsic to that object's having the magnitude that it does. Such relational talk is simply a convenient way of tracking certain substantive real-world relations, among either objects or magnitudes, depending upon how one conceives the measurement theory. There is no support in any of this for a relational conception of the magnitudes analogous to the relational conception of propositional attitudes, according to which having a particular mass (length, temperature, etc.) is a matter of standing in a certain relation to a real number.

5.6. MEASUREMENT THEORY AND MEASURE PREDICATES

Numerical measurement, we noted earlier, predates by millennia the development of numerical measurement theory, which investigates theoretically the empirical and mathematical conditions that make numerical measurement possible. Yet it would seem that both the practice of numerical measurement as well as the use of measure predicates to attribute specific quantities of magnitude to objects must presume at least a rudimentary grasp of some of the basic truths of numerical measurement theory, e.g., that there is an ordering on the quantities of any given magnitude. For how otherwise could one possibly understand what it is to measure numerically a particular magnitude, say the weight of some object, or what is meant by a sentence that attributes a particular numerical quantity of some magnitude to an object? But if this is so, does it not also follow that the semantics of measure predicates must incorporate in some fashion this rudimentary knowledge? For how else could a speaker understand just what someone is saying when he or she ascribes one of these predicates?

Consider the following *measure phrases*, which are used to specify quantities of physical magnitudes:

(1)   *a mass of 5 kilos*
    a weight of 10 lbs
    a temperature of 98.6° F
    a length of 10 feet
    a duration of 10 seconds
    a volume of 2 liters
    an area of 7 acres
    an age of 15 years
    a pressure of 3 atmospheres
    a resistance of 200 ohms
    a force of 3 joules
    a hardness of 4 on Moh's scale
    a pungency of 25,000 Scoville units

Each of these (numerical magnitude) measure noun phrases takes the same form: the head of the noun phrase specifies a *magnitude* (mass, weight, temperature, etc.), while the prepositional phrase, which is the grammatical complement of the head, specifies a *quantity* (amount, degree, etc.) of that magnitude.[13] The prepositional phrase does this by specifying both a real number and a particular numerical measurement scale for the specified magnitude, where the specified number is the representative, *on the specified scale*, of the specified quantity of that magnitude. A (numerical magnitude) *measure predicate* is formed by adjoining a measure noun phrase to a stative verb (typically a verb of possession such as *have*, but also verbs such as *exert, maintain*) or to a resultive verb such as *fall to, increase to, grow to*, etc., each of the latter of which might be analyzed in terms of coming to be in a certain state.[14] The predicates so formed can then be used to attribute to an object (or in some cases, to an event) a specific quantity of some magnitude: having a mass of 5 kilos, having a duration of 10 seconds, exerting a force of 3 joules, growing to 6 feet, etc.

Measure predicates are probably best construed as expressing the property of having the particular quantity q of a specified magnitude M, where this quantity is represented by a real number N that is its representative on the specified scale ϕ_M for M. Thus, for example, the measure sentence *x has a volume of 3 liters* would assert simply that x has a quantity q of volume equal to or greater than 3 liters, and this sentence would be true if and only if this were the case. But if understanding a sentence is a matter of knowing its truth conditions, then understanding measure sentences does not require knowing any numerical measurement theory. It will be enough simply to know what it is to have a volume equal to or greater than 3 liters. One needn't know anything about the function ϕ_M that maps quantities q into positive real numbers N on the liter scale or anything about how the standard liter volume is defined. One would have to know that specific real numbers are the representatives on specific scales of specific quantities of a given magnitude. But knowing this is consistent with not appreciating what it is about the

[13] Measure noun phrases can also take the form of compound nouns N_1 N_2 (e.g., a 2-liter volume, 25-lb weight), where N_2 specifies some object by means of one of the magnitudes it possesses (a volume, a weight), and N_1 specifies the quantity (amount, degree, etc.) of the magnitude that this object possesses, as represented on the specified numerical measurement scale.

[14] Some magnitudes have an associated pseudo-transitive verb phrase (*weighs 8 kilos, lasts 10 seconds*, etc.), where the verb specifies the magnitude, and the object noun phrase specifies the quantity (amount, degree, etc.) of that magnitude, again, as represented on the specified numerical measurement scale.

structure of the positive reals that enables them to serve as representatives of quantities. It is even consistent with not appreciating that there are other, equally good scales for measuring volume. The latter is probably something that we come to appreciate only when we are confronted in everyday life with alternative measurement systems, e.g., discovering early on that our height can be measured in both inches and centimeters, our weight in pounds, kilos, and stones. Until such time, we don't normally think of the quantity's numerical representative as the representative of a *non*-numerical quantity. Rather we think of these predicates as simply expressing the property of having a particular *numerical* quantity of the specified magnitude. We think of Jones as having the weight in lbs that he does, say 160 lbs, not in the sense of having a weight that can be represented in those terms, but in the sense of actually having that numerical weight in lbs, as if weight in lbs were an intrinsic property of Jones.

But does this imply that our use of measure predicates does not presume any understanding of the numerical measurement theory that these predicates presuppose? Consider the workaday case in which someone measures a certain magnitude of an object, say its weight, using an appropriate measuring instrument (a weight scale), and then reports the result of this measurement by means of a sentence containing an appropriate measure predicate, e.g., *the tomato has a weight of 0.95 lb*. A measurer counts as having correctly measured and correctly reported the measured weight just in case the tomato weighed does in fact have a weight of 0.95 lb, i.e., has a weight whose numerical representative is 0.95 on the lb scale. Someone hearing the measurement report counts as having understood the report only if he knows that the tomato was reported to have a weight of 0.95 lb, i.e., knows that the tomato was reported to have a weight whose numerical representative is 0.95 on the lb scale. But what is it to know this? Clearly it is not enough to know that the complement sentence 'the tomato was reported to have a weight of 0.95 lb' is true. For someone might know that without understanding the measurement report. Maybe this person has independent evidence that the person reporting the tomato's weight is a reliable truth-teller. Presumably, to understand the report, one must know certain of the report's entailments, specifically, that if the tomato has a weight of 0.95 lb, then it is heavier than one that weighs 0.90 lb and lighter than one weighing 1.00 lb, that it weighs the same as the combined weights of two tomatoes weighing 0.50 lb and 0.45 lb, and so on. For suppose that a hearer was able to confirm that the tomato was said to have a weight of 0.95 lb, but was unable to confirm any of these entailments. Surely we would not count this person as having understood the report. To understand the measure sentence, one needs to know one's way around the representational system that the measure sentence presumes. In the case of extensive magnitudes such as weight, that involves understanding that there is a ordering of objects with respect to their weights, that the weights of objects exhibit basic additive properties, and so on. Put another way, to count as understanding measurement talk about weights, the person needs to be able to reason surrogatively using the relevant representation scheme for weights, but such ability, it should be clear, does not presume any understanding of the empirical conditions that make such reasoning possible and that numerical measurement theory proposes to explain. Nor does it seem to require knowing anything about the mapping of quantities into their numerical representatives. So there is little reason, it seems, to suppose that the semantics of measure sentences incorporates much, if any, of the numerical measurement theory that the use of such sentences presupposes.

5.7. THE KNOWLEDGE AFFORDED BY MEASUREMENT THEORY

The import of measurement theory, we have seen, lies primarily in the justification and explanation that it provides for established measurement practices, thereby enabling us to understand more clearly the empirical content of our measurement claims. Measurement theory accomplishes this by providing solutions to both the representation problem and the uniqueness problem, but it is important in the present context to be clear about the sort of understanding, more specifically the knowledge, that it provides. A solution to the representation problem establishes that there exists a mapping of the relational structure that models the represented empirical phenomena into the relational structure that models our natural language representations of those phenomena, a structure that respects (preserves, counter-preserves, or maybe interprets, in the sense explained) the properties and relations of the former structure. A solution to the uniqueness problem characterizes the relative uniqueness of all such mappings by specifying a class of admissible transformations, all of which preserve empirical content. But the solutions to the representation and uniqueness problems do *not* provide a reductive explanatory account of the empirical properties and relations that are respected (preserved, etc.), and hence represented, in representations of the represented empirical domain. Thus, for example, one can know the relations that are respected in the measurement scales used to represent temperature, weight, IQ, and so on, without having the foggiest idea what, reductively speaking, these properties are. Measurement theory only provides knowledge of the empirical *structure* of the represented empirical phenomena (and, of course, of the mapping of such structure into the structure of acceptable representations of that structure). Such knowledge is a prerequisite to any explanatory account of the represented empirical phenomena, since the empirical structure of the phenomena, as revealed by measurement theory, will levy adequacy constraints on proposed explanatory accounts of the represented properties and relations. An explanatory account will be empirically adequate only if it entails that the phenomena have the empirical structure that the measurement theory attributes to those phenomena. But an account of the empirical structure of the represented phenomena is not an account of the nature of such phenomena. There is, quite simply, more to empirical science than measurement theory!

But while there is clearly more to empirical science than measurement theory, there might not be much more to the *metaphysics* of the measured properties than measurement theory, at least not in the case of propositional attitudes. For if one knew the empirical structure of the attitudes, one might have answers to many of the questions that have traditionally puzzled philosophers about the attitudes, questions that a philosophical account of the attitudes might be expected to answer. In particular, an account of the empirical structure of the attitudes might explain whether, as a matter of metaphysical necessity, propositional attitudes have the philosophically salient properties that we take them to have, specifically, whether they have the semantic and inferential properties that we take them to have. Such an account might also explain why we attribute propositional attitudes using the predicates that we do, why propositional attitudes (or their natural language attributions) exhibit the philosophical puzzles that they do, and so on. An account of the empirical structure of the attitudes would provide such an understanding, because such an account specifies certain empirical conditions that as a matter of metaphysical necessity propositional attitudes must satisfy if we are to be able to attribute them using the predicates that we do. Such an account might also enable us to see just what sort of cognitive computational architecture possession of propositional attitudes requires, whether, for example, possession of propositional attitudes requires what Fodor and his collaborators (Fodor and Pylyshyn 1988; Fodor and McLaughlin 1990) call a 'classical' architecture, such that proposed connectionist cognitive architectures can be ruled out on metaphysical grounds. Now, obviously there is going to be a lot that falls beyond the purview of a measurement-theoretic account of the attitudes. It would tell us nothing about the intrinsic nature of the attitudes beyond the fact that they have the empirical structure that they do. And it would tell us nothing about the lawlike generalizations of common-sense psychology that advert to the attitudes. But it is not clear that any of this is, or ever has been, of any particular philosophical, as opposed to psychological, interest.

6

The Basic Measurement-Theoretic Account

6.1. WHY PROPOSITIONAL ATTITUDE PREDICATES MIGHT BE MEASURE PREDICATES

Many may find it far-fetched to suppose that propositional attitude predicates might, like the numerical predicates by which we attribute physical magnitudes, be a kind of measure predicate. It will seem to them improbable that common-sense talk of propositional attitudes would employ basically the same predication scheme as that employed in talk of physical magnitudes. What, after all, would be the point of adopting such a scheme? And how could such a scheme have ever developed? Surely it is implausible to suppose that talk of propositional attitudes is modeled, even implicitly, on numerical magnitude predicates. Common-sense talk of the attitudes, after all, might well predate all talk of weights, lengths, and other measures.

There are nonetheless a number of reasons for thinking that propositional attitudes predicates *might* be measure predicates, not the least of which are the following striking similarities that these predicates bear to numerical magnitude predicates. First, like the numerical terms that figure in numerical magnitude predicates, the *that*-clauses in propositional attitude predicates appear to be singular terms. One can quantify over them (e.g., *John believes something, there is something John believes*) and form *wh*-questions that question the argument position occupied by the *that*-clause (e.g., *what does John believe*). Second, just as the numbers that are the referents of the numerical terms in numerical magnitude predicates function as representatives of the magnitudes that these predicates attribute, the referents of *that*-clauses appear to function as representatives of the attitudes that they attribute. At least, *that*-clauses serve to individuate different attitudes of the same type in just the way that numerical terms serve in numerical magnitude predicates to individuate one quantity of a magnitude from other quantities of the same magnitude. Third, just as the referents of the numerical terms in numerical magnitude predicates, the referents of *that*-clauses in propositional attitude predicates appear to be abstract particulars; at least many, if not most, philosophers who have thought about the matter have considered them such, even if it continues to be a matter of debate just what sort of abstract object they might be. Fourth, the scheme by which these representatives are specified, like that by which the numerical representatives of quantities are specified, is both productive and systematic, in such a way that the domain of representatives can be effectively enumerated by a recursive procedure. Fifth, the individuation of propositional attitudes by their representatives, like the individuation of quantities of magnitudes by theirs, depends, at least in part, on their place within a relational structure that has these representatives as its domain. Put another way, they are the representatives that they are, in part because of their relations to one another. It is this exploitation of structural relations among the representatives that presumably explains why different natural languages, say English or German, can assign different representatives to the same propositional attitude and yet nonetheless preserve the same empirical relations among propositional attitudes, in much the way that different numerical scales can assign different numbers to the same quantity of a magnitude and yet nonetheless preserve the same empirical relations among quantities.

Finally, both sorts of predicate seem to be quite similar extensions, each within their respective domains, of a pervasive common-sense predication scheme. On this scheme, we characterize the capacities, skills, traits, and dispositions of persons, animals, and even inanimate objects by reference to relations to objects or events that are in some sense the focus or target of these capacities, skills, traits, and dispositions. Thus, people can be flag wavers, firefighters, stock traders, psychologists, proctologists, devil worshipers, furniture buyers, risk takers, English speakers, opera lovers, bus drivers, skirt chasers, and so on, while animals can be anteaters, nest builders, bloodsuckers, disease carriers, and so on, and inanimate objects can be can-openers, posthole diggers, earth movers, pile drivers, dishwashers, typewriters, word processors, and so on. Such characterizations might be termed 'two-dimensional' inasmuch as the individual's capacities (skills, traits, etc.), and hence indirectly the individual, are individuated along two orthogonal dimensions, one having to do with the object or event that is the focus or target of the individual's capacities, the other having to do with the particular relation that the individual bears to that object or event, such that two capacities or individuals can be similar with respect to both dimensions, similar with respect to one but not the other, or different with respect to both.

Such two-dimensional characterizations, it should be noted, carry no behavioral implications. A firefighter might be a firefighter and yet never have fought any fires; surely some firefighters have spent their entire careers in the firehouse, simply waiting for the bell, just as there are car salesmen who have never sold a car. Nor does such a characterization seem to entail any particular behavioral disposition. To describe someone as a firefighter is rather to attribute to the person a fire-related skill or capacity, which he may or may not have had an occasion to exercise, may or may not be presently disposed to exercise. Matters here are little different, it would seem, from those that have led Chomsky to describe linguistic ability as a competence rather than, as Skinner would have it, a behavioral disposition.

The point of drawing attention to the pervasive two-dimensional predication scheme employed by our ordinary characterizations of persons, animals, and inanimate objects is to suggest that both numerical magnitude predicates and propositional attitude predicates might very well be natural *extensions*, in their respective domains, of this common-sense scheme. Consider first numerical magnitude predicates (e.g., *has a mass of 5 kg*). The scheme that we employ in predicating a specific quantity of some physical magnitude of an individual is similar to the common-sense predication scheme in that it effects the predication by specifying a relation that this individual bears to an object. But both object and relation are importantly different. The 'object' here is the real number that is, on the specified scale, the *representative* of the predicated quantity of some magnitude (e.g., 5 on the kg scale), and the relation is a non-causal *indexing* relation that the individual bears to this representative, where this indexing relation identifies the physical magnitude in question (e.g., mass). The novelty of this particular extension of the basic common-sense scheme is twofold. First, an indexing relation replaces the usual causal relation of the basic scheme, though arguably some common-sense two-dimensional predicates, e.g., *is a pinchpenny* or *is a flag waver*, make metaphorical use of a causal relation almost as a kind of indexing relation, specifically as a kind of personality-indexing relation. Second, numerical magnitude predicates exploit the relational structure of the real numbers that are the representatives of quantities of magnitudes, something that predicates of the basic scheme are unable to do. By exploiting this structure we are able not simply to specify particular quantities of a magnitude by reference to their real number representatives, in the way that the members of a baseball team might be identified by the numbers on their jerseys; we are also able to draw conclusions about the relative quantities so specified, e.g., that one is greater than another but less than a third, that one is equal to the sum of two lesser ones, and so on. The numbers that are the representatives of specific quantities of some magnitude thus function as more than proper names of these quantities; they are *quantitative* specifications of them that reflect the empirical relational structure within which specific physical magnitudes find their place.

The two-dimensional predication scheme that we employ in attributing to individuals those psychological states or properties that we call 'propositional attitudes' is one in which we first pick out something that we might think of intuitively as a 'state of affairs', typically a possible or at least conceivable, if not actual, state of the world,[1] and then specify a particular sort of relation (believing, desiring, hoping, imagining, etc.) that the possessor of the propositional attitude bears to the specified state of affairs. Thus, for example, to say of someone that she believes that the US economy is presently in recession is to specify both a particular state of affairs, viz., that of the US economy's being presently in recession, and a relation that this person is said to bear to that state of affairs, viz., her believing it (as opposed to doubting, wanting, or fearing it). The relation specifies the psychological state type, while the state of affairs specifies a particular type of the specified state type. Of course, if one is to understand this psychological attribution, i.e., if one is to understand just what psychological state or property is being attributed to this person by this attribution, then one must understand both the specified state of affairs and the specified relation that the possessor of the attitude is said to bear to that state of affairs, just as one must understand, for example, both what pianos are and what it is for them to be tuned if one is to understand what is being claimed when we describe someone as a piano tuner. These are matters that will be spelled out later in some detail. The important point here is that the predication scheme that we employ in attributing propositional attitudes to individuals seems to be basically the same sort of two-dimensional scheme that we employ in attributing capacities, skills, and dispositions to individuals. Yet there is here, as there is with numerical magnitude predicates, a sophisticated extension of the common-sense scheme. The states of affairs that figure in the specifications of propositional attitudes are *representatives* of propositional

---

[1] Clearly states of affairs need not be actual states of the world. One can have beliefs about all sorts of non-existent states of affairs, and many, indeed most, desires are for non-existent states of affairs.

attitudes in much the way that real numbers are representatives of physical magnitudes: they are so in virtue of their place in a relational structure that has states of affairs as its domain. And in a manner analogous to the way that the numerical magnitude predicates exploit certain structural relations defined on the real numbers, the predication scheme employed by propositional attitude predicates exploits certain structural relations that obtain both among the states of affairs that are the representatives of propositional attitudes and among the natural language descriptions of these states of affairs. Thus, for example, it is in virtue of the relation between the state of affairs of the *economy*'s being presently in recession and the state of affairs of *something*'s being presently in recession, a relation that can be represented in inferential terms, that I am able to predict with considerable confidence that if Jones believes that the economy is presently in recession, then she also believes that something is presently in recession (and furthermore that she will *ceteris paribus* admit as much).

If the predication schemes employed by propositional attitude predicates and numerical magnitude predicates are both extensions of the basic common-sense scheme which we use to characterize other persons and objects, and if these two extensions both exploit a relational structure defined on the representatives of propositional attitudes and physical magnitudes, respectively, then there is reason to take seriously the suggestion that propositional attitude predicates, like numerical magnitude predicates, might be a kind of measure predicate. This suggestion gains added strength from the argument presented in Chapter 4.4 that some recently proposed semantic theories for the sentences by which we attribute propositional attitudes are effectively committed, by their distinction between semantic and psychological objects of the attitudes, to treating these predicates as a kind of measure predicate. For, as we saw, once one draws this distinction, then one needs to explain how the former manage to track the latter and how native speakers are able to exploit the fact that the former tracks the latter to obtain information about the psychological states of the person to whom a propositional attitude is attributed, and such an explanation is tantamount to providing a measurement theory for these predicates.

These several similarities that propositional attitude predicates bear to numerical magnitude predicates don't establish that the former are measure predicates, but they are, I think, strongly suggestive of this possibility. Surely this possibility is no less plausible than the Received View. For that view would have us believe that common-sense psychology is a kind of proto-computational psychology, developed long before the advent of computers or computer science, one in which we can read our cognitive computational architecture off the two-dimensional predication scheme employed by the predicates by which we attribute propositional attitudes. The Received View's cognitive architectural construal of the two-dimensionality of propositional attitude predicates seems much less plausible once we realize how widespread the basic two-dimensional predication scheme really is. Surely no one would be tempted to discover in this basic scheme for characterizing capacities and skills a transparent window into the causal-functional, cognitive architecture underlying these capacities and skills! And just as surely there is little reason to embrace a similarly relational construal of the skills and capacities that our ordinary descriptive practice attributes to individuals (animals, and inanimate objects), simply on the basis of the two-dimensional predication scheme that we employ to characterize them. Our use of such a scheme reflects a deeply entrenched tendency to think of ourselves and our internal mental states in terms of our functional relations to the world about us, a tendency that is surely born out of both our preoccupation with the practical consequences of our actions and our ignorance of the internal structures causally responsible for these actions.

6.2. MEASURING PROPOSITIONAL ATTITUDES

Some find it implausible that propositional attitude predicates might be a kind of measure predicate on the grounds that this would seem to entail that we *measure* the propositional attitudes of ourselves and others, that we use propositional attitude predicates to report the results of such measurings. As one incredulous philosopher once put the objection to me, 'Do you REALLY believe that we *measure* propositional attitudes?', to which I answered, 'Yes, though we don't measure them in quite the sense that you probably have in mind!' We measure propositional attitudes, I want to argue, in basically the same sense in which thermometers measure temperature, produce scales measure weight, and tachometers measure engine revolutions: we are biological devices that are generally reliable in ascertaining and reporting the propositional attitudes of ourselves and others, and this reliability is best explained in measurement-theoretic terms.

It is a commonplace among cognitive ethologists that members of many different species of animal make (and use) all sorts of measurements in the

course of their everyday lives, whether it be in keeping track of the distance
and bearing of their nest or burrow, or in determining the time of day
or the time interval at which food becomes available at a source, or in
determining whether a challenge to a rival is likely to be successful or whether
a prey is within striking distance.[2] In many cases, the measurements involve
little more than pairwise comparisons with respect to some magnitude
(e.g., whether a rival is bigger or stronger), but in other cases, notably
in navigation and foraging behavior, the measurements are often quite
subtle, involving precise measurement of solar azimuth angles, distance run,
time intervals, and the like. Cognitive ethologists consider the cognitive
processes that eventuate in such behaviors to involve measurement because
these behaviors presume that the animal has the capacity to determine the
relevant physical magnitudes, and this capacity is seemingly best explained
in measurement-theoretic terms, specifically in terms of certain cognitive
processes whose reliability in computing the relevant magnitudes is to be
explained in measurement-theoretic terms. Roughly, the cognitive processes
in question operate on perceptual inputs to produce outputs that preserve
the relevant structural properties of the magnitudes measured. Many of our
own behaviors are similarly the product of cognitive processes that involve
various sorts of measurement. Thus, for example, the mundane decision to
cross a street, against the light and in front of oncoming traffic, rather than
waiting for the light, involves a calculation of both the speed and distance
of oncoming traffic and the time required to cross the street. Similarly, our
ability to navigate across a completely darkened but familiar room, without
ever bumping into furniture, presumes not only that we have a map-like
representation of the location of the furniture but also that in the course of
moving across the room we are able to keep track of our location relative
to these obstacles. This in turn presumes that we are able to determine with
reasonable accuracy such crucial variables as our instantaneous velocity and
elapsed time in order to be able to maintain an instantaneous position vector.
We sometimes *mis*judge certain situations in ways that are also best explained
in measurement-theoretic terms, as for example when people routinely
misjudge distance across an empty expanse or the relative temperatures of
objects with different coefficients of thermal conductivity. Of course, most

---

[2] Gallistel (1990) provides a fascinating summary of his and other researchers' work on a wide
range of different measurement activities in non-human animals, all of which serve to enable the
animal to adapt its behavior to the environment in which it lives. Measuring propositional attitudes
no doubt plays a similar role in our social lives.

of our measuring activity never rises to the level of conscious thought—as, for example, when we simply step over a puddle rather than jumping or going around it, or when undertaking to lift or move an object we exert a force proportionate to its *anticipated* weight or resistance, based on the object's appearance, sometimes with unpleasant consequences—but we are measuring nonetheless, for this is the best explanation of the success of these activities.

So the idea that we, like non-human animals, might be assiduous measurers of the world around us does not seem at all far-fetched. But is there any reason to suppose that we measure propositional attitudes? Of course, we do frequently judge certain individuals, including ourselves, to have certain propositional attitudes. In some cases these judgments are explicit and are reported as such; in other cases, perhaps most cases, they are merely implicit in our actions with regard to an individual to whom we would, if asked, attribute certain attitudes. And we do come to these judgments as a result of certain sorts of characteristic experiences. In some cases it is as a result of direct interaction with the individual to whom we attribute these attitudes or as a result of our being at the end of a chain of communication with someone who has had such direct interaction; in other cases it is as a result of imputing to the individual such attitudes as we or others similar to that individual would have in those circumstances. But admittedly we don't normally think of ourselves as coming to these judgments as a result of our having measured the propositional attitudes that we judge someone to possess. Yet this, I want to argue, is precisely what we do: we *measure* propositional attitudes. Of course, we do not use external measuring instruments; rather, in the usual case at least, we simply observe the behavior of the person whose attitudes we are measuring, also listening to anything he or she may say. But one can hardly conclude from this that there is no measurement going on here, any more than one can conclude that a paving contractor makes no measurements when he estimates the cubic yards of asphalt cement required for a driveway job because he didn't lay a tape to the job or even step it off. The paving contractor measures the job, but he does so, as he would put it, by 'eyeballing' it. His measurements are intuitive, like a good counterman at the local deli who weighs an order as he catches the slices in his hand as they fall from the slicing machine and then judging that he has the requested weight in hand verifies his measurement on a certified scale. What makes the actions of both contractor and counterman instances of measurement is that in both cases the reported judgment is the outcome of a process that *reliably* preserves the relevant measurement-theoretic relations between empirical and numerical domains. That such processes *are* reliable in this way, often astonishingly so, can easily be demonstrated by independent measurement. Arguably the same is true in the case of attitude measurements: What we do amounts to our *measuring* attitudes because in coming to these judgments we engage in cognitive processes that *reliably* preserve certain measurement-theoretic relations between the empirical domain of the attitudes themselves and the representational domain of their natural language representatives. That these processes *are* reliable can be independently verified both by others' measurements, specifically by our mutual agreement as to the propositional attitudes we judge someone to possess, and by our success in using the resulting representatives of the measured attitudes to predict the behavior of their possessor. It is easy to overlook the general reliability of our attitude measurements if we focus on the problematic cases that occupy our conscious thought rather than on the mundane cases that are the stuff of ordinary social interaction. When I pull up to the gas pump, the station attendant doesn't wonder to himself whether I want gas, he simply asks, 'what'll you have?', or words to that effect.

Whether, as I believe, we measure attitudes is not then a question that can be answered in any simple fashion, perhaps by looking for the employment of certain measuring instruments or procedures, or by asking whether we would be pre-theoretically inclined to describe ourselves in these ways. It is rather a matter of whether there is any significant *explanatory gain* to be had from describing ourselves and our practice of attributing propositional attitude in measurement-theoretic terms. I claim that there is. In particular, I would claim that it enables us to make sense of our propositional attitude attributions and the use to which we put these attributions in reasoning about the behavior of those of whom we make them. The idea that we are devices that measure propositional attitudes also enables us to explain the curiously immediate, almost perceptual, character of our judgments regarding the propositional attitudes of others: although we do sometimes struggle consciously to come to such a judgment, in the usual case we simply find ourselves to judge that a person has a particular propositional attitude, much in the way that we find ourselves to judge that an object has a particular perceptual property. It is as if, like thermometers, we continuously and rather passively record the propositional attitudes of those around us—no doubt a useful trait for social creatures like ourselves for whom the behavior of others (and ourselves) can have dramatic consequences for our well-being.

6.3. GOALS AND STRATEGY

If propositional attitude predicates are indeed a kind of measure predicate, then it should be possible to provide a measurement-theoretic account of the attitudes analogous to that for physical magnitudes. Such an account, were it complete, would presumably include (i) a specification of the representing relational structure that models the structure of our natural language representations of propositional attitudes—an analogue of the numerical relational structures that model the structure of our natural language representations of physical magnitudes, (ii) a specification of the represented empirical relational structure that models the structure of propositional attitudes themselves—an analogue of the represented empirical relational structures that model the structure of physical magnitudes, (iii) a characterization of the set of morphisms, or perhaps Hodges-style interpretations, that map the represented empirical structure into the representing relational structure which is its image, and (iv) the proof of a representation theorem and a uniqueness theorem for this set of morphisms, or interpretations, so characterized. Because much of our puzzlement about the attitudes focuses on propositional attitude attributions, the account should include (v) an explanation of why we should have developed the particular attribution practices that we have, and (vi) why we should expect the various puzzles (failures of substitution, Kripke puzzles, etc.) that have so dominated philosophical theorizing about the attitudes. One might even go on to speculate, as some philosophers have done, as to (vii) the intrinsic nature of propositional attitudes that would explain why they have the empirical structure that they do, bearing in mind that such empirical speculation would not, strictly speaking, be part of a measure-theoretic account of the attitudes.

The initial task confronting us in developing a measurement-theoretic account of the attitudes is that of specifying the two relational structures that are models, respectively, of the empirical structure of propositional attitudes and the structure of their natural language representations, since only when these specifications are in hand will we be able to accomplish the various other explanatory tasks that would define such an account. Philosophers of language have already done much of the work required for specifying the structure of our natural language representations of the attitudes. But the same cannot be said for the empirical structure of the attitudes themselves. The causal connections of propositional attitudes with their behavioral manifestations (and with sensory inputs and other mental states) are not sufficiently direct as to provide the sort of direct empirical evidence about the structure of the attitudes that, for example, the practice of mass measurement with a pan balance can afford someone interested in the structure of that extensive magnitude. Most of what we know, or *assume* we know, about the structure of the attitudes has been inferred from our representations of the attitudes, and these inferences are based on unproven, possibly erroneous assumptions about the representation relation that maps propositional attitudes into their natural language representations. Inferential knowledge about the empirical structure of the attitudes is likely all we can have, at least for the foreseeable future, but we can try to enhance the reliability of the inferences upon which hypotheses about the structure of the attitudes are based, principally by being explicit in our hypotheses both about the structure of our representations of the attitudes and about the representation relation that maps one structure into the other. We can only hope that these obviously interrelated hypotheses can be successively refined and ultimately justified in the light of their demonstrated joint explanatory powers.

The basic strategy to be pursued here will be this. I shall begin by developing a specification of the representing relational structure of our natural language represent propositional, developing a characterization of (i) the representational domain that is presumed to embed the natural language representatives of propositional attitudes, and (ii) the properties and relations definable on this representational domain that are seemingly exploited by these predicates. Once this is done, I shall turn to the task of specifying the represented empirical relational structure of propositional attitudes themselves, developing a characterization both of the empirical domain of propositional attitudes and of the empirical properties and relations defined over that domain. In developing this specification I shall assume that there is a measurement practice in place that utilizes persons like ourselves to measure and then attribute by means of propositional attitude predicates certain as yet unspecified properties and relations of third parties (and ourselves). I shall further assume that our surrogative reasoning using our natural language representations of propositional attitudes is largely reliable, so that it is plausible to hypothesize that the representation relation *respects*, in the sense explained in the previous chapter, the properties and relations of the empirical structure of the attitudes. Once the specification of these two structures is in hand, I shall then turn to the various explanatory tasks that the proposed measurement-theoretic account of the attitudes must address.

6.4. THE STRUCTURE OF NATURAL LANGUAGE REPRESENTATIONS OF PROPOSITIONAL ATTITUDES

6.4.1. The Representational Domain

A measurement-theoretic account of propositional attitudes presumes that our natural language representations of the attitudes can be modeled by a formal relational structure consisting of a representational domain of objects and certain properties and relations defined on that domain. This domain into which propositional attitudes are mapped must be capable of representing the properties and relations of propositional attitudes that are in fact respected in the mapping of propositional attitudes into their natural language representations. It must also get the individuation conditions on propositional attitudes right. Different propositional attitudes are presumably represented by different objects in the domain, in much the way that different temperatures (lengths, masses, etc.) are represented by different numbers on a given numerical scale.

The expression 'propositional attitude', which we owe to Russell, suggests that the objects that constitute the representational domain might be taken to be *propositions*, where by 'proposition' here we mean simply a semantically evaluable abstract object of some sort that is language-independent and has its truth conditions essentially. On this propositionalist construal of the representational domain, propositions would be for the representation of propositional attitudes what numbers are for the representation of physical magnitudes. As with the numerical representation of physical magnitudes in the reals, propositional attitudes of different attitude type (belief, desire, etc.) would share a single representational domain of propositions, but the maping of propositional attitudes into that domain might vary with attitude type. The properties and relations that are respected by these different mappings into the representational domain of propositions, and hence the representational structures which specify these properties and relations, might also vary. The attitude type itself of a propositional attitude that has as its representative a particular proposition would not be explicitly specified by that representative, any more than is the magnitude type of a particular quantity of a physical magnitude explicitly specified by its numerical representative. Rather the attitude *verbs* of the sentences that are our natural language representations of propositional attitudes (*believes*, *desires*, etc.) or nominalizations of such verbs (*belief, desire*, etc.) would identify the attitude type of the propositional attitude being represented, just as, for example, the head of a measure noun phrase (e.g., *mass* in the case of *having a mass of 5 kg*) serves to identify the magnitude type of the quantity for which the representative number, e.g., 5 on a kilogram scale, is the representative.

It is doubtful, however, that propositions could be the objects that constitute the representational domain, since on virtually any proposed construal, they are not sufficiently fine-grained to capture the individuation conditions on propositional attitudes. The objects that constitute the representational domain must be individuated no less finely than the sentences that are used to express propositional attitudes, since failures of substitutivity in propositional attitude contexts argue convincingly that propositional attitudes are sometimes individuated at least that finely.[3] We might consider adopting instead the view of Carnap (1947), who believed that propositional attitudes might be more aptly called 'sentential attitudes', and take objects in the domain to be sentence types. It would be no objection to this sententialist proposal that the domain so characterized might for some attribution purposes be too fine-grained, such that there might be more than one sentence type that was the representative of one and the same propositional attitude, since a solution to the uniqueness problem might define classes of such objects all of which are equivalent with respect to the propositional attitude that they represent. But the sententialist proposal nonetheless seems unsatisfactory on at least two counts. First, a sententialist characterization of the domain seems still *in*sufficiently fine-grained. The problem here is not simply that the sentences embedded in an ascription's *that*-clause are sometimes syntactically ambiguous, e.g., *the men can fish*, since one might reasonably hold that such sentences token more than a single sentence-type, viz., $[_{IP}[_{DP}the\ men][_{I'}[_{I}can][_{VP}[_{V}fish]]]]$ and $[_{IP}[_{DP}the\ men][_{I'}[_{VP}[_{V}can][_{DP}\ fish]]]]$. The problem is rather that embedded tokens of one and the same sentence type, e.g., *he's sick*, may in different contexts of utterance attribute different propositional attitudes, depending, for example, upon the referents assigned to referring expressions. This might not be a problem if the attitudes so attributed could always be attributed by means of a second, uniquely individuating sentence type, viz., one whose interpretation exhibits no contextual dependence (e.g., Quine's eternal sentences), since such attitudes could be represented by such uniquely

---

[3] For discussion of these points, see Richard 1990, and Larson and Segal 1995.

individuating sentence types. But Perry (1979) has demonstrated that such sentence-types are not available for many propositional attitudes, notably many of those attributed by means of sentences containing self-referring indexicals. Moreover, any such proposed substitution would be subject to the usual substitution puzzles. A second difficulty with the sententialist proposal is that it does not capture the fact that our natural language representations of propositional attitudes have determinate semantic (propositional) contents, and furthermore have them essentially (which is *not*, as we will see, to say that propositional attitudes themselves have determinate contents, much less have them essentially). But sentence types do not always have determinate semantic contents, so it would appear that a purely sententialist characterization of the representational domain will not do either.

If we could make sense of the notion of semantically interpreting sentence types (as opposed to tokens), we could take entities in the representational domain to be semantically interpreted sentence types. This would circumvent some of the individuation problems just discussed. But how would such interpreted sentence types be represented? It won't do simply to represent them as sentence types and then add—parenthetically, as it were—that these types are semantically interpreted, since this would fail to preclude different propositional attitudes being mapped to one and the same entity in the domain. Nor will it do, in the absence of a proposal for how contexts for semantic interpretation are to be formally represented, to take such sentence types to be ordered pairs $< s_i, c_j >$, where s_i is a sentence type and c_j the context for semantic interpretation for (a token of) s_i. We could, however, seemingly achieve substantially this result by doing what both Richard (1990) and Larson and Segal (1995) do, namely, take entities in the representational domain to incorporate both semantic values and lexical/syntactic material. Arguably, the resulting entities—RAMs in Richard's case, ILFs in Larson and Segal's case—are fine-grained enough to capture the individuation conditions on beliefs, at least when modified in ways discussed below.[4] And they achieve this without having to invoke Fregean senses, modes of presentation, or

---

[4] Whether, and just how, RAMs and ILFs differ depends how in the case of RAMs sentence types and Russellian propositions are construed and how in the case of ILFs semantic values are construed. Ludlow (2000: 33) suggests that under their 'ordinary' construals ILFs are more 'austere' than RAMs inasmuch as the former, unlike the later, eschew properties. At first blush, ILFs would also seem to be more fine-grained than RAMs, inasmuch as they incorporate the full syntactic structure at LF, whereas RAMs incorporate only minimal syntactic structure, but any added individuative power that might thus accrue to ILFs may be offset by the structure of the Russellian propositions incorporated in RAMs.

other kinds of intensional entities. A representational domain consisting of such hybrid entities would be able to individuate those propositional attitudes that either a purely propositionalist account or a purely sententialist account would find problematic, precisely because these hybrid entities incorporate the respective individuative resources of *both* sorts of account.

The answers just scouted to the question of how best to characterize the objects that constitute the representational domain are, of course, just the answers that philosophers of language have proposed to the question of how best to characterize the referents of the *that*-clauses of propositional attitude reports. This is hardly surprising, and not simply because any measurement-theoretic account of the attitudes will be concerned to capture their individuation conditions. It is a crucial tenet of any measurement-theoretic account of propositional attitudes that attitude attributions using sentences of the form *x [attitude verb] that S* attribute a particular propositional attitude to x by explicitly relating x to an object that is, in the representational domain, the representative of that attitude (just as, for example, weight attributions using sentences of the form *x weighs N pounds* attribute to x a particular weight by explicitly relating x to a number N that is on the pound scale the representative of that weight). On such accounts, the propositional attitude attribution is true just in case x possesses a propositional attitude of the attributed type that has this object as a representative. But these, formally speaking, are just the truth conditions that philosophical and semantic theories have traditionally associated with propositional attitude reports. According to such theories, sentences of the form *x [attitude verb] that S* are true just in case x bears the appropriate sort of relation to an object that is the referent of the *that*-clause. The measurement-theoretic construal differs from the traditional philosophical/semantic construal only in how it conceives of this object: on the former, it is the representative of the attitude, while on the latter, it is an actual constituent of the attitude—the so-called 'object' of the attitude (e.g., the belief). Recent proposals for the semantics of propositional attitude attributions that distinguish between 'semantic' and 'psychological' objects of the attitudes, such as Richard 1990 and Larson and Segal 1995 (see Chapter 4.4 above), effectively assume a version of this measurement-theoretic construal inasmuch as the semantic object that is the reference of the *that*-clause is taken to 'track' the psychological object, i.e., is taken to be its representative. These proposals differ from the measurement-theoretic proposal developed here in not providing any account of the tracking relation.

Assume for the moment that Larson and Segal's (1995) interpreted logical form (ILF) semantics for belief sentences of the form *x believes that S* is correct. Then we would know from the T-sentence which their semantics associates with such sentences that the representative, in the representational domain, of the propositional attitude ascribed to x is the ILF $[\![S]\!]$ of the sentence S that is embedded in the belief sentence's *that*-clause, as interpreted in the context of utterance of the attitude attribution. The technical term *believes* that appears on the right-hand side of the T-sentence, which Larson and Segal's proposed semantics leaves unexplicated and which in Chapter 4.4 I represented as *believes** in order to distinguish it from its homophonic counterpart in the object language, can be now understood as follows: to believe* an ILF is simply to be in a belief state that has the ILF $[\![S]\!]$ as its representative in the representational domain of the relational structure that is the model of our natural language representations of propositional attitudes. So construed, ILFs are *not* mental representational structures to which the possessors bear some psychological relation; rather they are simply abstract representatives of the psychological states that we call 'propositional attitudes'.

There is nevertheless a problem with Larson and Segal's proposed semantics for propositional attitude reports: ILFs *also* appear not to be sufficiently fine-grained to properly individuate attributed attitudes. As I noted in Chapter 4.4, Larson and Segal, following Larson and Ludlow (1993), point out that it might be true that Jones believes that John F. Kennedy went to /hahvahd/, but false that he believes that Kennedy went to /harverd/, perhaps because Jones once heard Kennedy say that he'd gone to /hahvahd/, but, being unfamiliar with Boston Irish speech, thought that this must be a second school different from the well-known /harverd/. But on their proposed semantics, both reports have the same truth conditions, viz., both are true just in case Jones believes* $[\![$ *John F. Kennedy went to Harvard* $]\!]$. Larson and Ludlow propose to handle this difficulty by taking the phonological form of lexical items to be present at the LF-level of syntactic description and hence present in the ILF. In other words, ILFs are taken to be 'phonologically annotated', with the consequence that distinct ILFs would be assigned to the above belief ascriptions. It is questionable whether Larson and Ludlow's proposal is compatible with current linguistic theory, which, to the extent that it assumes the existence of LF at all, assumes that the phonological properties of sentences are not represented at LF. But this is not the only difficulty with their proposed treatment of /hahvahd/-/harverd/ cases. There are cases where it will not suffice to assume that the constituent lexical items of ILFs are annotated by just their phonological forms. Sometimes the pragmatic properties of the sentence embedded in the belief sentence's *that*-clause will be relevant. Consider Mark Antony's eulogy for the slain Julius Caesar in Shakespeare's *Julius Caesar*. Mark Antony might have uttered the sentence, 'I believe Brutus to be an honorable man', where the belief that Mark Antony would thereby have expressed would *not* be the belief that Cassius would presumably have expressed by that same sentence. Even orthographic properties of the embedded sentence can be relevant. Imagine the case of Jones, a devotee of e. e. cummings, who reads a devastating critique of a poet referred to as 'E. E. Cummings', but not realizing the target of this critique to be his beloved cummings, comes to believe that this Cummings, unlike his namesake, is an artless poseur. Larson and Segal acknowledge the problem, concluding that what is needed is a more refined theory of ILFs, one that views ILFs as phrase markers annotated not only by semantic properties, but also by phonological, pragmatic, and even orthographic properties:

> It is this complex, totally interpreted form that would be the true object of an attitude report. These revised ILFs would differ from what we currently have only in being more complex. They are tree structures with nodes consisting of clusters of properties. Each terminal node will possess phonological and orthographic properties, as well as semantic ones. And at least the S node will be annotated with pragmatic properties, assigned by the pragmatics module in the specific context of utterance.
>
> (Larson and Segal 1995: 454)

Larson and Segal's proposal that we simply annotate ILFs with such additional properties as are necessary to capture the truth conditions on propositional attitude reports acknowledges the potential representational richness of the entities that are the representatives of propositional attitudes. Virtually *any* feature of an utterance of the sentence embedded in the attribution's *that*-clause is potentially individuative of the attributed attitude, provided only that any such feature could potentially serve to distinguish what the possessor of the attributed attitude would take to be different states of affairs (e.g., the state of affairs in which Kennedy went to /hahvahd/ but not /harverd/). Such features might include: (i) syntactic and morphological properties of the uttered sentence; (ii) the intended semantic interpretation, given the context of utterance, of the uttered sentence and its constituents; (iii) the inferential and semantic relations that the uttered sentence bears to other sentences, again given the context of utterance; (iv) the phonological properties of the sentence as uttered; (v) the pragmatic properties of the sentence as uttered in the context of utterance; and even (vi) the orthographic properties in the case of written expressions.

Given that any such feature is potentially relevant to the individuation of propositional attitudes, there seems to be little reason to describe the representatives of propositional attitudes as ILFs, even as fully 'annotated' ILFs, since the objects so annotated are not the interpreted LFs of any proposed linguistic theory. The representatives of propositional attitudes might be better conceived and described simply as *semantically and pragmatically interpreted utterance forms* ('IUFs', for short), for that quite simply is what they are, viz., utterances of sentences, virtually *any* linguistic property of which is potentially individuative of the represented attitude.

The tentative conclusion that it is IUFs that are the representatives of propositional attitudes is very much in the spirit of Davidson's (1968) account of *saying that*.[5] On that account, which provided the original inspiration for ILF accounts such as Larson and Segal's, indirect speech reports of the form 'x says that S' report what x said by presenting a sentence, namely S, the utterance of which in the context of the indirect speech report *samesays* what x said. In other words, the utterance of this sentence serves as a *representative* of what x said. Where the present measurement-theoretic account parts company with Davidson's account is in rejecting the latter's paratactic construal of the logical form of indirect speech reports. Their logical form is not, as Davidson claims, a relation between x and the demonstrative *that*, which the reporter uses to demonstrate an utterance that is the representative of (i.e., samesays) what x said. Rather, the logical form is a relation between x and the complement clause *that S*. The indirect speech report expresses a relation between x and the IUF, specified by the utterance in context of the sentence embedded in the *that*-clause, that is the representative of what x said. The semantics for sentences of the form *x says that S* gives as the truth conditions of such sentences that x said something that has as its linguistic representative the reporter's utterance of S (in the context of the report). The details of the formal semantics for the *that*-clauses that figure in indirect speech reports and propositional attitude attributions is not important here; however, presumably the complementizer *that* serves in *that S* constructions as a term-forming operator that maps the embedded sentence S into a homophonic name of the utterance of S that is the representative of what x said. (That the

---

[5] Cf. Davidson (1989: 16): 'Just as numbers can capture all the empirically significant relations among weights and temperatures in infinitely many different ways, so one person's utterance can capture all the significant features of another person's thoughts and speech in different ways'.

complementizer in *that*-clauses functions in this way would explain how it is possible for the referents of such clauses to be true, false, necessary, possible, plausible, and so on.) The semantics for sentences of the form *x says that S*, however, says nothing about how this representative manages to be the representative of what x said, just as the semantics for propositional attitude reports of the form *x believes (desires, etc.) that S* says nothing about how the referents of the *that*-clauses in these reports manage to be the representatives of the reported attitudes. The measurement-theoretic account is effectively *presumed*, but not explicated, by the semantic theory for these predicates, just as it is in the case of numerical measure predicates for the magnitudes.

It will not be an objection to the present proposal that the representational domain so characterized is too fine-grained, so that there might be more than one IUF that is the representative of a particular propositional attitude, since once again, as was the case with the sentientialist proposal discussed earlier, a solution to the uniqueness problem might simply define classes of IUFs all of which are equivalent with respect to the propositional attitude that they represent. Nor, so far as I can see, are there any serious worries here about the individuation conditions on IUFs. We may not at present be able to specify fully these conditions; however, we are able to recognize 'minimal pairs' of propositional attitude attributions each of the members of which could be used to attribute a different propositional attitude, and our ability to recognize such pairs evidences our knowledge of the salient linguistic dimensions along which propositional attitudes, and hence their IUF representatives, are individuated. Thus, we know that within the representational domain of a single attitude type, propositional attitudes, and hence their IUF representatives within that domain, are individuated in terms of semantic, syntactic, phonological, pragmatic, and even orthographic features of the embedded sentence as actually uttered. Our tacit knowledge of the properties in terms of which the representatives of propositional attitudes and hence the represented attitudes themselves are individuated can presumably be made explicit in just the way that other aspects of our tacit linguistic knowledge have been made explicit, namely through linguistic theorizing. So if one were worried about the individuation of IUFs, one presumably could, using the results of such theorizing, replace IUFs by an *n*-tuple of the potentially relevant linguistic features of utterances of the sentences that can be embedded in the *that*-clauses of propositional attitude sentences.

But if, as I am here arguing, the measurement-theoretic representatives of propositional attitudes are indeed IUFs, we do not normally think of these representatives in such language-theoretic terms. Rather we conceive of them in terms of the states of affairs towards which propositional attitudes are in some sense directed or related. Think, for example, of the desire shared today by many investors, which we might characterize by saying that they want to recoup their losses in the stock market crash of 2001–2. We think of ourselves as picking out these investors' desire by referring to a particular state of affairs, viz., one in which they recoup their losses in that market crash. More specifically, we conceive of ourselves as picking out these investors' desire by referring to this state of affairs *under a particular description*, viz., as a recouping of losses rather than, perhaps, as simply the earning of a *very* substantial return on current investment. It is not at all clear just what, ontologically speaking, these representative states of affairs could possibly be. They cannot always be states of the actual world, not even of possible worlds, sometimes not even of logically possible worlds—our desires, after all, are rarely for what is actual, and we can both desire the necessarily non-existent and believe the impossible. Perhaps these states of affairs are best conceived as notional constructions out of the constituents of actual states of affairs. But however they are to be conceived, the intuitive construal of the representatives of propositional attitudes as states of affairs seems to amount to little more than a seemingly harmless ontological *reification* of the IUFs that I am proposing are the measurement-theoretic representatives of propositional attitudes. That is to say, the intuitive construal *reifies* the IUF in the form of a concrete, but possibly non-existent (possibly necessarily non-existent) state of affairs which would satisfy the IUF, were that state of affairs to exist, where this state of affairs is as described by the sentence for which that IUF is, in the context of the sentence's utterance (whatever that happens to be), the IUF. This intuitive construal presumably makes these representatives more easily grasped and utilized in our surrogative reasoning about propositional attitudes than they might otherwise be. The availability of this reifying construal, I shall argue later, also serves as the intuitive conceptual link between the IUF and the propositional attitude for which it is the representative. Propositional attitudes are individuated with respect to certain characteristic behavioral relations that they bear to these states of affairs.

6.4.2. Properties and Relations of Representatives of Propositional Attitudes

If the representatives of propositional attitudes were propositions, then the properties and relations defined over these representatives that are the images of the properties of and relations among propositional attitudes might be taken to be just the truth conditions of and the inferential relations among these representatives, where the former might be given by a truth-conditional or model-theoretic semantics and the latter by a Boolean algebra augmented with quantificational apparatus and modal operators.[6] If, however, the representatives are IUFs, then the properties and relations defined over these representative IUFs will include properties and relations in addition to the semantic/inferential ones that would be associated with a propositional construal of the representational domain. These will include the various syntactic, phonological, pragmatic, and even orthographic properties and relations of IUFs, any of which could, as we have seen, be individuative of the propositional attitudes for which these IUFs are the representatives. The properties and relations might also include relations of productivity and systematicity defined over the domain.

But just as physical magnitude predicates do not exploit all properties and relations definable on the reals (i.e., not all such properties and relations receive an empirical interpretation), propositional attitude predicates presumably do not exploit all the properties and relations definable on the IUFs that constitute the representational domain. Certainly there is no a priori reason to assume that every such property or relation is the image of some empirical psychological property or relation. Nor is there any reason to suppose that the properties and relations defined over the representational domain that are exploited are fully exploited. There is, for example, no a priori reason to suppose that from the clearly nonfinitary character of the representational domain it follows that there is, even 'in principle', as some would have it, an infinite number of beliefs or desires. Productivity in the representational domain does not necessarily entail productivity in the empirical domain. And clearly the inferential relations that obtain among the entities in the representational domain are not fully exploited either. One may be able, for example, to infer safely that a subject's beliefs are closed under the empirical image of rules such as existential generalization, simplification, and perhaps *modus ponens*; however, one cannot safely infer that a subject's beliefs are closed under the empirical image of all rationally acceptable rules of deductive inference. Subjects' belief sets notoriously are not so closed. Just what sort of closure subjects' belief sets exhibit is clearly an empirical matter, to be determined by empirical research of the sort discussed in Chapter 3.6 above.

---

[6] For a sketch of such a propositional account, see Swoyer 1987: 281–3.

More generally, the point here is that while we can specify the properties of and the relations among the IUFs which constitute the representational domain, it is an open empirical question just which of these properties and relations are the image of properties and relations of propositional attitudes.

While propositional attitude predicates most often exploit features of utterances that are expressible by the ILFs of the sentences uttered, viz., their syntactic, semantic, and inferential properties and relations, they can, as we have seen, exploit features of IUFs that are not so expressible. There are no doubt many different properties of, and relations defined over, IUFs that could be exploited here, just as there are (uncountably) many relations definable on the reals that could be exploited in numerical measurement. But as a matter of the pragmatics of language use, the only features that are *likely* to be exploited are those that are likely to be correctly interpreted by those to whom attitude reports are addressed, which presumably explains why so few features other than those captured by ILFs are in fact exploited. (This may explain why ILF theorists have thought that propositional attitude reports express a relation to an ILF, or to a modestly annotated ILF.) Given the purposes for which attitudes are generally attributed, there is little point in being so subtle in the properties of the representative utterances which one produces that few, if any, in one's audience can figure just what attitude is being attributed.

The relational structure that models our natural language representations of propositional attitudes differs importantly from the relational structures employed in the numerical measurement of physical magnitudes, not only in the character of that structure, i.e., its domain and the properties and relations defined over that domain, but also in the fact that, as we have seen, virtually any property or relation defined over the IUFs that constitute the domain of this relational structure can in the appropriate context of use be exploited in the natural language representation of a propositional attitude. We can determine which of the properties and relations of IUFs can in principle be exploited by constructing minimal pairs of *that*-clauses (e.g., the /hahvahd/-/harverd/ case), each of which could, in an otherwise identical context, be representatives of different propositional attitudes. But to say this is still not to answer the question of which properties and relations are *in fact* exploited. There may be no categorical answer to this question, as there is in the numerical measurement of physical magnitudes. It depends crucially on the context in which the attitude report is used. Sometimes it is only those semantic properties of the IUF that specify the state of affairs that is the so-called 'object' of the attributed attitude, e.g., when I attribute to someone the belief that 'Tully is bald', without thereby intending to convey any information whatever as to how this person conceives of or would describe this state of affairs, even whether this person knows Tully by this name. In other cases, however, the propositional attitude attribution is intended to convey just such information, perhaps with a considerable degree of detail, e.g., when I attribute to someone the belief that Kennedy went to /hahvahd/ but not to /harverd/.

The variability with context of utterance in the properties and relations of IUFs that are exploited by our natural language representatives of propositional attitudes requires an account of the representation relation, between the empirical relational structure of the attitudes and the representing relational structure of our natural language representatives of those attitudes, that accommodates (and explains) such variability. It also requires an account, presumably pragmatic in nature, both of speakers' ability to exploit differentially in different contexts the various properties and relations of IUFs, and of the audience's ability to recognize just which properties and relations are being exploited, so as to be able to understand the propositional attitude attribution. In order to develop such an account we must first develop a preliminary characterization of the empirical structure of the attitudes, since only when we have such a characterization will we be in a position to see how IUFs are able to serve as the natural language representatives of propositional attitudes.

6.4.3. Recap

So to recap the foregoing account of the structure of our natural language representations of propositional attitudes, the representational domain consists of *semantically and pragmatically interpreted utterance forms* (IUFs, for short). These IUFs, which are the measurement-theoretic representatives of propositional attitudes, are the IUFs of sentences that could, grammatically speaking, be embedded in the *that*-clauses of the sentences by which we standardly attribute propositional attitudes. IUFs have all the properties and relations of utterances of the sentences for which they are IUFs, including semantic, inferential, syntactic, phonological, pragmatic, and even orthographic properties and relations. IUFs can be reified in an ontologically harmless way as states of affairs, more specifically as the state of affairs (under the description provided by the IUF) that would satisfy the IUF, were that state of affairs to exist. Not all the properties and relations of IUFs are the image of properties and relations of the propositional attitudes for which they are representatives. Just which properties and relations of an IUF are exploited in a propositional attitude attribution (i.e., exploited in the sense of being the image of properties and relations of propositional attitudes) depends on the specific context of utterance of the sentence employed in the attribution.

6.5. THE EMPIRICAL STRUCTURE OF THE ATTITUDES: WHAT ARE NATURAL LANGUAGE REPRESENTATIONS OF THE ATTITUDES IMAGES OF?

One of the principal tasks for a measurement-theoretic construal of propositional attitude attributions is to specify the empirical structure of the attitudes that has its image in the representational structure just described. As is the case with other sorts of measure predicates, competent users of propositional attitude predicates are typically unable to specify this structure. It will therefore have to be reconstructed inferentially, from a consideration of (i) the empirical evidence on which attitude attributions are based and the explanatory and predictive tasks to which they are put, and (ii) the structure of our natural language representations of the attitudes, on the assumption that the relevant properties and relations of propositional attitudes about which we reason surrogatively using those representations are *respected* (in the sense explained in Chapter 5.3) by those representations.

6.5.1. Inferring the Empirical Structure of the Attitudes

Suppose that we were faced with the task of determining the empirical structure represented by a particular kind of nautical chart, say a Mercator projection. If we had no previous experience with such charts, we would not begin by consulting a published key, because the ability to use such keys presumes considerable competence in interpreting the charts for which they are keys, and, in any event, the most basic information about the mapping from charted domain to chart, e.g., the empirical relations respected by the projection scheme employed by the chart, is not provided by its key. Rather we would probably begin by doing what those learning to use such charts typically do: we would observe how knowledgeable mariners use them. And from our observations, we would learn that Mercator nautical charts are used primarily in local navigation, e.g., for maintaining an updated plot of one's position relative to known landmarks that are represented on the chart, for determining distance and compass bearing from one known point to another, and so on. We would learn that straight lines drawn on the chart represent rhumb lines (i.e., lines of constant compass heading), that the local distance scales at any point on the chart are the same in all directions from that point, even though these scales vary over the chart as a function of latitude. We would also learn that such charts not only represent various known landmarks (e.g., shorelines, harbors, islands, bridges, radio towers, buoys, hazards to navigation such as shipwrecks), but also such things as water depth in an area, the nature of the holding ground in anchorages, and light sequences for lighted aides to navigation. In thus learning how such charts are used, we would learn not simply which entities in the charted area were paired one-to-one with which chart symbols, but also which empirical properties and relations possessed by or obtaining among these entities were respected by the Mercator projection scheme that such charts employ, and hence what sorts of information about the charted area users are able to recover from such charts. From this we could also come to know about the relative uniqueness of such projections, specifically about admissible formal transformations that would preserve their represented empirical content. We would also come to know about the characteristic distortions inherent in such projections, e.g., that such projections grossly exaggerate the relative size of areas in the higher latitudes, with the consequence that on a Mercator projection of the western hemisphere, Alaska and Brazil appear to cover about the same area, when in fact the area of the former is only about one-fifth that of the latter.[7]

The task of determining the empirical structure of propositional attitudes, which has an image in the structure of their natural language representations, should presumably proceed analogously. We should begin by considering how we commonly *use* the propositional attitude attributions which are these representations. In so doing, we should be able to reconstruct inferentially, with the help of certain crucial enabling assumptions which I'll endeavor to make explicit and eventually justify, the empirical structure of the attitudes.

---

[7] Cartographers often complain with some justification that the almost exclusive use of Mercator projections in American classrooms gives us a distorted perception of the world. One might wonder whether the particular natural language representations of propositional attitudes that we use might not similarly distort our perception of propositional attitudes, perhaps leading us to think of them as intrinsically linguistic in nature, encouraging us to think that they possess many of the linguistic properties of their representatives.

6.5.2. Propositional Attitude Attributions and their Use

Propositional attitude predicates, it goes without saying, are used by speakers to attribute propositional attitudes. In situations where we the recipients of these attributions have some confidence in their reliability, we use these natural language representations of propositional attitudes in reasoning *surrogatively* about the mental life, behavior, and environment of the possessors of these attributed attitudes. Thus, for example, we reason surrogatively from an attribution that represents Jones as believing that *Kennedy* went to Harvard to the conclusion that he believes that *someone* went to Harvard, via a valid rule of inference (viz., existential generalization) defined over the representational domain that includes a representative of the premised attitude. Most fundamentally, we use attitude attributions prospectively to predict the behavior and concomitant mental states of the possessors of attributed attitudes, and retrospectively to explain, and sometimes to justify, rationalize, or criticize, exhibited behavior and manifested mental states. We also use such attributions to draw conclusions about the environment of the possessor of an attributed attitude, sometimes even in cases where the attitude in question, typically a belief, is known to be incorrect.[8] Propositional attitude attributions can be used successfully in these ways because propositional attitudes bear certain characteristic relations to intentional behavior, concomitant intentional states, and the environment that will support the surrogative reasoning that eventuates in such predictions, explanations, and conclusions. The relations in question support such reasoning because they find an image in the relevant properties and relations defined on the representational domain. These relations are causal in the case of their relations to behavior and the environment, while in the case of relations to other intentional states, including other propositional attitudes, the relations may also be constitutive in the sense that to possess the one, e.g., believe that Jones is at the door, just is to possess the other, e.g., believe that someone is at the door. At least, so far as I can see, no one has offered any compelling reason for thinking that these relations are anything other than causal or constitutive.

Certainly the relations of propositional attitudes to behavior and the environment are not, as logical behaviorists supposed, analytic. Talk about

---

[8] The late Pauline Kael of *The New Yorker* was a reliable movie reviewer, not because her aesthetic judgments were infallible, but rather because they were reliably skewed in a way that permitted cognizant readers to recalibrate her judgments to their individual tastes.

propositional attitudes is not a disguised way of talking about dispositions to behave in certain ways in certain environments. And similarly, it would seem, for those causal and constitutive relations that propositional attitudes bear to other intentional states. Yet even if these relata are causally related, and hence are materially distinct from one another, they might nevertheless be 'internally' related in the sense that propositional attitudes might not be able to be, conceptually speaking, the things that they are, viz., propositional attitudes, without bearing the contingent causal relations that they do to behavior, other concomitant intentional states, and the environment. Propositional attitudes might be similar in this respect to sunburns, on the one hand, and topical sun-screens, on the other: they cannot be the things that they are without having the specific causal relations that they do to certain characteristic causes and effects.

Now, to say that propositional attitude attributions can be used successfully in the ways that they are because propositional attitudes bear certain internal relations to behavior, concomitant mental states, and the environment is not yet to say anything specific about the empirical structure of the attitudes that explains why they can be so used. We need to specify this structure, showing how it enables the *specific* sorts of surrogative reasoning that we are able to accomplish by means of these natural language representations of the attitudes. Let us begin this task by looking at the particular sorts of relations that propositional attitudes bear to behavior, concomitant mental states, and the environment. Having done this we can then turn to the crucial question of the empirical structure of propositional attitudes that has as its image the representational structure described in the previous section.

6.5.3. Propositional Attitudes, their Behavioral Manifestations, and IUFs

It is the empirical structure of propositional attitudes that enables them to be usefully represented two-dimensionally in the way that they are, namely, as relations to IUFs (or more intuitively, as relations to the states of affairs that would satisfy IUFs), just as it is the empirical structure of capacities, skills, and traits that enables them to be usefully represented two-dimensionally in the way that they are, namely, as relations to objects or events in the world. In the case of capacities, skills, and traits, the relations in question, we noted, are not behavioral, at least not in a way that any behaviorist would recognize. Firefighters don't fight every fire they come across; they can sit in front of their fireplaces like anyone else. But there is nevertheless a predictable behavioral aspect to a firefighter's relation to fires. Firefighters do, after all, *fight* fires (which explains, of course, why they are called 'firefighters'), and what they do in fighting fires is a predictable behavioral manifestation of their firefighting skills. But firefighters fight only those fires that they believe ought to be fought and only to the extent that they are physically able to do so, and what firefighters do in the course of fighting a fire reflects their beliefs about how best to accomplish their task given their firefighting goals, such that the causal relation between their skills and their behavior is mediated by these beliefs and abilities. Yet even though the causal relation between the capacity, skill, or trait and the behavior that manifests it is thus mediated, capacities, skills, and traits nonetheless have predictable behavioral manifestations. This is because the mediating mental states and physical abilities that someone knowledgeable of the capacity, skill, or trait in question would expect to be present in the possessor of the capacity, skill, or trait are in point of fact normally present. Thus a suitably knowledgeable observer can as a result both predict the behavior in relevant circumstances of persons having certain capacities, skills, and traits and also infer a person's capacities, skills, and traits from the behavior manifested in such circumstances. A knowledgeable basketball fan, for example, can both predict with reasonable accuracy the play of a skilled player and also determine with similar accuracy the skill of a unfamiliar player through observation of his or her play. Much the same is also true of propositional attitudes. There is no single behavior or set of behaviors characteristic of those who believe, for example, that the economy is presently in recession. But those who believe this will, in the usual case, *manifest* their belief behaviorally in fairly predictable ways, specifically in ways that are suitably related behaviorally to the state of affairs that they take to exist, which explains why we identify the belief in question as the belief that 'the economy is presently in recession'. Just what those who believe the economy is presently in recession will do or say depends crucially on such other propositional attitudes as may mediate between this belief and its manifesting behavior. For example, those with limited financial reserves who worry that their jobs may be in jeopardy will typically reduce their spending on consumer goods, especially if they believe that the recession will be protracted, while those without such worries may actually increase their spending in an effort to take advantage of the lower prices that recessions typically bring. And, of course, virtually all who believe the economy to be in recession will typically affirm as much if asked, except perhaps in situations where they think it imprudent to admit to such a belief. In such situations they may even behave in ways that are calculated to mask their belief. But such dissembling aside, people tend to manifest their beliefs and other propositional attitudes behaviorally in predictable ways. Were this not the case, and if we didn't also recognize many behaviors for the manifestations of specific propositional attitudes that they are, it is difficult to imagine how we could ever come to know the propositional attitudes that others hold.

That the particular way in which a propositional attitude is manifested behaviorally depends on the possessor's other propositional attitudes suggests that it is *sets* of relevantly related propositional attitudes, rather than individual propositional attitudes, that produce the behaviors that we take to manifest particular propositional attitudes. Propositional attitudes, taken separately and by themselves, are generally not causally sufficient to bring about any behavior. In the usual case, desires or beliefs alone eventuate in no behavior whatever; they have to be suitably paired one with the other if they are to eventuate in behavior. This is not to deny that propositional attitudes are the causes of the behaviors that we take to manifest them. Rather, it is just to say that the relation between a particular propositional attitude, say a belief (or a desire), and the behavior that manifests it is mediated by other propositional attitudes, including the desire (or belief) that is the other member of the belief-desire pair. That we take these behaviors to manifest one particular member of this set of propositional attitudes presumably reflects both our interests and our presumptions: we presume a certain background of propositional attitudes, either because we take them to be widely shared or because we have independent reasons for attributing these attitudes to the person in question, and it is against the background of these other propositional attitudes that this person's behavior is seen as the manifestation of some particular propositional attitude, not among these presumed attitudes, that is the focus of our interests. Our success in recognizing a behavior to be the manifestation of a particular attitude depends on our being able to 'factor out' the respective contributions of the mediating attitudes. In certain situations, this is quite easy; the attitude is transparent in the behavior. In other situations it is less so, such that our success in recognizing the behavior as the manifestation that it is will depend crucially on our having a good grasp on the agent's other propositional attitudes, either because we know the person well or because we are correct in assuming we share with this person these mediating propositional attitudes and thus know the sort of behavior that those propositional attitudes would give rise to. To the extent that we fail to have a firm grasp on these mediating attitudes, typically as a result of different life experiences, different socioeconomic and cultural backgrounds, or different constitutions (maybe we are even members of different species), then to that extent we may fail to recognize the manifesting behavior for what it is, viz., the manifestation of a particular propositional attitude or set of attitudes. But the basic point remains that when viewed against a background of generally shared propositional attitudes, propositional attitudes can be paired with certain behaviors that we recognize to be, as a matter of empirical fact, their manifestation. And these behaviors will bear the sort of relation to the state of affairs that we take to be the attitude's representative that will justify individuating that attitude in terms of that state of affairs.

Let us remind ourselves of the sorts of behavior that we take to manifest possession of various sorts of propositional attitude. In the case of desiring and other desire-like propositional attitudes such as wanting, preferring, and wishing, the behaviors that manifest such attitudes are typically behaviors that are intended to bring about the desired state of affairs, i.e., the state of affairs that satisfies the IUF that is the representative of that attitude. Thus, for example, if I desire that a window be opened, then behavior that manifests that desire will characteristically be behavior intended to bring about that state of affairs. The behavior in question may involve actually walking to the window and opening it, or it may be verbal behavior intended to cause others to bring about a desired state of affairs, as, for example, when I say to you, 'Please open the window', intending thereby to get you to open the window. Of course, a behavior can also manifest a desire without being intended to bring about the desired state of affairs (as, for example, when I say to myself, 'I wish that the window were open', not intending thereby that I or anyone else be caused to bring about that state of affairs). In such cases, what is said manifests the desire simply by expressing it verbally, though arguably it does so because such expressions of one's desire are commonly uttered with the intention of causing someone, perhaps one's own self, to bring to about the desired state of affairs, thus explaining why we are justified in taking this expression as an expression of that desire rather than of some other propositional attitude. The behaviors that manifest behaviorally more attenuated desire-like propositional attitudes such as hoping (wishing, longing, etc.) typically don't involve behavior intended to bring about the hoped-for state of affairs. Rather the behaviors that manifests these attitudes are generally verbal expressions that simply specify the hoped-for state of affairs, though they can also involve certain non-verbal behaviors that also express the attitude, such as acting as if the hoped-for state of affairs were going to come about, as for example when someone waits by the phone, hoping that a loved one will call. The propositional attitudes that give rise to such behaviors count as desire-like, despite the fact that they don't give rise to behaviors intended to satisfy the attitude, because like desires they can be satisfied by certain states of affairs coming to exist, and when they are satisfied the behaviors that manifest them typically cease.

The behaviors that manifest believing and other belief-like propositional attitudes such as knowing, presuming, assuming, speculating, and even bald imagining are not intended to bring about the states of affairs that are their representatives, since the possessor of these attitudes takes them already to exist, even if only hypothetically. Rather the behaviors that manifest these attitudes are behaviors intended to bring about certain other states of affairs. Belief and other belief-like propositional attitudes modify and shape these goal-directed behaviors in ways that in the usual course of events makes it more likely that the goals towards which these behaviors are directed will be achieved. The belief-like attitudes are manifest in the particular character that this goal-directed behavior assumes: the behavior is reasonable, appropriate, etc. as a means of achieving the desired goal only on the assumption that the agent has certain belief-like attitudes. Thus, for example, I cross a completely darkened room in order to throw a light switch on an opposite wall, moving circuitously first in one direction and then another as I cross the room, until finally I am in a position to reach out with my hand and throw the unseen switch. I move in the way that I do because I have certain beliefs about the location of furniture. My behavior manifests these beliefs inasmuch as my circuitous behavior would be appropriate given my intended goal only if the furniture were where I believed it to be, i.e., only if the state of affairs of the furniture's being where it is satisfies the IUF which is the representative of the belief in question. Otherwise my path across the room could be expected to take a different course. Of course, my attempt to cross the room without falling over any of the furniture may be undone by someone's having relocated some of the furniture without my knowledge, but even the behavior that I exhibit in these unsuccessful attempts manifests my beliefs about the location of furniture no less than do the successful attempts.

To say that propositional attitudes have a predictable behavioral manifestation is not to deny that the possessors of propositional attitudes sometimes fail to exhibit the behavior that we would take to manifest their attitudes. But when such behavior fails to be manifested, we assume that there is an explanation of this failure, one that explains why the expected behavior was not exhibited. That these explanations typically advert to the presence of countervailing attitudes (e.g., 'she didn't betray what she knew of the matter when her friend brought it up in conversation, because she thought he would become upset') underscores the mediating role of other propositional attitudes, but the mere fact that such explanations *are* expected underscores our expectation that a person's propositional attitudes will be manifested behaviorally in fairly specific ways appropriate to the context in which that person finds him or herself. It is in virtue of this fairly predictable relation between the attitude and its manifesting behavior that we are able to specify, and individuate, propositional attitudes in terms of the states of affairs that are their representatives, even though there is *not*, as analytic behaviorists would have it, an analytic relation between the attitude and the behavior. The internal relation is not between the attitude and the behavior, but between the attitude and the state of affairs to which the behavior is related in ways that depend on the attitude's type.

The foregoing explains how an IUF manages to be a representative of some particular propositional attitude. The propositional attitude that has a particular IUF as a representative will, with the mediation of certain other propositional attitudes, produce the predictable behavior that is taken to manifest the attitude, and this behavior bears a quite specific relation to the state of affairs that satisfies that IUF. In the case of desire-like propositional attitudes, the characteristic behavior that manifests one of these attitudes is behavior that has as its goal bringing about that state of affairs. It is behavior that would, *ceteris paribus*, be rational (reasonable, make sense, etc.) if that behavior were intended to bring about that state of affairs. In the case of belief-like propositional attitudes, the behavior that manifests one of these attitudes is behavior that would, *ceteris paribus*, be rational (reasonable, make sense, etc.) given the subject's goals if that state of affairs were to exist. Schematically, the IUF that is the representative of a propositional attitude (1) specifies a state of affairs, where this state of affairs is (2) behaviorally related to the attitude in the attitude-type specific ways just described, and hence in virtue of (1) and (2), this IUF can (3) serve as the representative of the propositional attitude (See Figure 6.1 below).

So it turns out that logical behaviorists were right to think that there are certain characteristic behaviors associated with the possession of particular propositional attitudes, but the relation between attitude and behavior obtains only in the context of certain predictable mediating propositional

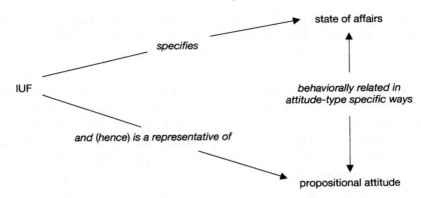

Figure 6.1. How Propositional Attitudes are Related to their Representative IUFs.

attitudes. Thus, as critics of logical behaviorism were quick to point out, carrying an umbrella normally manifests a person's belief that it might rain, but it does so only on the presumption that the person, like most of us, desires not to get wet, believes that an umbrella is a means of achieving the desired state of affairs in the event of rain, and so on. There is a internal relation between attitude and behavior, but it is a relation that the attitude bears to the behavior only insofar as the behavior is specified in terms of its relation to the state of affairs that is the attitude's representative.

In view of the internal relation between a propositional attitude and the characteristic state of affairs-related behavior that manifests it, propositional attitudes might be described as *aptitudes*, i.e., states that are *apt* to produce certain characteristic effects, specifically the characteristic state of affairs-related behavior that manifests them.[9] To say that propositional attitudes are such states is to say both that these states are suited for this purpose, i.e., they are the sorts of states that *can* in fact produce such behavior, and that in the appropriate contexts they do as a general rule produce such behavior in their possessors, though in other contexts they may not.[10] Thus conceived, propositional attitudes might be thought of as dispositions inasmuch as they dispose their possessors to certain characteristic behaviors. But

---

[9] The English word *attitude*, which derives from the Latin *aptitudo* (meaning fitness or suitability), still carries as one of its dictionary senses 'a state of readiness to respond in a characteristic way'.

[10] For further discussion, see Armstrong (1968: 82) who similarly argued that 'the concept of a mental state is primarily the concept of *a state of the person apt for bringing about a certain sort of behavior*' [his emphasis].

they are clearly *not* the behavioral dispositions that logical behaviorists such as Ryle took them to be. To attribute a propositional attitude to an individual is not to assert that a behavioral conditional of the form 'if [environmental condition], then [behavior]' is true of that individual. These aptitudes that are the attitudes are genuinely efficacious internal states that *cause* the characteristic behaviors that manifest them. But they cause these behaviors only in conjunction with the appropriate mediating attitudes. Moreover, these states, unlike behavioral dispositions, are apt to produce more than simply the behaviors that manifest them. They are also apt to produce certain other mental states, including both other propositional attitudes and certain affective mental states such as anger, shame, fear, happiness, worry, pleasure, and disappointment. To say this, however, is not to deny that the possessors of propositional attitudes sometimes fail to possess these expected concomitant states. But when the possessor of a propositional attitude fails to exhibit the expected concomitant mental states, we assume, as we do in the analogous behavioral case, that there is an explanation of this fact. And once again, these explanations typically advert to the presence of certain countervailing attitudes that are thought to explain the absence of these concomitant states (e.g., 'she wasn't the least bit embarrassed upon learning that she'd been found out, because she believes that she was perfectly within her rights in acting as she did'). That these explanations typically advert to the presence of other, countervailing attitudes suggests that the relation between the attitude and its concomitant states, like the relation between the attitude and the behavior that we take to manifest it, is mediated by other propositional attitudes.

Given the conceptual salience of the internal relation between propositional attitudes and the characteristic states of affairs-related behaviors that manifest them, it is hardly surprising that we typically specify propositional attitudes in terms of certain states of affairs which are implicated in the behaviors that we take to manifest them. Desires are desires *for* the obtaining of certain states of affairs, and behaviors that we take to manifest particular desires are behaviors that aim to bring about the desired states of affairs. Similarly, beliefs are beliefs *about* the obtaining of certain states of affairs, and behaviors that we take to manifest particular beliefs are behaviors that are modulated and shaped in ways that reflect the believed obtaining of these states of affairs. Thus, for example, we specify a certain internal state as the desire to talk with a friend because the state is apt to produce behavior that has as its goal the bringing about of the desired state of affairs. And we specify another internal state as the belief that the friend in question can be reached at a certain telephone number because the state is apt to modulate or shape goal-directed behaviors in ways that render the success of these behaviors dependent on the actual obtaining of the believed state of affairs, e.g., by causing a person who desires to talk by telephone to this friend to dial this particular telephone number rather than some other.

All propositional attitudes, I want to argue, are similarly specified in terms of behaviorally related states of affairs. Wishes, hopes, and preferences, like desires, are always *for* certain states of affairs, and the behaviors that we take to manifest these sorts of attitudes are behaviors that aim to bring about the mentioned states of affairs or at least endorse the prospect of their coming to exist. Assumptions, presumptions, speculations, and even bald imaginings, like beliefs, are always *about* certain states of affairs, and the behaviors that we take to manifest these are behaviors that are modulated or shaped in ways that suggest that a subject takes these states of affairs to exist. To say that we specify propositional attitudes in terms of certain behaviorally related states of affairs, I want to emphasize again, is not to deny that many of our beliefs and desires eventuate in none of the behavior that we would take to manifest these attitudes. We can, and often do, keep our attitudes to ourselves. The point here is simply that we do in fact specify the attitudes in these terms, and we are able to do this because there is the following internal relation between the attitudes and their specifying states of affairs: the attitudes are just those internal mental states that are apt to produce behavior that is appropriately related to the states of affairs that satisfy the IUFs that are these attitudes' representatives. Of course, to say that propositional attitudes are such states is not to deny that propositional attitudes (believings, perceivings, rememberings, etc.) are not also type-individuated in terms of specific kinds of causal antecedents for the state (e.g., being in the state as a result of some perceptual event, as a result of reasoning), but such individuation conditions attach to the attitude-type specifying verb and not to the IUF-specifying *that*-clause.

6.5.4. The Empirical Structure of the Attitudes

The empirical structure of the attitudes, like the empirical structure of physical magnitudes, can be conceived of in two different ways: either as a formal relational structure consisting of individuals who possess propositional attitudes and certain first-order relations (including first-order monadic properties) defined over these individuals—the first-order nominalist construal favored by Davidson (1989)—or as a formal relational structure consisting of propositional attitudes themselves, construed as first-order properties of individuals, and certain second-order relations (including second-order monadic properties) defined over these attitudes. I shall adopt here the second of these two construals, and for basically the same sorts of reasons that motivated Mundy's (1987) and Swoyer's (1987) adoption of a property-theoretic measurement theory for physical magnitudes (see Chapter 5.5). Most notably, such a construal seems to square quite well with our intuitive conception of propositional attitudes as causally efficacious states which individuals can possess (come to possess, fail to possess, no longer possess, etc.) at a time; moreover, it does not commit us, as the first-order nominalistic construal does, to the implausibly strong existence claim that, for every possible propositional attitude, there actually exists some individual who possesses that attitude. If we adopt such a property-theoretic construal, the mapping of propositional attitudes into representative IUFs will be what I described in Chapter 5.3 as a *trans-type* mapping of the first-order properties that are propositional attitudes into the IUFs that are their images in the representational domain. The second-order properties and relations defined over propositional attitudes will have as images in the representational structure certain first-order properties and relations defined over these IUFs, where these latter will include both the semantic, syntactic, phonological, pragmatic, and perhaps even orthographic properties of IUFs, as well as such relations, including inferential relations, that obtain among IUFs.

If for each property and relation of IUFs there was invariably some distinct property or relation of propositional attitudes of which it was the image, then the task of reconstructing the empirical structure of the attitudes might be relatively straightforward. But this is not the case. Not all the properties and relations of IUFs are exploited, i.e., are 'empirically meaningful'. And of those that are exploited, not all are exploited on every occasion of use, nor even fully exploited on those occasions when they are exploited. Thus, for example, I may attribute to Jones the belief that 'the wealthy Cicero is destitute', intending thereby to draw attention to the falsity of Jones's belief, but not intending thereby to attribute to Jones a logically inconsistent belief different from the one that I would attribute by describing him as believing that 'Cicero is destitute'. Similarly, I may attribute to Jones the belief that Kennedy went to /harverd/, not intending thereby to attribute to Jones a belief different from the one that he might attribute to himself by describing himself as believing that Kennedy went to /hahvahd/. My choice of IUF may simply reflect the fact that the audience to whom my attribution is directed knows Harvard only as /harverd/, not as /hahvahd/, and I want to make sure they understand just what belief I am attributing to Jones. It may be irrelevant for the purposes of the attribution just how Jones would pronounce the name of Kennedy's alma mater. Of course, in other cases these very same properties of the IUF may be images of properties of the propositional attitude for which the IUF is the representative. Thus, for example, the phonological and orthographic properties of IUFs that are exploited in the /harverd/-/hahvahd/ and e. e. cummings-E. E. Cummings cases discussed earlier serve to specify certain (non-existent) states of affairs, viz., ones in which there exist two different institutions, /harverd/ and /hahvahd/, and two different poets, e. e. cummings and E. E. Cummings, which a knowledgeable person would otherwise be unable to specify by means of the *that*-clauses of their attitude reports if the IUFs expressed by these *that*-clauses did not exploit these properties. Here the use in the IUF of one phonetic or orthographic form rather than the other does mark a difference in propositional attitude, one that can manifest itself behaviorally in a number of different ways, including how the possessor of the attitude would verbally (or orthographically) express the belief. This difference in propositional attitude, which the different IUFs mark, is unquestionably a matter of the propositional attitudes in question having different causal properties. But to say that these IUFs mark different propositional attitudes with different causal properties is not yet to say anything specific about these properties, except that in the one case the properties are sufficient to produce the effects associated with believing that Kennedy went to /hahvahd/ while in the other they are sufficient to produce the effects associated with believing that Kennedy went to /harverd/. Our characterization of these propositional attitudes and their properties, in other words, remains purely functional, viz., as apt to produce certain characteristic effects.

The import of the foregoing examples is that distinct properties and relations of IUFs are not necessarily the images of distinct properties and relations of propositional attitudes. Rather, an IUF, with the particular individuating properties and relations that it has, serves to specify a state of affairs that satisfies that IUF. This state of affairs is in turn related to the propositional attitude that has this IUF as its representative by way of the behavior that this propositional attitude produces (in conjunction with other mediating propositional attitudes), where importantly this behavior may include the particular form of words that the possessor of the attitude would use to describe this state of affairs.[11]

But what, then, are the properties and relations of propositional attitudes that define the empirical structure of the attitudes (and hence find an image in the properties and relations of IUFs)? These properties and relations, whatever they turn out to be, will presumably be characterized in purely *distal* terms. For suppose *per mirabile* that we had a complete computational model for an individual, one that enabled us to predict, at least in principle, both the computational state changes and the physical movements of the individual, given a history of environmental stimuli to that individual. Included among these computational states would be various representational states, i.e., states that in one fashion or another encode information about distal states of affairs, since otherwise it would seem impossible to explain how the individual is able to adapt his goal-directed behavior to his environment. However, to say that the individual possesses such representational states is not to say anything about how this information is represented; in particular, nothing requires that there be a systematic natural language interpretation of these representations according to which they express the contents of the *that*-clauses of propositional attitudes that might plausibly be attributed to the individual. The situation might turn out to be as described by Dennett (see Chapter 3.8 above), where, for example, a chess-playing program can be plausibly described as wanting to get its Queen out early, yet no description of that program would at any level of *computational* description attribute to that program any explicit representation, i.e., data structure, that could plausibly be construed as representing or expressing the desired state of affairs.[12] The program's desire to get its Queen out early might turn out to

---

[11] The IUF that is the representative of a propositional attitude will in many, if not most, cases specify the state of affairs using words that are not those that the possessor of the represented attitude would use. In some cases the attributor simply cannot use the words of the possessor to specify the representative state of affairs, e.g., when someone undertakes to attribute to me the desire that only I could express by saying, 'I want wine with dinner'. In other cases the attributor may use a different form of words in order to make clear to the audience of the attitude attribution just what the representing state of affairs and hence the attributed attitude are, e.g., when someone attributes to Jones the belief that 'Cicero is bald', despite Jones's knowing Cicero only as 'Tully', because the audience knows Cicero only as 'Cicero', or when the words that the possessor would use are in a language that the audience doesn't understand. In still other cases the attributor may use a different form of words in order to comment critically on the attributed attitude (e.g., attributing to someone the belief that 'the wealthy Cicero is destitute', the desire to 'earn an unreasonably high rate of return on his investments').

[12] By 'computational description' here I mean a description that those engaged in actual computational modeling of cognitive processes would count as such, where such modeling is

be, as Dennett puts it (1977 [1981]: 107), 'in an entirely innocent way, an emergent property of the computational processes', by which we mean that desiring to get one's Queen out early would be a matter of having certain computational properties and representations, but the having of the former might not be in any practical sense a predictable or foreseeable consequence of the having of the latter.

There would seem to be two possibilities in the hypothetical situation in which we possess a complete computational model of an individual: either one can map the content of each propositional attitude possessed by that individual onto some computational data structure maintained by that individual that expresses the content of the associated attitude, or one cannot. Consider first the case, described by Dennett, in which one *cannot* map attitude contents onto data structures in the way envisioned by the Received View. In such a case we would have no discrete computational structures with which to identify (or correlate) propositional attitudes, and hence no salient computational properties and relations to identify as the properties and relations that find an image in the properties and relations of IUFs. The computational model would give us no particular handle on the properties and relations of propositional attitudes, since from the perspective of the model, propositional attitudes and their properties and relations would be, as Dennett would have it, innocently emergent from the computational processes. The properties and relations of propositional attitudes would have to be gleaned from the common-sense practice of predicting, explaining, and rationalizing behavior and thought in terms of propositional attitudes. Our rationale for attributing certain propositional attitudes with specific properties and relations to the individual described by this computational model would therefore be just the usual behavioral rationale that we have for attributing propositional attitudes with specific properties and relations to one another.

Consider next the case in which one *can* map contents onto data structures in the way envisioned by the Received View. Clearly these data structures would play a causal/computational role in the psychological economy of their possessors; moreover, they would have all sorts of properties and any number of different relations both to other data structures that are similarly interpretable as expressing the contents of their possessor's propositional

responsive to the usual computational concerns of resource availability, architectural constraints, etc. 'Desiring to get one's Queen out early' is definitely *not* such a description!

attitudes and to the sensory inputs and motor outputs of their possessor. But why suppose that these properties and relations would have, much less would have to have, images in the properties and relations of IUFs? Given the probable complexity of the computational processes defined over these data structures, processes that no doubt heavily mediate these various relations, there is no reason to suppose that the properties and relations of propositional attitudes that find an image in the properties and relations of IUFs are ones that would be salient, indeed even specified, in the computational model. For suppose that certain data structures could be taken to express the contents of their possessor's propositional attitudes, perhaps because these structures covary systematically with certain distal states of affairs (or perhaps because they exhibit what Fodor (1990b) describes as an 'asymmetric dependency' on such states of affairs). Propositional attitudes might then be taken to be, as the Received View would have it, relations to such data structures. But the *computationally* relevant properties of, and relations among, these data structures are almost certainly going to be ones that concern detailed features of the computational processes defined over these data structures rather than the rather gross distally characterized properties and relations that are relevant to their role in the common-sense practice of predicting, explaining, and rationalizing thought and behavior. The properties and relations in question might, for example, be those responsible for causing the data structure to be placed on a certain stack, stored in a certain register, transformed in ways that depend on structures located lower in the stack, stored in other registers, etc. The point here is that the computational properties and relations of the representations over which computational processes are defined are in all likelihood not going to be the properties and relations of propositional attitudes that define their role in common-sense practice. That practice abstracts away from all detail, including computational detail, of cognitive processing, focusing entirely on the effects of propositional attitudes on thought and behavior.[13]

The upshot, then, is that even if the contents of propositional attitudes were able to be paired with certain computational data structures, there is reason to expect that the *properties and relations* of propositional attitudes that find images in the properties and relations of IUFs would nevertheless turn out to be, in the manner Dennett (1977 [1981]) imagines, emergent

---

[13] The point here is just the one made in Chapter 3.5 about the computational implementation by a Marcus parser of the linguistic knowledge expressed by grammars made available by Chomsky's Extended Standard Theory.

from the properties and relations of these data structures. Common-sense propositional attitude psychology would thus turn out to be, as Newell (1981) insisted, an autonomous, non-computational level of psychological description and explanation. The theoretical entities, properties, and relations posited at the level of propositional attitude description (what Newell called the 'knowledge level') would not then reduce smoothly and transparently to the entities, properties, and relations posited at computational levels of description; indeed, as Dennett's talk of their being emergent properties suggests, they might not even be predictable in any practical way from these computational properties and relations. Propositional attitudes, their properties, and their relations would turn out not to be natural kinds from the perspective of lower-level computational description. They would turn out to be kinds only at the intentional level, just as certain geological entities, properties, and relations turn out to be kinds only at that level of physical description. Thus, on this second possible outcome, as on the first, the availability of a mapping of propositional attitudes onto their natural language representations would once again have to be gleaned, if gleaned at all, from our common-sense practice, from their role in predictions, explanations, and rationalizations of behavior and thought. So the question, then, in both cases is this: How are these the properties and relations of propositional attitudes that define the empirical structure of the attitudes to be gleaned from common-sense practice, and what sort of properties and relations are they?

If the properties and relations of propositional attitudes that define the empirical structure of the attitudes can only be gleaned from the common-sense practice of predicting, explaining, and rationalizing thought and behavior, then their characterization will be *functional* in nature, since this common-sense practice is concerned with propositional attitudes only insofar as they have certain characteristic effects (on behavior and thought) that are the focus of this practice. Of course, propositional attitudes have these causal properties and relations in virtue of the possessors of these attitudes having certain more basic, perhaps computational, properties; however, the latter do not play any role at all in the predictions, explanations, and rationalizations of common-sense practice. All that is relevant to that practice is that propositional attitudes be capable of producing certain characteristic effects that are specified, as we have seen, in terms of specific sorts of behavioral relations to the states of affairs specified by IUFs. The properties and relations of propositional attitudes must therefore be sufficient, in the context of mediating propositional attitudes, to produce these effects. There is no reason, it should be noted, to suppose that these properties and relations are in any essential way linguistic, any more than there is any reason to suppose that the properties and relations of physical magnitudes are in any essential way numerical. The most that can be presumed is that the structure of the properties and relations defined over propositional attitudes is relevantly homologous to the structure of the properties and relations defined over IUFs, which are the representatives of propositional attitudes.

But what, then, are these functional properties and relations that define the empirical structure of the attitudes? We can begin to get some idea by considering how propositional attitude attributions can be elaborated in order to respond to queries about just what attitude is being attributed. Consider, for example, how I might elaborate my attribution 'Jones believes that Tully was bald' in order to make clear just what I take Jones to believe. Under questioning, I might describe Jones more expansively as believing that 'Tully, whom Jones knows only as "Cicero", and of whom he knows only that he was a Roman orator and that he denounced Catiline (put another way: Tully whom Jones conceptualizes as "Cicero, the Roman orator who denounced Catiline"), is bald'. And in saying that Jones believes that he, Cicero, is 'bald', I might mean that Jones believes that Cicero has the property of exhibiting the loss of scalp hair associated with the condition known as 'male pattern baldness'. Under further questioning I might elaborate my initial attribution even further, making clear just how Jones conceives of Cicero (maybe Jones conceives of him only under the French spelling of his name: 'Cicéron'), Catiline (perhaps Jones knows him only as 'Lucius Sergius Catilina'), Roman orators, and denouncings. Presumably such elaborations of our context-sensitive common-sense attributions are limited only by our specific knowledge of (or beliefs about) the attributed attitude. It is not clear whether for any attitude attribution of the usual context-sensitive sort there exists a 'maximal' elaboration of that attribution, one that specifies fully and completely (and in a context-independent way) the attributed attitude. Probably there is not. Nevertheless, these richly elaborated attributions seem to provide some insight into the functional properties and relations that define the empirical structure of the attitudes. They do this by providing a rich specification of the representative state of affairs to which an attributed propositional attitude is behaviorally related, one that makes clear in a way that the usual attributions typically do not just what the characteristic effects of the attributed attitude are likely to be on the possessor's behavior and his concomitant intentional states. On the basis of such an elaboration, we would know, for example, how Jones is likely to verbalize his belief, just what sorts of individuals he is likely to count as bald, as orators, as denouncers, what he thinks being bald, an orator, or a denouncer comes to, and so on.

So from these elaborations we can begin to see just what sorts of functionally specified properties and relations the empirical relational structure of the attitudes is likely to define on the domain of propositional attitudes. Specifically, these elaborations give us a pretty clear idea of how the possessor of an attitude is likely to conceive of the state of affairs that the IUF specifies, i.e., how the possessor would individuate that state of affairs relative to other states of affairs which we might take to be the same (or different), how he would describe it, and so on. They would also give us a pretty clear idea of how the possessor of an attitude is likely to behave relative to this state of affairs, behavior that in the case of desire-like attitudes is intended to bring about the state of affairs, or that in the case of belief-like attitudes is shaped or modulated by the state of affairs. They would also give a clear idea of the (concomitant) mental states that would be expected to accompany the attitude. From these elaborations we would also know what IUFs the possessor would in different contexts count as equivalent specifications of the attitude.

On the basis of elaborations of the sort just described, we can conclude that the *properties* that define the empirical structure of the attitudes are those second-order properties of propositional attitudes that find an image in the linguistic properties of IUFs that specify the states of affairs (and their descriptions) to which propositional attitudes are behaviorally related in the ways described earlier in this chapter. These properties are just those second-order properties of propositional attitudes that are causally responsible for the possessor of an attitude behaving as he does with respect to the specified state of affairs, saying what he does, individuating the state of affairs that is the representative of the attitude in the way that he does, coming to hold the other, concomitant mental states that he does, and so on.

The *relations* that define the empirical structure of the attitudes are just those second-order relations that find an image in the inferential relations among IUFs that are the representatives of propositional attitudes. These imaged relations no more have to be themselves inferential than do the imaged properties have to be linguistic, and for just the same reason: all that is required is that the empirical structure of the attitudes be homologous in the relevant way to the representational structure of IUFs. The relations among propositional attitudes that have as images inferential relations among IUFs will be *material* relations of some sort, specifically causal or constitutive relations, or relations of identity or similarity. Suppose, for example, that the inferential relation between the IUF ⟦[[old men] and women] are at risk of infection⟧ (understood as indicated by the brackets) and the IUF ⟦women are at risk of infection⟧ is the image of a relation between two propositional attitudes, perhaps beliefs, that have these IUFs as representatives. The relation between these attitudes, which the inferential relation marks, is one that will be manifest in the characteristic behavioral effects of the two attitudes: those behaviors that characteristically manifest the attitude that has the former IUF as its representative will include all those behaviors that characteristically manifest the attitude that has the latter IUF as its representative. Functionally speaking, then, the former attitude has the latter attitude as a constituent, in the sense that to be a state apt to produce the effects characteristic of the former is *eo ipso* to be a state apt to produce the effects characteristic of the latter. Similarly, the inferential relation that instantiates the inference rule of modus ponens would be the image of the empirical fact that subjects who have (or come to have) attitudes that have as images IUFs which are instances of the rule's antecedents, viz., p and $p \rightarrow q$, will normally have (come to have) an attitude that has as its image an IUF that is an instance of the rule's consequent, namely, q.

While many properties and relations defined over IUFs are the images of second-order empirical properties and relations defined over propositional attitudes, others are not. Or if they are, they are only partial images. In some cases, the failure of such properties and relations to be such an image can be explained in terms of the pragmatics of language, as, for example, might be the case if the property or relation was not sufficiently salient to those to whom propositional attitude attributions are addressed for it to be exploitable. In other cases, the failure might be explained in terms of certain performance limitations on the part of the person to whom the propositional attitudes are attributed. The failure of belief to be 'closed under logical consequence', as some mistakenly put it, is often explained in just these terms. Subjects, we are told, lack sufficient memory or computational capacity. But the well-known difficulties that subjects have with various reasoning tasks such as the Wason selection task and the so-called THOG problem (see Johnson-Laird and Bryne 1991, and Braine and O'Brien 1998b) suggest that the failure of deductive closure is not to be explained in terms of performance limitations. The inferences that subjects draw, as well as the inferences that they don't draw, are not well predicted on any plausible assumptions about memory and computational capacity. Certain inferences that would appear to be relatively inexpensive with respect to the memory and computational resources that they require typically don't get made, while certain other inferences that are relatively expensive typically do. Alternative explanations in terms of non-standard logics, mental models, and so on have been proposed, but arguably each of these effectively concede that the inferential relations defined over the representational domain specified by propositional attitude ascriptions are at best partial, no doubt idealized, images of the relations defined on the empirical domain. This should hardly be surprising, if, as I am arguing, the attitudes are simply states apt to produce certain characteristic effects and as such need not be the sort of states, much less entities (such as sentences) that stand in inferential relations to one another. At most one might expect the representational structure specified by propositional attitude ascriptions to capture the empirical structure of the attitudes only roughly, and then only under significant idealization. That our inferential representation of the empirical relations among propositional attitudes should be thus rough and idealized has no deleterious effect on the reliability of our common-sense practice of predicting, explaining, and rationalizing thought and behavior for the simple reason that the practice itself has evolved in such fashion as to be employed only for reasoning tasks where the representation is generally reliable. In this respect we are like mariners who by practice and circumstance generally use Mercator projection nautical charts only for local navigation, where they are quite reliable, but rarely for navigation over long distances, where the distortion associated with this projection scheme is quite significant. That experimental research has sometimes seemed to discover an unexpectedly rich inferential structure in the propositional attitudes of subjects may simply be an artifact of the competence of experimental subjects in manipulating the very familiar measurement-theoretic scheme for representing propositional attitudes. In circumstances where the attributed attitude is so etiolated as to amount to little more than an aptness for both uttering the words that we take to express the attitude and reasoning about the implications of these words, it would hardly be surprising if subjects fell back on the inferential relations defined on the representational domain, such as they were able to determine them, in deciding what 'entailed' propositional attitudes to impute to themselves and to others.

6.5.5. Recap

So here, then, is the picture that emerges of the empirical structure of the attitudes, a structure that is represented by a relational structure defined over IUFs, which are the natural language representatives of propositional attitudes. The structure consists of a domain of propositional attitudes, understood as first-order properties (states) of their possessors, with certain second-order functional properties and relations defined over them which find an image in the first-order properties and relations defined over IUFs. The functional properties of propositional attitudes that define the empirical structure of the attitudes are the properties of being able to produce the characteristic effects, both on behavior and on thought, that we identify with, indeed use to identify, specific propositional attitudes. These properties include such properties as being able to produce the behavior that manifests the attitude, being able to express verbally the attitude, being able to discriminate the state of affairs (and hence the IUF) that is the representative of the attitude, being the cause of certain other intentional states (including both other propositional attitudes and also certain affective intentional states), and so on. The functional relations that define the empirical structure of the attitudes are certain material relations, both causal and constitutive, among propositional attitudes, as well as relations of similarity and identity. These relations include cases in which coming to have certain propositional attitudes causes the possessor of these attitudes to come to have certain other attitudes. They also include cases in which one propositional attitude is constitutive of another in the sense that having the first is *eo ipso* to have the second inasmuch as the characteristic effects of the first include those of the second.

6.6. INFORMAL SKETCH OF A REPRESENTATION THEOREM

A completed formal measurement-theoretic account of propositional attitude predicates would prove a representation theorem. That theorem would establish the existence of a mapping of propositional attitudes into their natural language representatives that respects (in the sense explained in Chapter 5.3) the properties and relations of propositional attitudes that we exploit in our surrogative reasoning regarding propositional attitudes and their effects. We are not currently in a position to prove a representation theorem, because we lack adequately developed formal characterizations of both the represented empirical relational structure of the attitudes and the representing relational structure of their IUF representatives. Nevertheless, we can be reasonably confident that there does in fact exist a structure-respecting mapping of the sort that a representation theorem would establish, and we can, I think, see roughly how a proof of the required representation theorem might be expected to go. Let us consider each of these in turn.

Our confidence that there is a structure-respecting mapping of propositional attitudes into their natural language representatives rests on our success in predicting the behavior of others by attributing to them certain propositional attitudes that we take to be the causes of their behavior.[14] This success does not entail the existence of the attitudes, for there are notorious examples of false theories that are very good predicting devices. But predictive success is presumptive evidence both for the existence of the entities which these predictions presuppose and for the empirical faithfulness of a chosen scheme for representing these entities and their prediction-relevant properties. But if this is so, then there is good reason to think both that propositional attitudes exist and that there exists a structure-respecting mapping of the attitudes into their natural language representatives that enables us to predict successfully the behavior of others using these representatives.

But if there is such a mapping, how might the proof of a representation theorem go? What we know is that such a proof will establish that there exists a (trans-type) mapping from the empirical relational structure of propositional attitudes into the relational structure of our natural language representatives of propositional attitudes, a mapping that respects the properties and relations of propositional attitudes to which we advert in reasoning surrogatively about propositional attitudes and their effects. The relational structure of our natural language representations of propositional attitudes, we said, is a structure consisting of a domain of IUFs, which are the representatives of propositional attitudes, and certain first-order properties and relations defined over that domain. These properties include the syntactic, semantics, phonological, and pragmatic properties that linguistic theory would attribute to IUFs, and perhaps certain orthographic properties of IUFs, while the relations include the inferential relations that a semantic theory and a logic

---

[14] Eliminativists such as Churchland (1981) have endeavored to challenge this basic premise of the argument, arguing that the touted successes of common-sense predictive practice are more apparent than real. But Fodor (1987: 3) is surely right that these predictive successes are real; indeed, these successes are ubiquitous to the point of being practically invisible in the course of our everyday lives.

for natural language would attribute to those IUFs. The empirical relational structure of the attitudes, we said, is a structure consisting of a domain of propositional attitudes, construed as first-order properties of individuals, and certain second-order properties and relations defined over this domain. The second-order properties are the functional properties of being apt to produce, in the appropriate circumstances, both the behaviors that manifest the attitude (including verbal behavior) and the mental states (including both other propositional attitudes and certain affective states) that are its usual mental concomitants, while the second-order relations are just those causal and constitutive relations that propositional attitudes bear to one another, to behavior, and to certain affective intentional states.

We are not, I said, presently in a position to provide the formal characterizations of either the relational structure of the attitudes or the relational structure of their natural language representatives suitable for the proof of a representation theorem. But we do have a reasonably good idea of the properties and relations that define the latter of these two relational structures, and there is certainly reason to suppose that advances in both linguistic theory and the logic of natural language will eventually provide a suitable formal characterization of these properties and relations. We are, however, in considerably less good shape as regards the structure of the attitudes. We are clearly not in a position to characterize the properties and relations that define this structure in terms of their intrinsic neurophysiological or even computational nature, and in any event there is no reason to suppose that a characterization in these terms would be a characterization of the relational structure of *propositional attitudes* rather than of the underlying neurophysiological or computational states that realize them. There is no reason to suppose that the domain of such realizing states would be individuated in a way that corresponded even remotely to that of propositional attitudes. So our only real option here, then, would seem to be to characterize the relational structure of the attitudes *functionally*, in terms of the states of affairs to which they are behaviorally related in the attitude-type specific ways described in section 6.5.3 above. But if it is a functional characterization of the properties and relations of propositional attitudes that we are after, then we need only consider elaborations of propositional attitude attributions of the sort described in section 6.5.4 above. For such elaborations, if sufficiently developed, will provide a fairly detailed characterization of the functional properties and relations of propositional attitudes relevant to surrogative reasoning about the attitudes.

The Measure of Mind

Suppose we had both the linguistic theory and a logic for natural language sufficient to provide a formal characterization of the relational structure of our natural language representatives of propositional attitudes. And suppose we also had rich elaborations of a sufficient number of representative common-sense propositional attitude attributions so as to be able to develop a formal specification of functional properties and relations that define the empirical structure of the attitudes. We would then be able to specify two intensional relational structures, $\Re_\Lambda$ and $\Re_P$, where these are the intensional relational structure of our natural language representatives of propositional attitudes and the empirical intensional relational structure of the attitudes, respectively. $\Re_\Lambda$ would consist of a domain of IUFs with certain first-order properties and relations, given by linguistic theory and the logic of natural language, defined over them. More precisely, $\Re_\Lambda$ would be an ordered triple $<\Lambda, {}^f\lambda_i, {}^\vee>$, where Λ is the domain of IUFs and the ${}^f\lambda_i$ are first-order n-adic relations (including first-order monadic relations, or properties) defined on Λ, and ${}^\vee$ a unary function on ${}^f\lambda_i$ that assigns to each ${}^f\lambda_i$ an extension in Λ. $\Re_P$ would consist of a domain of individuals who are the possessors of propositional attitudes, certain first-order monadic functional properties of these individuals which are the propositional attitudes, and certain second-order functional properties and relations of these first-order properties. More precisely, $\Re_P$ would be an ordered quadruple $<I, {}^fP_i, {}^s\rho_i, {}^\vee>$, where I is a domain of individuals who are the possessors of propositional attitudes, ${}^fP_i$ the first-order properties of I that are the attitudes, and ${}^s\rho_i$ the second-order relations defined on ${}^fP_i$ that are the functional properties and relations of propositional attitudes, and ${}^\vee$ a unary relation on ${}^fP_i$ and ${}^s\rho_i$ that assigns an extension in I to every member of ${}^fP_i$ and an extension in ${}^fP_i$ to every member of ${}^s\rho_i$.

Suppose that we had specifications of both $\Re_\Lambda$ and $\Re_P$. How would we go about demonstrating that there is a mapping of $\Re_P$ into $\Re_\Lambda$ that respects the second-order relations ${}^s\rho_i$ defined on the ${}^fP_i$ (the attitudes)? Let us suppose for purposes of argument that for any IUF of a common-sense attitude attribution there is a 'maximal elaboration' of that IUF, i.e., an elaboration of that IUF which cannot be further elaborated (in the sense that further elaborations would not be individuative of different propositional attitudes).[15] Then the proof would proceed in two steps. First, it would

---

15 The supposition that there are such maximal elaborations is thoroughly dispensable. It is enough simply that the IUFs of common-sense attributions can be elaborated sufficiently to display the functional properties and relations of the attributed attitudes relevant to our surrogative reasoning regarding the attitudes and their effects, which seemingly they can. Even if it turned

establish that the first-order relations $^f\lambda_i$ defined on those IUFs that are maximal elaborations of the IUFs of common-sense attitude attributions respect the second-order relations $^s\rho_i$ defined on the ^fP_i that are the attitudes. Second, it would establish that the first-order relations $^f\lambda_i$ defined on non-maximally elaborated IUFs respect some contextually determined proper subset of the second-order relations $^s\rho_i$ respected by the maximal elaborations of these IUFs, specifically, just those second-order relations that, in the context of attribution, these IUFs represent the attitude as having. Together these two steps in the proof would establish what needs to be established, namely that there is a mapping of the structure of the attitudes into the structure of their natural language representatives that respects the second-order relations of propositional attitudes that common-sense propositional attitude attributions represent them as having.

The proof envisioned here would proceed similarly to a proof that non-quantitative physical magnitude predicates such as *has a heavy mass* or *has a very low temperature* respect certain empirical properties and relations of the relevant physical magnitudes. First, one would prove a standard representation theorem for the scales that quantitative predicates such as *has a mass of 5 kg* or *having a temperature of 25 degrees Centigrade* employ. Then having done that, one would show that the relation that non-quantitative predicates bear to the scales for which one has proved a representation theorem is such that these predicates respect certain properties and relations of the physical magnitudes measured by these scales. This second task, which is basically a problem in the semantics of such predicates, involves construing them as predicating some unspecified quantity of the magnitude the numerical representative of which falls within a contextually determined interval on the scale for which the representation theorem has been proved. The relations (including monadic properties) of physical magnitudes that are thus respected by such natural language representations include the property of having just such an unspecified but bounded quantity of the magnitude, of having a quantity of the magnitude greater than any magnitude whose representative falls below the interval, and so on (for details, see Schwarzschild and Wilkinson 2002).

The strategy for proving a representation theorem for maximally elaborated IUFs seems reasonably straightforward. Such elaborations provide a functional

---

out that detailed elaborations of IUFs failed to display all such properties and relations, the most that would follow is that our representation theorem would fail to cover some of the second-order relations of propositional attitudes that the first-order relations defined over IUFs respect.

specification of the second-order relations $^s\rho_i$ of propositional attitudes. Such a specification can be taken to be correct inasmuch as our generally successful surrogative reasoning about propositional attitudes and their effects adverts directly to such relations. So there is no issue here about whether propositional attitudes actually have the functional characterized relations $^s\rho_i$ that maximally elaborated IUFs attribute to them, since propositional attitudes are not otherwise independently specified. And because there is not such an issue, there is also not an issue as to whether these relations are respected by the first-order relations $^f\lambda_i$ defined over these maximally elaborated IUFs. There would be an issue if we were constrained to provide a *non*-functional, presumably structural specification of the $^s\rho_i$, since then one would have to establish that these were respected by the functionally specified $^f\lambda_i$. (This, incidentally, is *precisely* where a measurement-theoretic version of the Received View would run into a problem: it proposes to identify propositional attitudes with certain sentence-like mental structures, though without having any detailed story as to how such structures might produce the various effects associated with propositional attitudes, and in terms of which propositional attitudes are individuated.) So from these maximal elaborations of IUFs, we can be confident that we have a correct functional characterization of the properties and relations of propositional attitudes, even if we know little or nothing of the structures that have those functional properties and relations. In effect, propositional attitudes are purely functionally defined states. So there is really not that much that has to be offered by way of a proof of a representation theorem—propositional attitudes just are states that have the functional properties and relations attributed to them by maximally elaborated IUFs.[16]

The second step in a proof of a representation theorem, I said, would establish that the first-order relations $^f\lambda_i$ defined on the non-maximally elaborated IUFs of common-sense attributions respect a contextually determined proper subset of the second-order relations $^s\rho_i$ respected by maximally elaborated IUFs. Specifically, it would establish that these first-order relations respect just those second-order relations that, in the context of attitude

---

[16] The situation here is really no different from the case of physical magnitudes where the relevant properties and relations of the magnitudes are similarly defined in a way that abstracts away from all structural commitments. The relevant properties and relations are defined functionally in terms of their measured effects. In both cases the properties and relations are ones that objects in the empirical domain presumably have in virtue of having certain other non-functional properties and relations.

attribution, an IUF represents the attributed attitude as having, such that we can reason surrogatively in terms of IUFs about propositional attitudes with these second-order relations. Consider, for example, the attitude attribution, 'Jones believes Tully is bald'. The relations of the attributed attitude that are respected in the clearly non-maximally elaborated IUF [] *Tully is bald* [] would include such properties as being such as to cause those behaviors that are manifestations of the attitude (perhaps such properties would cause Jones to assert that Tully is bald, to identify Tully as a promising candidate for a hair replacement, and so on). They would also include relations to certain other IUFs, e.g., the IUF that is the representative of the belief that someone was bald. But the respected relations might not include the property of being such as to cause Jones to utter the words 'Tully is bald' or 'I believe that Tully is bald'. Jones may believe that Tully is bald, but know Tully only as 'Cicero', or he may speak only French, in which case he might express his belief by saying 'Cicéron est chauve'. The relations respected in this IUF would not include all those respected in any particular elaboration of this IUF; rather they would include just those relations that are respected by *all* elaborations of this IUF, which is the representative of the attributed attitude. In effect, then, what a common-sense attitude attribution attributes to the possessor of the attitude is an attitude that is a member of an equivalence class of attitudes, all of which share certain relations, namely those that are respected by all elaborations of the attitude's representative IUF. Propositional attitude predicates such as *believes Tully is bald* or *wants to meet the girl next door*, then, turn out to function semantically in a manner analogous to physical magnitude predicates of the sort *has a large mass* or *has a very low temperature*. Both sorts of predicate pick out an equivalence class of first-order properties (beliefs, wants, mass, temperature, etc.) all of which share certain second-order properties and relations that are roughly specifiable in terms of properties and relations of the measurement-theoretic representatives of these first-order properties.

6.7. THE UNIQUENESS PROBLEM: WHEN HAVE WE ATTRIBUTED THE SAME PROPOSITIONAL ATTITUDE?

Numerical measurements of physical magnitudes permit certain transformations of scale that preserve the measured empirical properties and relations. Thus, for example, properties and relations respected on an interval scale (e.g., temperature) are preserved under linear transformations. If proposition-al attitude predicates are genuine measure predicates, then presumably there will be certain non-trivial transformations defined on the representatives of propositional attitudes that preserve the empirical properties and relations of represented attitudes that are respected in the mapping of propositional attitudes into these representatives. A solution to the uniqueness problem for propositional attitude measurement would provide a characterization of these transformations. So the question here is this: Under what transformations defined on the representational domain are the empirical properties and relations of propositional attitudes preserved?

The representatives in the representational domain of propositional atti-tudes are IUFs. Admissible transformations will presumably relate different IUFs as representatives of one and the same propositional attitude. Such transformations could conceivably relate representatives of different types of attitude; however, admissible transformations seem always to preserve attitude-type.[17] There is no a priori reason why this should be so; however, failure to preserve attitude-type would clearly impugn a realist construal of our common-sense taxonomy of attitude-types. For suppose that admissible transformations turned out to systematically relate two different attitude-types. That would surely be good grounds for concluding that these two attitude-types were not different psychological kinds, and for just the sorts of reasons that lead us to conclude that the Celsius and Fahrenheit scales do not measure different kinds of physical magnitude.

If admissible transformations preserve attitude-type, then natural language representations of propositional attitudes that are related by admissible transformations will differ only in the IUFs that they assign to a particular propositional attitude of some specific attitude type. So what, then, are the admissible transformations that map IUFs into IUFs, all of which are representatives of the same propositional attitude? Intuitively, admissible transformations are ones which relate IUFs that, to use Davidson's (1968) terminology, 'samesay' one another. But what precisely is the relation between IUFs such that one IUF 'samesays' another, i.e., such that one 'says the same thing' as another? Practically speaking, of course, we have a pretty clear sense of when two utterances (in languages we understand) say the same thing, and hence of when two IUFs are representatives of the same propositional

---

[17] Indeed, there seem to be no equivalences across different attitude-types, with the possible exception of believing that not p and doubting that p.

attitude. So the fundamental task for someone who undertakes to prove a uniqueness theorem for this domain is to formulate in explicit terms the criteria upon which such practical judgments are based.[18] This task is made difficult by the apparent context sensitivity of the samesaying relation. Thus, in one context my saying in English, 'Jones believes that Tully is bald' counts as saying the same thing as your saying in French, 'Jones croit que Cicéron est chauve', though in another context it does not, perhaps because in the latter context it is important not simply that some particular person, 'Tully' or 'Cicéron' as he may be called, is said to be bald, but also just how that person is picked out, e.g., as 'Tully' rather than as 'Cicéron'. The issue here, it should be noted, is not always a matter of how fine-grained the similarities have to be, such that in one context utterances expressing the same Russellian proposition count as samesaying one another, whereas in another context they won't, unless in addition they share the particular form of words used to express that proposition. It can sometimes be a matter of sharing certain similarities that do not include expressing the same proposition. Consider Loar's (1988) example of a diarist and his twin-Earth doppelgänger, both of whom write in their diaries the words: 'no swimming today; the water's too rough'. In the context that Loar describes, the two inscriptions count as saying the same thing, despite the fact that in the diaries of these two individuals the same words express different propositions, the one having to do with the roughness of H_2O, the other having to do with the roughness of a different compound XYZ. In the described context they count as saying the same thing, because both are expressions of a shared psychological state, viz., the state that is causally responsible for both the diarist and his twin-Earth doppelgänger not going swimming.

So how in the light of the context sensitivity of the samesaying relation are we to proceed? One strategy might be to begin by considering how we would characterize the samesaying relation over IUFs if we were to neglect just those pairs of samesaying IUFs that seemingly drive us towards the conclusion that the samesaying relation is context-sensitive. Such a characterization might turn out to capture a significant portion of our common-sense attributive practice, perhaps the great bulk of that practice. For certainly there are many

---

[18] I am presuming here that the samesaying relation is sufficiently systematic that it makes sense to talk of IUFs thus related as being *transforms* of one another, i.e., as a being related by a formally specifiable transformation. If this turned out not to be the case, then it would be forlorn to suppose that we can specify admissible transformations of the representational domain, and hence to suppose that we can provide a solution to the uniqueness problem.

cases where, in the absence of any specific knowledge of the context in which an attitude was attributed, we are quite willing to offer (or accept) what we assume to be a perfectly adequate alternative representative of the attributed attitude. Thus, for example, Kripke's (1979) Pierre cases notwithstanding, I would normally have no qualms about describing a French speaker as 'believing that London is pretty' based solely on his sincere avowal that, as he would put it, 'Londres est jolie'. I would also normally have no qualms about attributing to someone various beliefs about attorneys that this person expressed using the term 'lawyers'. It might turn out that once we had in hand a characterization of the samesaying relation in cases where context seems irrelevant, we would see how, with suitable adjustments, to go about extending that characterization to cover the context sensitive cases. Or perhaps we might conclude that the supposed context-sensitivity of the samesaying relation was overblown, or maybe even non-existent, with the result that the context-sensitive cases would not really be an issue for a specification of admissible transformations of the representational domain.

If we adopt this strategy, neglecting for the moment those cases that appear to involve context sensitivity, we might propose that two IUFs samesay one another, and hence can be representatives of the same propositional attitude, just in case the two IUFs are *synonymous*, in the sense of having the same meaning and hence being translations or paraphrases of one another.[19] More precisely, the proposal here is that the properties and relations of propositional attitudes that are respected in the representational domain of IUFs are preserved under a synonymy transformation on that domain.[20] Such a proposal enjoys considerable empirical support: in translating and paraphrasing attitude attributions, we presume, absent any evidence to the contrary, that sentences attribute the same attitude just in case the sentences, and in particular the sentences embedded in their *that*-clauses (which specify IUFs), are synonymous. Thus we count the English sentence *Jones believes that Cicero is bald* and the French sentence *Jones croit que Cicéron est chauve* as attributing one and the same belief to Jones, because we take the sentences, and more specifically the sentences embedded their *that*-clauses, to be

---

[19] Strictly speaking, it is the two *sentences* which these IUFs semantically and pragmatically interpret that are synonymous; however, for simplicity of exposition I shall speak of the IUFs themselves as synonymous, since nothing hangs on which description we choose.

[20] If the notion of synonymy seems problematic here, perhaps because one supposes that the notion of synonymy is not defined for proper names and hence not for sentences that contain proper names, then one could take the relevant relation here to be one of translation or paraphrase.

synonymous. The proposal is also intuitively plausible on general theoretical grounds: natural languages would seem to be the obvious analog in propositional attitude measurement of the different scales used in physical magnitude measurement, and synonymy is the salient equivalence relation that pairs sentences across natural languages. Of course, the belief that is represented by the English IUF ⟦*Jones is a lawyer*⟧ is typically the same belief as that represented not only by the French IUF ⟦*Jones est advocat*⟧ but also by the English IUF ⟦*Jones is an attorney*⟧. So there would seem to be no reason not to allow that the synonymy transformation could be *intra*-linguistic as well as *inter*-linguistic, in which case the proposal here is that the properties and relations of propositional attitudes that are respected in the representational domain of IUFs are preserved under *any* synonymy transformation on that domain.

But there would seem to be an obvious difficulty with this proposal. There seem to be many examples of propositional attitude attributions that are not invariant under a synonymy transformation. It may be true, for example, that someone believes, as this person would put it, that 'all lawyers are parasites', but false that this same person believes that 'all attorneys are parasites', despite the fact that the terms *lawyer* and *attorney*, at least as *we* use these terms, are synonyms. Similarly, it may be true that someone doubts that, as this person would put it, 'all doctors are physicians', or 'all furze are gorse', but not true that this same person doubts either that 'all doctors are doctors' or that 'all furze are furze', despite the fact that the terms *doctor* and *physician*, and *furze* and *gorse*, at least as we use them, are synonyms. And there are as well the 'Tully'-'Cicero', /harvahd/-/hahvahd/, and 'e. e. cummings'-'E. E. Cummings' type examples that I used earlier to motivate the decision to take IUFs as the representatives of propositional attitudes. In all these cases, substitution of synonyms (or in the case of proper names, co-designative names) does not always preserve the represented propositional attitude. The IUFs that result from substituting synonyms are sometimes representatives of different propositional attitudes.

None of the above examples would cut against our proposal that the properties and relations of propositional attitudes that are respected in the representational domain are preserved under synonymy on that domain, if the notion of synonymy were relativized to the idiolect of the person about whom the attitude attribution is made.[21] In the first of these examples,

---

[21] I see no particular difficulty in so relativizing the notion of synonymy, especially given the general skepticism within linguistic circles about the notion of a public language. Certainly linguists

the person has a belief that he would express by saying, 'all lawyers are parasites'. But in this person's mouth, the sentences *all lawyers are parasites* and *all attorneys are parasites* are not representatives of the same propositional attitude, precisely because in his idiolect the terms *lawyer* and *attorney* are not synonymous. This person would no doubt be quite happy to substitute for the sentence that he uses to express his belief any sentence that he took to be synonymous, but *all attorneys are parasites* is not such a sentence. In the last two examples, as the person uses the names /harverd/ and /hahvahd/, 'e. e. cummings' and 'E. E. Cummings', they are not co-designative. As this person uses these names, the members of each pair are taken to designate different institutions, different persons. So again it does not count against the proposal that the properties and relations of propositional attitudes respected in the representational domain are preserved under synonymy that this person is unwilling to freely substitute these names, provided that we understand the notion of synonymy as relativized to his idiolect. Indeed, so understood the proposal finds support in the fact that in all these cases, this person is not willing to substitute these terms freely, precisely *because* he does not take the terms to be synonymous (or co-designative). And precisely because this person does not, like us, take these terms to be synonyms, we will in most circumstances be reluctant to disquote his words and adopt them as our own, in making attitude attributions of him. For in so doing we run the risk of being taken to be representing him as believing that all *lawyers* are parasites, when in fact what he believes is that all members of a proper subset of those whom we refer to indifferently as 'lawyers' or 'attorneys', viz., the ones whom *he* calls 'lawyers', are parasites. The only contexts in which we might be willing to disquote will be ones where either the risk of misinterpretation is low or the consequences of misinterpretation insignificant. In other contexts, we will probably take pains to make it clear either by word or gesture that we are not disquoting the words that the believer uses to express his belief, thereby making it clear that a hearer is not licensed to substitute into the IUF that is the representative of his belief what by our lights are synonyms.

In each of the above examples we are unable to freely substitute what we take to be synonyms because as a result of ignorance, confusion, or mistake on the part of the person to whom the attitude is attributed, this person does not share our synonymy judgments. In the first example, the person

find no difficulty relativizing the notion of synonymy to regional dialects—more than a few lexicographers make their living mapping the boundaries of dialectical synonymies.

mistakenly thinks that lawyers are a particular kind of attorney, perhaps attorneys who specialize in civil actions; he thus concludes that the terms *lawyer* and *attorney* are not synonyms. In the last two examples, the person mistakenly thinks that the two different phonological or orthographic forms of the name designate different things, so that they could not be synonyms, even in the minimal sense of being designations of one and the same thing. In still other cases, the mistake is straightforwardly linguistic, as in the case of speakers who misconstrue the meaning of *nonplused*, taking it to mean something like 'not impressed', with the consequence that for these speakers the term is not synonymous with its standard dictionary definition. Such confusions on the part of the person to whom the attitude is attributed make it difficult, sometimes virtually impossible, for anyone who fails to share this person's confusion to specify a propositional attitude by means of an expression that presumes it. We would be uncomfortable, for example, describing a person simply as 'believing that all lawyers are parasites', when we discover that this person won't accept 'all attorneys are parasites' as an expression of his belief, because to do so would suggest that this person will behave and think in a way that in fact he won't. This person's unwillingness to accept what we take to be a synonymous expression of the belief makes it clear that he does not mean what we do by the expression 'all lawyers are parasites'. And for precisely this reason, we would be equally uncomfortable specifying this person's belief by means of any expression that we take to be synonymous with 'all lawyers are parasites', e.g., by the French sentence 'tous avocats sont des parasites'. In attempting to specify this person's belief without thereby embracing his confusion, we sometimes resort to paraphrases that *mention*, but don't use, the words that embody the confusion or mistake, or else we *use* the words but in a way that makes clear that our use differs from his, often by adding a parenthetical phrase that marks the difference. These paraphrases endeavor to make clear how the meanings that he attaches to these words differ from the meanings that we attach to these same words, thus explaining why in our attribution we are unable simply to disquote (or first translate and then disquote) his words, using his words as our own. But again there is nothing in these supposed counterexamples that counts against the proposal being considered here. These are simply cases in which we can't use the person's words as our own, because he uses them with a meaning that we do not. The problem raised by these cases, to the extent that they raise any problem at all, is just that of having to exercise some care in deciding how to express in our own words the words of another. But whatever IUF we do eventually fix on as the appropriate representative of this person's belief, we will count as an equally appropriate representative of that belief any IUF that interprets a sentence that we take to be synonymous with the sentence that this IUF interprets, where synonymy here is judged relative to *our* language or idiolect. Thus, for example, if we describe Jones as believing that all lawyers of a certain kind, namely those that bring civil actions, are parasites, then we will think that Jones can equally well be described as believing that all attorneys of a certain kind, namely those that bring civil actions, are parasites.

In some cases we may be unwilling to substitute freely synonymous sentences, not because of ignorance, confusion, or mistake on the part of the person to whom we are attributing an attitude, but because of ignorance, confusion, or mistake on our own part, i.e., on the part of us attributors, that is not shared by the person to whom we are attributing the attitude. We may be unwilling to attribute to someone the belief that attorneys are parasites on the basis of his sincere assertion, 'lawyers are parasites', not because this person fails to count *attorney* and *lawyer* as synonyms, but because we don't. And similarly, we might be unwilling in *any* context to attribute to someone the belief that Tully is bald on the basis of his sincere assertion, 'Cicero is bald', not because this person fails to know that Tully is identical with Cicero, but because we don't. In describing these beliefs we cannot simply disquote the person's expression of his beliefs, because, again, we don't use these words with the same meanings as him. But as in cases where the ignorance, confusion, or mistake is on the part of the person to whom we are attributing the belief, we can resort to paraphrases that make clear how the meanings that he attaches to these words differs from the meanings that we attach to these same words. And again there is nothing in these cases that counts against the proposal being considered here, viz., that the properties and relations of propositional attitudes are preserved under a synonymy transformation on the representational domain. For whatever the IUF that we choose as a representative of an attitude, any IUF that is *by our lights* synonymous with this chosen IUF will also by our lights be a representative of that same attitude. Thus, for example, if I am willing to attribute to a person the belief that Cicero is bald, but not the belief that Tully is bald, perhaps because I think that Cicero and Tully are two different individuals, then on the assumption that I know that *Cicéron* is the conventional translation into French of *Cicero* and *Tullius* the conventional translation into French of *Tully*, I will also be willing to attribute to that same person the belief that 'Cicéron est chauve', but presumably not the belief that 'Tullius est chauve', despite the fact that *Cicéron* and *Tullius* are co-designative.

So the general conclusion here seems to be this: the properties and relations of propositional attitudes that are respected in the representational domain are preserved under a synonymy transformation defined on the representational domain, but it is synonymy *defined relative to the idiolect of the attributor, whose representational domain it is.*

But where, then, does context sensitivity come in? So far we have not attributed any particular role to context in determining whether two IUFs in the representational domain are representatives of the same propositional attitude. That determination is simply by synonymy defined relative to the idiolect of the attributor. Context does play a role, but the role it plays has to do not with whether two IUFs samesay one another, but with what IUF (or set of samesaying IUFs) is taken to be, in the context of utterance, the proper representative of the attributed attitude. Context plays a role in cases in which the synonymy judgments of the person making the attitude attribution (the 'attributer') and the person to whom the attitude is being attributed (the 'attributee') fail to coincide, and where, furthermore, there fails to be any smooth mapping of terms from the idiolect of the one into the idiolect of the other that preserves the synonymy relations within the respective idiolects. In such cases the attributer has to figure out how to represent in his idiolect the attitude that the attributee would represent in another way, and he must do so in a way that guards against potential misunderstandings that can arise in an audience who may fail to share the synonymy judgments of *either* attributer *or* attributee. The attributer will presumably be guided in the IUF that he chooses as the representative of the attributed attitude by considerations having to do with what sorts of inferences, predictions, explanations, and so on he wants his choice of representative to license, and such considerations clearly involve considerable context sensitivity. But once the choice of representative IUF is made, then any other IUF that the attributer takes to be synonymous with that IUF will be an equally good representative from the perspective of the attributer, though not necessarily from the perspective of either an attributee or an audience who fails to share the attributer's synonymy judgments.

6.8. RECAP

On the proposed measurement-theoretic account, propositional attitude predicates are a kind of measure predicate. Propositional attitude sentences of the form *x [attitude verb] that S* attribute a propositional attitude of a given type (believing, desiring, etc.) to an individual by relating that individual to a formal object, an IUF, that is the measurement-theoretic representative of the attributed attitude. The attitude-type is specified by the sentence's main verb, the representative IUF by the utterance, in context, of the sentence embedded in the sentence's *that*-clause. The representative thus specified is able to represent the attributed attitude by virtue of being an element in a representing relational structure whose properties and relations *respect*, in the sense explained, the properties and relations of the represented empirical structure in which the represented (and attributed) attitude is an element. The properties and relations of the representing structure respect the properties and relations of the represented structure in virtue of the fact that the representing structure stands in a suitable morphism relation (e.g., a homomorphism) to the represented structure. The properties and relations of propositional attitudes relevant for surrogative reasoning about propositional attitudes and their characteristic effects thus find a faithful structural image in the properties and relations of IUFs. These images, however, are decidedly partial, both in the sense that not all properties and relations defined on the representational domain are exploited (i.e., they are not all empirically meaningful in the sense of being images of empirical properties and relations) and in the sense that such properties and relations as are exploited are not always fully exploited. Nevertheless, our natural language representatives of propositional attitudes do respect those properties and relations of propositional attitudes which are relevant to the various purposes to which attitude reports are put in surrogative reasoning about attitudes and their effects.

The intuitive idea behind the proposed measurement-theoretic account is that judgments about propositional attitudes are judgments about the applicability of certain measure predicates. Our rendering of these judgments amounts to a measurement claim because in coming to these judgments we engage in cognitive processes that reliably eventuate in IUF representatives that bear the appropriate measurement-theoretic relations to the attitudes that they represent. The reported judgment is the outcome of a cognitive process that reliably preserves the relevant morphism relation.

Propositional attitude predicates, like the numerical predicates by which we attribute quantities of physical magnitudes, turn out to be a sophisticated, but nonetheless quite natural, extension of a pervasive common-sense predication scheme. On that scheme we attribute capacities, aptitudes, skills, and traits to individuals, including animals and non-animate objects, by attributing to an individual a particular relation to an object or event that is in some sense the focus of the attributed capacity, aptitude, skill, or trait. The novelty of measure predicates is to exploit the relational structure of the set of objects to which individuals are related by these predicates—real numbers in the case of numerical magnitude predicates, IUFs in the case of propositional attitude predicates—so as to be able to attribute to an individual a particular member of a structured set of magnitudes, capacities, aptitudes, etc.

On the proposed measurement-theoretic account, propositional attitudes turn out to be causally efficacious internal states that are *apt* to produce both the intentional behavior that we take to manifest these attitude states and the other intentional states, including propositional attitudes, that we take to be these states' mental concomitants. To say that propositional attitudes are such states is not to offer a reductive functional analysis of propositional attitudes, but it is to say that propositional attitudes are specified functionally in terms of their aptness for producing certain characteristic effects, specifically the states of affairs-related behaviors that manifest them and the mental states that are their usual concomitants. Taken singly, these states that are the attitudes are not in themselves causally sufficient to produce either the manifesting behaviors or the concomitant mental states, but instead require for their causal efficacy the mediation of other attitudes.

Like the numerical measurement theories for extensive magnitudes upon which it is modelled, the proposed measurement-theoretic account of propositional attitudes distinguishes sharply between the attitudes and their representatives, and between the properties and relations that it attributes to the former and those that it attributes to the latter. Like numerical measurement theories, it rejects the notion, fundamental to the Received View, that properties and relations of the representatives, indeed of propositional attitude reports themselves, can simply be read back onto the attitudes. The account thus allows for the possibility that propositional attitudes might be monadic properties of their possessors, even though these properties are attributed by means of relational predicates. The account also allows for the possibility that propositional attitudes might turn out not to have the semantic properties and inferential relations of their natural language IUF representatives. Certainly nothing about our common-sense explanatory and predictive practice of attitude attribution requires that propositional attitudes have such properties and relations. It is sufficient simply that they be states apt, in the sense defined, for the production of their characteristic effects. But the proposed measurement-theoretic account of the attitudes is nevertheless thoroughly realist about the attitudes, just as numerical measurement-theoretic accounts are realist about physical magnitudes, even though on those accounts these magnitudes do not have the numerical properties and relations of their numerical representatives.

7

Elaboration and Explication of the Proposed Measurement-Theoretic Account

The measurement-theoretic account sketched in the previous chapter takes seriously, in a way that the Received View does not, the distinction between our natural language representations of propositional attitudes and propositional attitudes themselves. Specifically, the account takes it to be a matter for substantive inquiry to determine the precise character of the representation relation that maps propositional attitudes into their natural language representatives. Furthermore, it provides a well-understood theoretic framework, namely, that provided by measurement theory, for undertaking this inquiry. The account does not presume that the properties of, and relations among, these representatives can simply be read back onto the represented attitudes. Thus, the account allows for the possibility that the representatives of the propositional attitudes have semantic properties and inferential relations without propositional attitudes themselves having such properties and relations, just as our numerical representatives of physical magnitudes have numerical properties and relations without the represented magnitudes themselves having any such properties and relations. The account also allows for the possibility that the predicates by which we attribute propositional attitudes are relational without propositional attitudes themselves being relations. For all we know, propositional attitudes, which we represent linguistically by means of relational predicates, might turn out, like most physical magnitudes, to be monadic properties of their possessors.

Much remains to be done in order to complete the proposed measurement-theoretic account, but the general outlines of the account should be clear. We have in hand preliminary specifications of (i) the representing relational structure that models the structure of our natural language representations of propositional attitudes, (ii) the represented empirical relational structure of propositional attitudes themselves, and (iii) the structure-respecting relation that maps this represented empirical structure into the representing structure that is its image. We also have in hand (iv) a rough outline of representation and uniqueness theorems for this mapping relation. But a number of important questions remain. First, there is the general question of how well the account satisfies certain adequacy conditions that any proposed account of propositional attitudes and the natural language predicates by which we attribute them must satisfy. Second, there is the question of the implications, if any, of the account for the intrinsic nature of propositional attitudes. Third, there is the question of the implications of the account for the role of propositional attitude attributions in empirical cognitive science, specifically for the computational entailments of such attributions. And finally, there is the question of the implications of the account for various philosophical projects and views that might be thought to require a particular kind of account of propositional attitudes, perhaps one that is more specific in its structural commitments. Answering these questions may usefully elaborate and explicate the account, perhaps providing further impetus to the undoubtedly difficult task of providing a fully developed measurement-theoretic account of the attitudes.

7.1. THE EXPLANATORY ADEQUACY OF THE ACCOUNT

An adequate account of propositional attitudes should explain (i) what having a propositional attitude amounts to, in the sense of explaining what it is that we are attributing when we attribute a propositional attitude. It should also explain (ii) what are the salient properties of propositional attitudes, and if these are different from the properties that we take them to have, why that should be so. The account should explain (iii) why we have the particular predication scheme that we do for attributing propositional attitudes, both in the sense of explaining why that scheme is adequate to attribute the sort of properties that the proposed account takes propositional attitudes to be and in the sense of explaining how we might have evolved such a scheme, and (iv) why, or how it is that, propositional attitude attributions are able to play the particular role that they do in common-sense explanations of behavior and thought. The account should also explain (v) why we should expect the various semantic puzzles about propositional attitude attributions that have preoccupied philosophers since Frege, and it should do this consistent with the fact that on the proposed measurement-theoretic account, a propositional attitude attribution of the form 'x believes (desires, etc.) that S' is true just in case x is in a belief state (desire state, etc.) that has as a representative the IUF specified by the utterance in context of 'S'. Finally, the account should provide (vi) a plausible account of our construal of iterated attitude attributions, something that other accounts have found it difficult to do.

7.1.1. What Having a Propositional Attitude Amounts to

On the proposed account, what we attribute when we attribute a propositional attitude is an *aptitude* both for the behaviors that manifest the attitude and for the intentional mental states, including other propositional attitudes, that are its entailed mental concomitants, where, as we noted, just what are the manifesting behaviors or entailed mental concomitants in a particular context depends crucially on such other propositional attitudes as mediate the attitude's production of these behavioral and mental effects. To say that propositional attitudes are such aptitudes is to say that they are states of their possessors that are *apt* to produce these effects, both in the sense that they are states suited to produce these effects and in the sense that they do typically produce them. To say this is not to say anything at all about the intrinsic nature of propositional attitudes in virtue of which they are states apt to produce the effects that they do. This is a matter for empirical investigation and discovery (see section 7.2 below). It is rather to provide a purely functional characterization of these causally efficacious internal states that are the attitudes, a characterization that enables us to refer to these states in explanations, predictions, and rationalizations, even in the absence of any knowledge of their intrinsic nature. To say that propositional attitudes are aptitudes for their effects is also not to deny that propositional attitudes are type individuated at least in part by the characteristic ways in which their possessors come to have these aptitudes, but these ways are not the focus of the present measurement-theoretic account because they are not reflected in the representation scheme by which we individuate propositional attitudes of a given type. For on that scheme, we individuate propositional attitudes of a given type in terms of their characteristic states of affairs-related behavioral effects, where these states of affairs are those specified by the IUFs that are these attitudes' representatives. Thus, for example, what makes a particular propositional attitude one of believing that p, rather than one of assuming that p, has to do, at least in part, with how the possessor of that attitude came to be in that state, whereas what makes a particular belief the belief that p, rather than the belief that q, has to do with the states of affairs-related behavioral effects that it is apt to produce. At least different beliefs can be individuated in those terms, even if it might nonetheless be the case that believing that p rather than believing that q also has to do how I came to be in that belief state.

Thus characterized, the proposed measurement-theoretic account shares much in common with 'minimalist' accounts of propositional attitudes such as those proposed by Dennett (1987), Jackson and Pettit (1990), Horgan and Graham (1991), and Egan (1995), which emphasize the minimal character of the functionalist-theoretical commitments of propositional attitude attributions. The minimalism here is not simply that, as all functionalists would agree, such attributions entail no specific structural-architectural commitments, beyond having a structure or architecture capable of realizing the relevant functional properties; it is also that such attributions entail no specific commitments to any particular psychological theory of the functional organization of the possessor of the attributed attitude, such as might be articulated by either common-sense propositional attitude psychology or an elaborated scientific propositional attitude psychology. On the minimalist view, propositional attitude attributions are not in any interesting sense theoretical claims the understanding of which presumes or presupposes some sort of background psychological theory in which they find their place. In particular, propositional attitudes are not, as some functionalists have imagined (e.g., Lewis 1972; Block 1978 [1980]), implicitly defined by psychological theories that advert to them, perhaps by means of a Ramsification over the terms of the theory. Rather, propositional attitude attributions, like physical magnitude attributions, are simply low-level empirical claims to the effect that an individual has certain causal powers, specifically certain aptitudes for producing specific effects. Where the proposed measurement-theoretic account differs from the minimalist accounts mentioned above is that in its individuation of propositional attitudes of a specific type (e.g., beliefs), the account appeals to the empirical relational structure of that attitude type, just as the individuation of physical magnitudes of a specific type appeals to the empirical relational structure of that magnitude type, individuating attitudes of that type in terms of their characteristic states of affairs-related behavioral effects.

7.1.2. The 'Essential' Properties of Propositional Attitudes

On most contemporary philosophical accounts, including the Received View, propositional attitudes are (i) *causally efficacious* in the production of behavior and other mental states (including other propositional attitudes),

(ii) *semantically evaluable* as true or false, satisfied or not, depending on attitude type, and (iii) *inferentially involved* in the sense of standing in various inferential relations to one another. These accounts hold that propositional attitudes have these three properties essentially and not simply as a matter of empirical fact,[1] so it would seem reasonable to require of any adequate philosophical account that it should explain why it is that propositional attitudes, given their nature, should have these properties, or if propositional attitudes lack these properties, why it is that we philosophers have mistakenly supposed them to have them. Proponents of the Received View hold that propositional attitudes, or at least our capacity for such, are also (iv) *productive and systematic*, in ways that Fodor and his collaborators have endeavored to spell out (see, e.g., Fodor and Pylyshyn 1988; Fodor and McLaughlin 1990). If propositional attitudes, or our capacity for such, have these properties essentially and not simply as a matter of empirical fact, then any adequate philosophical account of the attitudes should explain them too.

On the proposed measurement-theoretic account, propositional attitudes are indeed causally efficacious in the production of behavior and other mental states, since on this account they are aptitudes for their behavioral and mental effects. But on the proposed account propositional attitudes are *not necessarily* semantically evaluable, and they are *not necessarily* inferentially involved. For it seems eminently possible that propositional attitudes might have all the causal powers that they do to produce their behavioral and mental effects and yet be devoid of both these properties, since nothing about these effects would seem to necessitate that the propositional attitudes which are their causes have these properties. Nor, so far as I can see, is there any compelling empirical rationale for thinking that they have either of these properties as a matter of contingent empirical fact (though see Chapter 7.2 below). There is what I described (in Chapter 6.5.3) as an internal relation between propositional attitudes and the states of affairs specified by the IUFs that are their representatives. But arguably there is *not* in this internal relation anything that would adequately ground the claim that propositional attitudes are themselves semantically evaluable or inferentially involved. The intentionality, the 'aboutness' or 'directedness' as some would put it, of the *behavior* that possessors of specific propositional attitudes characteristically exhibit with respect to these states of affairs does

---

[1] Fodor (1987: 10) claims that it is a further 'essential property' of propositional attitudes that 'the implicit generalizations of commonsense belief/desire psychology are largely true of them'. But contrary to what Fodor claims, it seems that a creature might fail to share our common-sense psychology but nonetheless possess propositional attitudes.

not entail either the semantic evaluability or the inferential involvement of the states that are the causes of this behavior. To be sure, our natural language *representatives* of propositional attitudes are semantically evaluable and inferentially involved. And the relations among these representatives respect the relations among the represented propositional attitudes. That we commonly take these properties and relations of the representatives to be properties and relations of propositional attitudes themselves is arguably of a piece with our uncritical tendency to take the numerical properties and relations of the numerical representatives of physical magnitudes to be properties and relations of the magnitudes themselves. Both testify to the fundamental role of these representational systems in our reporting, and indeed in our very conception, of propositional attitudes and physical magnitudes. We are unable to think of either propositional attitudes or physical magnitudes except in terms of their very familiar representatives and thus quite naturally come to think of each as actually *possessing* the salient properties and relations of their respective representatives.

The mistake here is of little consequence in the usual course of events, where our thought and talk is focused on the propositional attitudes (and physical magnitudes) possessed by particular individuals (and objects) and the import of their possession for behavior. But when our interests take on a more theoretical focus, as they do in philosophical discussion, especially when this discussion concerns the general nature of propositional attitudes, the mistake may no longer be innocuous. For we may be led to attribute quite implausible properties and relations to propositional attitudes, which in turn invariably lead, as we have seen, to rather bizarre metaphysical accounts of the 'objects' of propositional attitudes. We may be led to wonder, e.g., how causal relations among propositional attitudes could, as Fodor puts it (1987: 12), 'somehow typically contrive to respect their relations of contents'. As if causal relations among states of mind had somehow managed to shape themselves in the image of relations between their natural language representations! The analogous puzzle about the physical magnitudes would ask how they somehow contrive to respect certain arithmetic relations on the reals. In fact, what needs to be explained is just the converse, namely, why physical magnitudes can be represented in the domain of the reals, and why propositional attitudes can be represented in the domain of IUFs, which is precisely what a measurement-theoretic account undertakes to do.

Many philosophers will probably be willing to entertain the possibility that there are no inferential relations among propositional attitudes, that what we *represent* as inferential relations are, as we argued earlier, material relations among the internal states that are the attitudes. For nothing about our surrogative reasoning about propositional attitudes and their effects on behavior and thought would seem to demand the existence of inferential relations among the attitudes. It is enough simply that we are able to represent the relevant material relations among attitudes in such terms. But many philosophers, I suspect, will find it difficult to countenance the idea that propositional attitudes are not semantically evaluable. For we do in fact commonly speak of beliefs as 'about' specific individuals, properties, or states of affairs, of desires as 'for' these same sorts of things, of beliefs as 'true' or 'false', of desires as 'satisfied' or not. And this manner of speaking certainly seems to entail that propositional attitudes are in some important sense semantically evaluable. It would therefore seem only reasonable to expect that an adequate account of propositional attitudes would explicate the sense in which propositional attitudes are so evaluable, even if it were to turn out that they are not, as the Received View assumes, semantically evaluable in the same sense as are linguistic utterances.

But if propositional attitudes are semantically evaluable, in just what sense are they semantically evaluable? If they are the sort of (mediated) dispositional states that the present account of the attitudes as aptitudes takes them to be, then it is implausible to suppose that they have the sort of compositional constituent structure of which semantic values might plausibly be predicated, and thus no reason to think that one could explain their semantic evaluability in terms of a Tarski-style compositional semantics. At least it is implausible to suppose that these states have such structure essentially. Presumably we need a different sort of account.

One strategy for accounting for the semantic evaluability of propositional attitudes construed as dispositions, first proposed by Ramsey (1927) and then developed by Stalnaker (1984), focuses on the causal role of the attitudes in bringing about certain states of affairs:

Belief and desire, the strategy suggests, are correlative dispositional states of a potentially rational agent. To desire that P is to be disposed to act in ways that would tend to bring it about that P in a world in which one's beliefs, whatever they are, were true. To belief that P is to be disposed to act in ways that would tend to satisfy one's desires, whatever they are, in a world in which P (together with one's other beliefs) were true.

(Stalnaker 1984: 15)

This strategy leads to an account, which recent proponents have dubbed 'success semantics', according to which, as Bermudez (2003) explains it, propositional attitudes have the semantic properties that they do by virtue of their role in producing behavior that succeeds in bringing about certain desire-satisfying states of affairs:

True beliefs are functions from desires to actions that cause thinkers to behave in ways that will satisfy their desires . . . . The basic idea of success semantics is that the content of a belief is given by its utility condition, that is, the condition that would have to obtain for the various desires with which it is associated to be satisfied. In brief, true beliefs cause actions that satisfy desires.

(Bermudez 2003: 65)

The content of a desire is given by its satisfaction condition, that is, by the condition or state of affairs whose coming to obtain would satisfy the desire, in the typical case extinguishing both the desire and the behavior to which the desire has given rise. And just as true beliefs cause actions that satisfy desires, desires cause actions that satisfy those desires when those actions are shaped by true beliefs.

Critics have pointed out a number of seemingly serious difficulties with success semantics, especially if it is conceived of in the way that proponents often do, namely, as providing a reductive analysis of the semantic properties of propositional attitude contents, viz., truth (in the case of belief), and satisfaction (in the case of desire).[2] First, the account seems viciously circular. As Stalnaker puts the worry, 'Is this theory simply a shell game that hides the problem of intentionality under belief while it explains desire, and under desire while it explains belief?' (1984: 15). Thus, for example, Whyte defines a belief's truth condition as that which 'guarantees the fulfillment of any desire by action which that belief and desire would combine to cause' (Whyte 1990: 150), and a desire's fulfillment condition as 'that condition which is guaranteed to result from any action caused by that desire, if the beliefs with which it combines to cause the action are true' (Whyte 1991: 65). Proponents who don't wish to embrace a thoroughgoing Davidsonian-style holism of the attitudes thus find themselves faced with the task of breaking out of this circle without either abandoning the dispositional account of the attitudes that originally motivated the account, as Stalnaker arguably does when he introduces his notion of indication, or else falling into an untenable

---

[2] For a useful discussion of the difficulties, see especially Bermudez (2003).

behaviorist construal of desire satisfaction, as Bermudez arguably does when he identifies satisfaction with the cessation of behavior. Second, there seems to be what Stalnaker dubs the problem of 'fatal relativity', viz., of how on the success semantics account one is to avoid a radical indeterminacy in attitude contents if propositional attitudes are individuated solely in terms of their characteristic effects, and not also in terms of their environmental causes. Third, success semantics seems most plausible as an account of the semantic properties of belief and desire that bear a direct causal relation to behavior intended to satisfy concrete desires; it seems less plausible an account of such properties for belief and desire that bear only a tenuous relation, even in counterfactual situations, to such behavior.[3] Fourth, and perhaps most seriously, success semantics seems to conflate truth with utility, when it holds that, as Whyte (1990: 149) puts it, 'truth just *is* the property of belief that suffices for your getting what you want when you act on it'. In identifying truth with utility, success semantics would appear to open itself to a version of Moore's open question argument. Arguably, truth is one thing, utility another, such that far from truth just being utility, truth is what generally *explains* utility, which is why we have little difficulty imagining that acting on false beliefs might in some domains be the best way to get what we want, even if in most domains acting on true beliefs is more efficacious.

It is not clear whether these various difficulties can be surmounted without abandoning success semantics' fundamental goal of providing a reductive account of the apparent semantic properties of propositional attitudes. But there does seem to be another way of thinking about these properties, compatible with the proposed measurement-theoretic account, that both avoids these difficulties and also preserves the fundamental intuition that success semantics undertakes to explicate. This way involves assuming that propositional attitudes have the semantic properties that they do in virtue of the causal role of these attitudes in actions that succeed in bringing about certain desired states of affairs. The idea is simply this: beliefs count as true just in case the IUFs that are their representatives are true and hence the states of affairs that these IUFs specify actually obtain, such that actions shaped by these beliefs can in the usual course of events be expected to satisfy the desires

---

[3] It is considerations of this last sort that lead Bermudez (2003) to conclude that while success semantics may be plausible as an account of the semantic properties of the beliefs and desires of non-linguistic creatures, it is not plausible as an account of the beliefs and desires of linguistic creatures such as ourselves, which include, e.g., many non-instrumental beliefs and numerous second-order desires, few of which, he claims, play any causal role in the production of behavior.

that motivated these actions; desires count as satisfied just in case the IUFs that are their representatives are true (have come to be true) and hence the states of affairs that these IUFs specify obtain (have come to obtain), such that these desires are satisfied in the sense that they are satiated and thus in the usual course of events cease to exist and hence cease to give rise to actions intended to bring about the desired states of affairs. So conceived, propositional attitudes have the semantic properties that they do in virtue of their causal relations, via behavior, to these states of affairs. They may not have their semantic properties in the direct sort of way that linguistic entities *presumably* have theirs; rather they inherit them from the IUF-specified states of affairs to which they are behaviorally related. Whether this is inheritance enough to count them as genuinely possessing semantic properties depends upon how one conceives of truth itself, but whatever one's views on this matter, there is arguably enough here to explain (or explain away), in a manner consistent with the proposed measurement-theoretic account, our firm conviction that propositional attitudes do possess the semantic properties we attribute to them. To be sure, if possession of semantic properties requires a compositional constituent structure, then on this account propositional attitudes don't have semantic properties, but this again is a matter for a theory of truth, not an account of the attitudes.

Proponents of the Received View, we noted, hold that propositional attitudes, or at least our capacity for such, are productive and systematic. On the proposed measurement-theoretic account, our capacity for propositional attitudes might indeed be productive and systematic, but here too we must guard against inferring such features of this capacity from features of our scheme for representing propositional attitudes. That scheme is clearly productive and systematic in the sense that the domain of IUFs can be effectively enumerated by a recursive procedure and the constituents of IUFs stand in various systematic relations to one another in virtue of the fact that IUFs (and their constituents) stand in syntactic and inferential relations to one another. But there is no empirical warrant in this fact for the presumption that every IUF is the representative, even 'in principle', of some nomologically possible propositional attitude. To think otherwise would be analogous to supposing that the productivity of the reals provides empirical warrant for the presumption that every real number on, say, the centigrade scale is the representative of some nomologically possible temperature. Thus, any compelling argument for the claim that our capacity for propositional attitudes is both productive and systematic is going to have to rest on more than the productivity and systematicity of our scheme for representing the attitudes. One must establish that the recognized productivity and systematicity of the representational scheme are in fact the images of certain relevantly homologous relations among propositional attitudes, something that proponents of the Received View have yet to establish, have yet even to recognize the need to establish.

7.1.3. Why We Have the Particular Predication Scheme that We Do

The proposed measurement-theoretic account of the attitudes offers an explanation for why we have the particular predication scheme that we do for attributing propositional attitudes to individuals, both in the sense of explaining why that scheme is adequate to attribute the sort of properties to individuals that the proposed account takes propositional attitudes to be and in the sense of explaining how we might have evolved such a scheme. This scheme, I have argued (in Chapter 6.1), is an extension of the basic (two-dimensional) common-sense predication scheme that we often use to attribute aptitudes, capacities, dispositions, and skills to persons, animals, and even inanimate objects. On the basic scheme, we attribute one of these sorts of property to an individual by specifying a relation to an object or event, typically an action-specifying relation that this individual bears to an object or event that is the focus of the specified action. The scheme used to attribute propositional attitudes extends the basic scheme in a natural way: As with the basic scheme, we attribute a propositional attitude to an individual by specifying a relation that this individual bears to an object. But on this extension of the basic scheme, both relation and object are importantly different. The predication scheme no longer simply specifies an action-specifying relation (e.g., buying, selling, trading) and an object or event that is the target or recipient of that action (cars, stock, etc.). Rather it attributes a propositional attitude (e.g., believing that Fido is at the back door) to an individual by specifying a behavior-implicating relation that this individual bears to a state of affairs that is the 'object' of the attitude. The specified behavior-implicating relation determines the type of propositional attitude being attributed, e.g., a belief rather than a desire, while the specified state of affairs determines the particular subtype of the attributed attitude type, e.g., that what is believed is that Fido is at the back door rather than that the postman is at the front door. Attribution to an individual of a behavior-implicating relation to a state of affairs succeeds in attributing a propositional attitude to that individual, inasmuch as possession of a propositional attitude is a matter of possessing an aptitude for behavior of the specified sort. For the relation characterizes the way in which the possessor of the attitude is related behaviorally to the state of affairs, specified by its IUF representative, that is the 'object' to which the possessor of the attitude is behaviorally related. In the case of desire-like attitudes, the behavior that such propositional attitudes are aptitudes for is behavior intended to bring about those states of affairs, while in the case of belief-like attitudes, the behavior that such propositional attitudes are aptitudes for is behavior that, while directed towards other goals, is intended to be sensitive in its modalities to the believed states of affairs.

The predication scheme for propositional attitudes has significantly greater explanatory and predictive power than the basic scheme from which it presumably evolved. Knowing simply, for example, that someone is correctly described as a firefighter does not enable one to predict which fires this person is likely to fight or just what he is likely to do in fighting the fires that he does, since to know that a person is a firefighter is to know only that this person is apt or capable of performing a certain action, viz., fighting fires. Nor does the knowledge provided by an attribution 'x is a firefighter' offer much by way of an explanation of why a firefighter fights some fires but not others, or why he does one thing rather than another when fighting the fires that he does, since to explain a behavior by saying it is the behavior of a firefighter is merely to characterize it as the exercise of a particular aptitude, capacity, or skill.

Knowing a person's propositional attitudes, by contrast, provides considerably greater explanatory and predictive power. Knowing, for example, that a firefighter who is fighting a fire believes that a certain action on his part would prevent the further spread of the fire, one can with reasonable confidence predict that this firefighter will take that action (neglecting, of course, all the usual *ceteris paribus* qualifications). One can also predict that this firefighter would also believe that there is something he could do to prevent the further spread of the fire, and so on. And such knowledge would also enable one to explain this firefighter's action. Such enhanced explanatory and predictive power is attributable to three features of the predication scheme for propositional attitudes, the first having to do with the attitude-type specifying, behavior implicating relations that are specified by attitude verbs, the second having to do with the states of affairs to which these relations relate the possessor of the attitude, and the third having to do with the structural relations that the IUFs which states of affairs satisfy bear to one another. First, the attitude-type specifying relations employed by the scheme specify, as we said, aptitudes for quite specific sorts of states of affairs-related behaviors, viz., in the case of desire, behaviors directed towards bringing about certain specified states of affairs, and in the case of belief, behaviors whose modalities are sensitive to those states of affairs. These behaviors are more specific than the generic behaviors attributed by the basic scheme. Second, the states of affairs that are the objects of these behaviors are considerably more fine-grained than the objects of the basic scheme, so that one can individuate quite finely first the behaviors to which the attitudes characteristically give rise, and then second the attitudes themselves. This fine-grainedness is further enhanced by the possibility of exploiting for purposes of individuation virtually any of the properties of the IUFs that specify these states of affairs. These properties not only specify these states of affairs but can also serve to characterize the agent's way of conceptualizing and describing these states of affairs, thus enabling us to predict and explain an even wider range of related thought and talk on the part of the possessor of the attributed attitude. Third, the inferential relations among IUFs enable us to capture material relations (both causal and constitutive) among propositional attitudes, enabling us to explain and predict the mental concomitants of propositional attitudes.

It is not difficult to imagine how we might have evolved this particular predication scheme for attributing propositional attitudes to individuals. Clearly it is advantageous to social creatures like ourselves, who have to both compete and cooperate with one another, as well as be able to predict, explain, and rationalize (both to others and ourselves) the specific behavior and thoughts of others and ourselves. This requires a scheme for conceptualizing and characterizing our aptitudes for such behavior and thoughts. The basic (two-dimensional) scheme for attributing aptitudes, capacities, dispositions, and skills (described in Chapter 6.1) provides a rudimentary scheme of the required sort. It enables us to conceptualize and characterize the aptitudes, capacities, dispositions, and skills of agents in a manner that provides us with a handle on the *sort* of behavior and thought that an agent is capable of producing, indeed likely to produce over the long run, but it does not enable us to predict or explain an agent's behavior and thought with any specificity. Yet in our dealings with others, specificity often counts. It is sometimes not enough to know simply that someone is, for example, a firefighter; we may want to be able to predict and explain with some specificity how this person will behave or think in a particular situation. And to do this we need something better than the basic scheme. In particular, we need a scheme that individuates individuals in terms of their aptitude for specific behaviors and specific mental states. And because such aptitudes can vary over time, often as a function of the context in which the individual finds himself, we need a scheme that individuates the aptitudes themselves as aptitudes directed towards specific goals and sensitive to specific environmental conditions.

Given the competitive and cooperative advantages that more specific predictions and explanations of behavior and thought would bring, it would be natural for us to attempt to improve the basic scheme by extending it in ways that promised to remedy its deficiencies. Arguably our predication scheme for propositional attitudes represents just such an extension. Rather than having to think of ourselves as having just the brute aptitudes that the basic scheme is able to characterize, with this predication scheme for propositional attitudes we can come to think of ourselves as having a more complex kind of aptitude, more specifically as having two different sorts of such aptitudes, one desire-like, the other belief-like, that operate in conjunction with one another to produce behavior that is sensitive in its specifics both to our goals and to environmental contingencies that must shape our behavior appropriately, if we are to achieve these goals. The desire-like aptitude is focused on the specific goals of the behavior, while the belief-like aptitude is focused on specific aspects of the environment that must shape and modulate behavior if it is to achieve those goals. The predication scheme for propositional attitudes is able to effect this greater specificity and environmental sensitivity because by taking the objects of the attitudes to be states of affairs rather than simple objects or events, one is able to characterize with greater specificity the aptitudes that are the causes of behavior and thought. Moreover, one is also able to characterize in a way that previously one could not, viz., in inferential terms, the causal interactions and relations among these aptitudes. And once one begins to characterize the 'objects' of the attitudes as states of affairs, it is but a short step to treating them intentionally. For one would quickly realize that different persons might perceive, conceptualize, and hence describe one and the same state of affairs differently, with certain attendant consequences for their behavior. And having realized this, one would realize that propositional attitudes could be, an indeed should be, individuated not simply in terms of the state of affairs but also in terms of how the possessor of the attitude would perceive, conceptualize, and describe that state of affairs. And from here it would also be only a short step to the realization that the scheme could also be used to pick out propositional attitudes for which there were, perhaps necessarily, no actual states of affairs that were the 'objects' of those attitudes. Perhaps there would be only a linguistically describable one. The scheme could also be used to describe an etiolated sort of propositional attitude that had no associated behavior except for that involved in verbal expressions of the attitude.

The upshot, then, of this extension of the basic scheme is a considerably more precise and informative predication scheme that enables us to specify, in functional terms, aptitudes for a very wide range of very specific behaviors and thoughts, something we could never have done with the basic scheme. The predictive and explanatory gain achieved by this extension is very much of a piece with that achieved by the move from qualitative to quantitative measures of physical magnitudes. Our ancestors' genius was to realize how to extend the basic two-dimensional predication scheme so as to achieve the desired increase in predictive and explanatory power. At some distant point in the past, they presumably recognized that their own behavior and the behavior of others depended on certain relatively enduring internal states that were causally efficacious in the production of this behavior. But they lacked the knowledge that would enable them to characterize these states in terms of their intrinsic properties. Their genius was to realize that these efficacious states could be characterized (and individuated) in terms of certain states of affairs to which these internal states were behaviorally related in quite specific, characteristic ways—ways that depend on the particular kind of internal state being attributed.

7.1.4. Role of Attitude Attributions in Common-sense Causal Explanations

Propositional attitudes are causally efficacious both in causing behavior intended to bring about a particular state of affairs that is the 'object' of a desire (or some desire-like propositional attitude) and in shaping or modulating behavior in ways, based on beliefs (or belief-like propositional attitudes), that are intended to facilitate the bringing about of a desired state of affairs. Propositional attitudes are also efficacious in the production of other mental states such as affective mental states and other propositional attitudes. On the proposed measurement-theoretic account, propositional attitudes are efficacious in these ways, precisely because they are aptitudes, i.e., states that are apt, for the production of such effects. And on this account, common-sense causal explanations that advert to propositional attitudes explain such effects as the result of possessing the aptitudes in question: the possessor of certain propositional attitudes is said to have done what he did, simply because he

possessed the relevant propositional attitudes, i.e., possessed certain states apt
to produce the effects to be explained.[4] Thus, for example, we might explain
why a particular public figure wrote an op-ed piece in the *New York Times*
critical of US foreign policy in the Middle East by saying that this individual
believes that the policy is both morally indefensible and also threatens US
interests in the region and wanted to express this belief publicly.

Behavioral explanations typically do not specify causally sufficient conditions for the behavior to be explained. Like virtually every sort of causal
explanation, they invariably focus on certain causal factors to the exclusion of
others. Just which factors get mentioned depends on the explanatory interests
that the explanation is intended to serve. According to Dretske (1988),
explanations that advert to propositional attitudes specify what he calls the
'structuring causes' of behavior. Specifically, they specify certain properties
of subjects, aptitudes according to the present proposed account, that are
causally sufficient in the presence of the appropriate triggering event(s) to
produce the behavior or mental state to be explained, much in the way
that the presence of oxygen can be causally sufficient in the presence of
an appropriate triggering event such as the striking of a match to produce
a fire. As such, explanations that advert to propositional attitudes explain
why the possessor of the attitude behaved or came to think one way rather
than another. Thus, for example, I can explain why Smith ran out of the
building rather than remained inside, by citing her belief that the building
was on fire. If, by contrast, I wanted to explain why she ran out of the
building when she did, I might advert to what Dretske calls the 'triggering
cause' of her behavior, viz., her smelling smoke. Propositional attitudes are
able to serve the particular explanatory interests that they do, viz., provide
the structuring causes of behavior and thought, because they are relatively
enduring properties of their possessor that guide behavior and thought in
predictable ways across a range of different contexts.

---

[4] Some explanations that advert to propositional attitudes are non-causal, specifically those that
justify the claim that a subject possesses one propositional attitude in terms of his possession of
another. Thus, I might assert that Jones believes that someone stole the silver because he believes
that Smith stole it. But I am not thereby asserting that Jones' believing the latter *causes* him to
believe the former. We would not accept 'Jones believes that Smith stole the silver' as a possible
answer to the question 'What *caused* Jones to believe that someone stole the silver?' Rather we would
expect an answer such as 'he found the lock on the silver cabinet jimmied' or 'he discovered that
someone had pawned the silver'. On the proposed account, believing that someone stole the silver
is related to believing that Smith stole the silver by material constitution rather than by cause (and
this relation is represented by an inferential relation between the IUFs that are the representatives
of these two beliefs). The constitutive relation warrants the justificatory claim.

Although propositional attitudes are structuring causes of behavior, the coming to have one of these structuring causes can be the proximal event that triggers the behavior. At least, coming to have a propositional attitude can serve, along with other propositional attitudes, to explain why the possessor of the attitude did what she did, both in the sense of why she did what she did rather than something else and in the sense of why she did what she did when she did it. Thus, for example, we might explain why Smith ran out of the building when she did by describing her as having run out of the building because she came to believe that the building was on fire. Her coming to believe what she did seems to do double duty here, as both a structuring cause and a triggering cause. It is not just that a propositional attitude can do this double duty, but arguably one of the propositional attitudes that explains why the possessor of the attitudes did one thing rather than another *has* to be serving in such a capacity, even if the explanation doesn't make that explicit. One could, for example, explain Smith's running from the building by saying that she did this 'because she smelled smoke', where her smelling smoke is clearly the triggering cause of her behavior. But if we ask why her smelling smoke was able to cause her to do what she did, it has to be because that led her to believe that the building was on fire. Smelling smoke is a plausible explanation of Smith's behavior only on the assumption that this caused her to come to have a propositional attitude that in the context was sufficient to cause her to do what she did, rather than something else, at the time when she did it. Smelling smoke plays the causal role that it does only through the intermediation of some propositional attitude, which presumably explains why the relevant generalization to draw regarding Smith's behavior is not that whenever she smells smoke, she runs out of the building she is in, but rather that whenever she comes to believe that the building she is in is on fire, she runs out. Smith presumably sticks around like anyone else when she burns a meal.

There are cases in which we explain our behavior in terms of our having certain propositional attitudes, but in which we cannot point to anything, not even our coming to have one of these attitudes, that might plausibly be said to be the triggering cause of our behavior. Thus, for example, I may get up from my desk and go turn on the television. Asked why I did what I did, I may explain that I knew that a Yankee game was in progress and wanted to know the score. There looks to be no triggering cause here. But perhaps one will insist that it was really my remembering that there was a game in progress, not simply my knowing that to be the case, that explains my behavior, in which case there was a triggering event that led to my behavior. My remembering that there was a Yankee game in progress was the triggering event for my behavior, what I remembered one of the structural causes of that behavior. Maybe one is right in insisting that behavior must have a triggering cause. But surely it is noteworthy that in cases where a subject seems to have just the propositional attitudes sufficient to cause someone to act in a particular way and yet that subject fails to act, we never consider the possibility that the lack of action might result from the lack of a triggering cause. Our first inclination in such cases is to attribute to the subject certain countervailing attitudes that cause her not to act as expected, or failing that to deny that this subject has the attitudes that we assumed she had. But if behavior requires a triggering cause, why don't we also consider this possibility, perhaps hypothesizing that all behavior is triggered by an unseen 'act of will'? Whether or not behavior requires a triggering cause, perhaps only in the guise of a coming to have a certain propositional attitude, it seems clear that we think of propositional attitudes as sometimes causally sufficient for the production of their effects. The proposal that attitudes are aptitudes is fully consonant with this conception of the attitudes, for on that proposal propositional attitudes are states apt to produce certain effects, both in the sense that they are the sorts of states that *can* in fact produce such effects and in the sense that in the appropriate contexts they do as a general rule produce these effects. If metaphysical considerations necessitate that behavior have a triggering cause, perhaps because all effects require such, this is not something that one discovers from an inspection of our intentional explanations of behavior. The only time triggering causes get trotted out is when we want to explain why someone did what they did when they did. Such an explanation clearly requires that we advert to an event by reference to which we can date the behavior, but it isn't obvious that we should conclude from this that behavior requires a triggering cause and hence that propositional attitudes are not causally sufficient by themselves to produce their effects.

7.1.5. Puzzles about Propositional Attitude Attributions

Proposed accounts of propositional attitudes and their attribution are invariably evaluated in terms of their success in solving certain well-known puzzles that have emerged in the course of philosophical theorizing about these matters.[5] Most of these puzzles have to do with the interaction of three component

---

[5] A number of these puzzles are discussed in Richard 1990.

aspects of proposed relational accounts: (i) the nature of the 'objects' to which the possessors of propositional attitudes are said to be related by the psychological relation expressed by the attitude verb, (ii) the truth conditions of attitude attributions, and (iii) the pragmatics of attitude attribution. The puzzles have their source in the difficulties, discussed in Chapter 4, of finding a single kind of object (e.g., proposition, sentence, mental representation) to which the possessor of the attitude might plausibly be said to be psychological-ly related and which correctly predicts both the truth conditions of attitude attributions and the common-sense individuation conditions on proposi-tional attitudes. Typically these puzzles arise only against the background of specific assumptions about the truth conditions of attitude attributions, specifically the semantic values that a semantics for such attributions assigns to the *that*-clause and its constituents. Thus, for example, it is found puzzling on the assumption that proper names are directly referential that it can be true that Lois Lane believes that Superman can leap tall buildings, yet apparently false that she believes that Clark Kent can do so, since on this assumption the two names would presumably have the same semantic value. The puzzle here is born of the collision of two otherwise well-supported convictions, the the-oretically motivated conviction that because the two proper names have the same semantic value, the two belief attributions should have the truth-value, and the common-sense intuitive conviction that because Lois Lane claims to believe the one thing but not the other, the two attributions differ in truth value. The typical 'solution' to such a puzzle is to abandon one or the other conviction: either one attempts to explain away the common-sense intuition, typically by appeal to the pragmatics of attitude attribution, or one proposes different semantic values for the *that*-clauses that embed the names and hence for the two predicates that embed the *that*-clauses. The problem, however, is that proposed 'solutions' typically give rise to other, equally difficult prob-lems. Thus, for example, one may propose that the *that*-clause designates something more fine-grained than a proposition—perhaps a particular such as Richard's (1990) RAM or Larson and Segal's (1993) ILF (see Chapter 4.2), such that the *that*-clauses in the two attributions, the one containing the name *Superman*, the other containing the name *Clark Kent*, turn out to have different semantic values, so that it is no longer puzzling that the attributions could have different truth values. Proponents find support for such solutions in the fact that the proposed semantic values for the *that*-clauses seem to get the individuation conditions on propositional attitudes right. But if moving to a more fine-grained object as the semantic value of the *that*-clause solves the original substitution puzzle, it creates others. It seems implausible that exotica such as RAMs or ILFs could be objects to which the possessors of the attitude could possibly bear a psychological relation (and hence could explain the causal role of propositional attitudes in thought and behavior). It is just this sort of worry that eventually forces both Richard (1990) and Larson and Segal (1995) to abandon the traditional notion of a single object of the attitudes and to distinguish between semantic and psychological objects of the attitudes (see Chapter 4.4). And with this distinction comes the problems that are arguably the precursors of a measurement-theoretic account of the attitudes, namely, those of explaining how the semantic object manages to track the psychological object and how users of attitude attributions are able to understand attributions that presume this tracking relation.

But regardless of whether one abandons the traditional notion of a single object of the attitudes in favor of a distinction between semantic and psychological objects, there remains the problem of the apparent context-sensitivity of the truth conditions of attitude attributions, which is not at all addressed simply by introducing a more fine-grained object as the semantic value of the *that*-clause. For whatever one takes to be its semantic value, one still needs to explain how it is that a single propositional attitude predicate, e.g., *believes that Tully is bald*, can be true of an individual in one context of utterance but not in another, though seemingly without the semantic value of any of the terms of the *that*-clause having changed and without the individual to whom the belief is attributed having changed his belief.

The proposed measurement-theoretic account explicitly embraces the conclusion to which a number of philosophers concerned with the semantics of attitude attributions, including Richard (1990) and Larson and Segal (1995), have found themselves driven: the *that*-clause of the attitude sentence designates a *representative* of the attributed attitude, not the attitude itself or, as relationalists would have it, some particular that is the (psychological) 'object' of the attitude. On the proposed account, the representative so designated is an IUF, which, as we have seen, has available to it the individuative resources necessary to individuate propositional attitudes as finely as our common-sense intuitions demand. Thus, for example, the account can explain as well as any other account the Frege puzzles involving failures of substitution. To attribute to Lois Lane the belief that Superman can leap tall buildings is not necessarily to attribute to her the belief that Clark Kent can leap tall buildings, since the two *that*-clauses designate different IUFs, which are not necessarily representatives of one and the same belief. And this individuation is achieved without having to assume anything more about the semantics of *that*-clauses than that they designate IUFs.

But how, on the proposed measurement-theoretic account, are we to explain the context sensitivity of attitude predicates? The answer is this: an IUF is the representative of a propositional attitude by virtue of its specifying the state of affairs to which that propositional attitude is behaviorally related in the manner characteristic of an attitude of that type. The IUF specifies this state of affairs by *describing* it. Thus, for example, Smith's belief that Tully is bald has as its representative the IUF designated by an utterance of the *that*-clause *that Tully is bald*, and this IUF specifies the state of affairs to which Smith is related behaviorally in the way characteristic of beliefs by describing that state of affairs in those terms, viz., as the state of affairs in which Tully is bald. But as with any description, context will determine what behavior-implicating state of affairs counts as satisfying the description. In some contexts, how the believer would conceptualize or describe the state of affairs will be irrelevant to the truth of the description, in which case the belief attribution will be true even if Smith knows Tully only as 'Cicero'. In other contexts, perhaps because the point of the attribution is to convey to a listener just how the believer would express her belief, this same belief will be false.[6]

Kripke's (1979) Pierre and Paderewski puzzles present a different sort of challenge to proposed accounts of propositional attitudes. Arguably, these puzzles don't have anything in particular to do with either the semantics of attitude attributions or the nature of the attitudes themselves. Rather they seem to have to do with difficulties that arise when we undertake to describe in our own words the beliefs of individuals who don't share with us relevant assumptions about the states of affairs these beliefs are about. In the Pierre case, for example, we cannot simply translate into English the French sentence 'Londres est jolie' that Pierre would use to express his belief about the city he knows only by the name 'Londres' and then disquote the resulting English sentence 'London is pretty' and embed it in the *that*-clause of a belief sentence, given that for reasons that Kripke explains, Pierre would also assent to the English sentence 'London is not pretty'. For to do so would suggest

---

[6] The idea here echoes a proposal of Bach (1997), according to which we should think of the *that*-clauses of belief reports not as singular terms that designate the objects of belief but as descriptions of them, for in so doing we will be able to explain the context-sensitivity of belief reports. Bach, I think, is correct in believing that the context-sensitivity of the truth conditions for attitude attributions is of a piece with the context-sensitivity of the truth conditions for descriptions, but he is mistaken in believing both that *that*-clauses aren't singular terms and that what is described is an object, the belief, to which the possessor of the attitude is related.

incorrectly that Pierre is guilty of believing a logical contradiction, viz., that London is both pretty and not pretty, when in fact his mistake is the logically innocent one of simply not knowing that Londres and London are one and the same city. The puzzle here, to the extent that there is one, is one of not being able to express in our own words just what Pierre believes, given that he uses the names *Londres* and *London* differently than we do.

Kripke's Paderewski case offers a similar example, though one in which there are seemingly no issues of translation. In this case, Jones, as we might call him, asserts of a well-known pianist named *Paderewski*, 'Paderewski is a great musician', and of a well-known politician named *Paderewski*, 'Paderewski is not a great musician', not realizing the pianist and the politician are one and the same person. We cannot simply disquote Jones' assertions and embed them in the *that*-clauses of belief attributions, since to do so would, as in the Pierre case, suggest incorrectly that Jones believes a logical contradiction, viz., that Paderewski is and is not a great musician. The puzzle, again, is how to describe Jones' beliefs in a way that is both faithful to his beliefs and yet absolves him of believing a logical contradiction. We might try to describe Jones as believing that, as we might put it, 'there are two distinct individuals of the same name, the one Paderewski, the pianist, who is a great musician, the other, Paderewski, the politician, who is not a great musician', though arguably the belief that we are here attributing to Jones is neither (nor both) of the two singular beliefs that Jones presumably expresses when he asserts what he does.

The puzzle posed by Kripke's Pierre and Paderewski cases is not peculiar to attitude attributions. It arises equally for verbs of saying, when we undertake to say exactly what Pierre and Jones *said* in uttering the sentences that they did. So the puzzle isn't just about attitude attributions. But given that the puzzle does arise for attitude attributions, one might expect an account of attitude attribution to have something to say about this puzzle, if not simply to convince us that the puzzle is not damaging to the account.

If we consider Kripke's two cases, it is clear that the source of the problem is to be found in the fact that in trying to say in our words what it is that Pierre and Jones believe, we are stymied by our different beliefs about relevant features of the world: Pierre believes that the city he calls 'Londres' and the city he calls 'London' are two different cities, whereas we believe they are one and the same; Jones believes that Paderewski the pianist and Paderewski the musician are two different individuals, whereas we believe that they are one and the same. We would have no difficulty expressing in our words Pierre's and Jones' beliefs if we shared their beliefs. But we don't, and hence we find ourselves forced to various artifices such as using foreign words or words in scare quotes to formulate the *that*-clauses that express what Pierre and Jones believe.

Cases such as Kripke's present a practical problem for attitude attribution practice, but it is not clear that they present any particular problem for an account of propositional attitudes and their attribution, unless that account is committed to something that entails that such problems should not arise. This might very well be the case for a relational account of the attitudes that construes the *that*-clause in an attitude attribution as a singular term that designates the object of the attitude, especially if that account assumes that the logical structure of the object is given by the logical form of the sentence embedded in the attribution's *that*-clause. For on such account it would seem that whatever formulation we might settle on as an expression in our own words of what Pierre and Jones believe, that formulation would not designate the actual objects of their beliefs. We could never say truly in our own words what it is they believe, which certainly seems counterintuitive. But nothing in the proposed measurement-theoretic account would seem to preclude our being able to formulate in our own words what it is that Pierre and Jones believe, because what the *that*-clause in a belief attribution specifies is a merely representative of the attributed belief, and as such it can be more or less precise, more or less specific, as a representation of that belief. In most cases, nothing would require that these representatives preserve the logical form of the sentences by which Pierre and Jones would express their beliefs. Of course, in certain cases it might be important precisely what words (in their language) Pierre and Jones would use to express their beliefs, in which case any suitable representative of those beliefs would minimally have mentioned their very words. But the existence of such cases does not impugn the truth of belief attributions that in other circumstances specify the attributed belief by means of a less precise representative. To think otherwise would be analogous to thinking that it couldn't be true to say of an object that it was hot because that object could have been more precisely described as having a temperature of $230°C$.

7.1.6. Iterated Propositional Attitude Attributions

Iterated propositional attitude attributions have been a notorious source of difficulty for accounts of propositional attitude attributions that, like Frege's, propose to explain failures of substitution in intentional contexts by appeal to the notion that in such contexts expressions change their semantic values.

For such accounts need to articulate and justify the principle according to which these hypothesized changes occur in multiply embedded contexts. Thus, for example, if like Frege one holds that referents of the terms of the sentence embedded in the *that*-clause of (1) are the customary senses that Lois associates with those terms, then what referents are to be assigned to the terms that appear in the lower *that*-clause in (2)?

(1) Lois believes [that Clark Kent is not Superman].
(2) Sue believes [that Lois believes [that Clark Kent is not Superman]].

Is it the customary senses that Lois associates with those terms, or is it the customary sense that Sue associates with those terms, or is it perhaps some (mysterious?) third thing, which following Frege we might call the 'indirect referent' of the customary sense of those terms.[7]

The present measurement-theoretic account seems to handle iterated propositional attitude attributions perfectly well, assigning just the truth conditions that we would expect. On the proposed account, iterated attributions, like simple, non-iterated attributions, attribute to some individual a propositional attitude that has as its representative the IUF expressed by an utterance of the sentence embedded in the attribution's *that*-clause, but with this difference: the IUF thus expressed itself attributes a propositional attitude, where this attitude itself has as its representative the IUF expressed by an utterance of the sentence embedded in that attribution's *that*-clause (and so on, for as many iterations as the original iterated attribution requires). Thus, for example, sentence (2) attributes to Sue a belief state that has as its representative the IUF expressed by an utterance of (1) in the context of (2), where (1) in turn attributes to Lois a belief state that has as its representative the IUF expressed by an utterance of (3) in the context of (1), and hence also of (2):

(3) Clark Kent is not Superman.

But this difference that distinguishes iterated from non-iterated attributions is not a theoretically significant difference. The truth conditions for both sorts of attribution are the same: the attribution is true just in case the individual to whom the attitude is attributed has a propositional attitude, of the type specified by the attribution's main clause verb, that has as its representative the IUF expressed by an utterance of the sentence embedded

---

7 For a discussion of the difficulties with each of these options, see Richard 1990: 69–75.

in the attribution's *that*-clause. There is no theoretically significant difference in the fact that the IUF expressed by the sentence embedded in the *that*-clause of the iterated attitude attribution specifies a mental state of affairs, specifically, that some individual possesses some propositional attitude. This is just one of many different sorts of states of affairs to which the possessors of propositional attitudes can be behaviorally related in the ways already described. There is no problem analogous to one that confronts the Fregean, because on the proposed measurement-theoretic account, expressions do not change their semantic values in the intentional contexts created by attitude verbs. The iteration of attitude verbs presents no special problems, because the representational domain of IUFs is unchanging across all of the intentional contexts created by this iteration of attitude verbs: it remains unchangingly that of the person making the attribution. And as in non-iterated attributions, the appropriate choice of representative IUF, and of the sentence that expresses this IUF, will depend on a number of different factors, including who the attribution is addressed to, the beliefs of the attributor, and so on, such that in different contexts the same *that*-clause might express different representative IUFs, while in other contexts, different *that*-clauses might express the same IUF.

7.2. THE INTRINSIC NATURE OF THE ATTITUDES

Philosophers have offered a number of different accounts of the intrinsic nature of propositional attitudes. Most influential in recent decades, of course, has been the Received View, according to which propositional attitudes are relations to mental representations that express the propositional content of the attitude. So conceived, propositional attitudes are mental representations that play a causal role in the production of behavior and other mental states. Just what causal role these mental representations play is said to vary as a function of the attitude type, so that, for example, the representations that are beliefs play one sort of causal role, while the representations that are desires play another. Proponents of the Received View have been quite explicit about the empirical character of the view; as Fodor (1978 [1981]: 202) puts it, 'the theory that propositional attitudes are relations to internal representations is a piece of empirical psychology'.

The proposed measurement-theoretic account of the attitudes, according to which the attitudes are aptitudes, i.e., states apt to produce their characteristic effects, is non-committal as to their intrinsic nature. The

account does require that propositional attitudes have the empirical relational structure that it attributes to them, and having such a structure is an
essential (and hence necessary) property of those psychological states that
are the attitudes. But having such a structure is consistent with a wide
range of different realizations of this structure, including that propositional attitudes might turn out, like the physical magnitudes, to be monadic
properties of their possessors rather than, as the Received View would have
it, discrete representational structures to which the possessors of propositional attitudes bear a functional/computational relation. The proposed
account is equally non-committal about both the nature and the role of
representations in an empirical account of the intrinsic nature of the attitudes.

In principle, the proposed account is consistent with propositional attitudes
having the intrinsic nature that the Received View attributes to them, though
for reasons spelled out in Chapter 3, it is empirically implausible that
propositional attitudes are relations to mental representations of the sort
that this view presumes, specifically that they are relations to sentence-
like computational data structures with certain characteristic inference-like
computational processes defined over these data structures, where the data
structures express the propositional contents of the associated attitudes.

There is, nevertheless, good reason to presume that, as a matter of empirical
fact, possession of a propositional attitude requires certain representational
abilities on the part of the possessor, since it is otherwise difficult to imagine
how propositional attitudes could play the causal roles that they do in the
production of behavior and thought. Desire states, for example, are causally
efficacious in causing us to act in ways intended to bring about certain
non-existing states of affairs, yet it is hard to see how such states could be
thus efficacious without the possessor of such states being able to represent in
some fashion the desired states of affairs. Similarly, belief states are causally
efficacious in modulating our behavior in ways that make our behaviors
more likely to achieve their goals, yet it is hard to see how such states
could be thus efficacious without the possessor of such states being able to
represent the believed states of affairs. But it is difficult to see just what, if
anything, these facts entail regarding the supposed representational nature of
propositional attitudes themselves. If propositional attitudes are conceived of
as aptitudes, i.e., as a kind of mediated disposition for certain characteristic
effects, then possession of a propositional attitude would presumably be a
matter of 'being related to a representation' only in the loose sense that the

computational structures and processes that realize the attitude would include certain representations, but without the attitudes themselves being identified with these representations, or with relations to these representations. The attitudes are analogous in this respect to various other aptitudes, e.g., for chess-play or for mathematics, which presumably require for their possession and exercise the concurrent possession of various representations that are part of their implementing substrate, though without being identified with them.

Nevertheless, even if representations figure in an account of propositional attitudes only insofar as they are constituents or properties of their computational realizations, one would still expect an empirical account of the intrinsic nature of propositional attitudes to provide some account of these representations and their role in the computational processes that realize the attitudes. For arguably one could not understand the attitudes as the aptitudes that they are without seeing how these aptitudes are had in virtue of these underlying computational processes upon which they supervene. It is precisely an account of these underlying processes that enables us to understand what possession of particular propositional attitudes comes to in particular creatures or species, say ourselves, even if such an account might take an entirely different form in the case of different individuals or different species. Thus, for example, an empirical account of what it is for an ant to know at every point in its lengthy foraging trajectories the relative location of its nest is *not* to provide a philosophical analysis of what it is to possess such knowledge, an analysis which might advert to various other constitutive propositional attitudes. Rather it is to provide an account of the computational structures and processes (and maybe ultimately the neural structures and processes) that realize this knowledge. Such an account would include an account of whatever representations the ant maintains of its location relative to its nest.[8]

Once we recognize that any empirical account of the intrinsic nature of the attitudes is going to be an account of the computational structures and processes that realize the particular attitudes that we have, then there is going to be even less reason to suppose that such representations as may be implicated in such an account will be of the sort envisioned by the Received View. For there is simply no reason to suppose that such a computational account will traffic in distally interpretable data structures with certain inferential processes defined over them. Such representations

---

[8] For a detailed discussion of this example, see Gallistel 1990 and also the next section of this chapter.

as the account might postulate will no doubt bear a heavily mediated relation to behavior, such that it would be something of a miracle if these representations turned out to be distally interpretable. To think otherwise is effectively to assume that the cognitive processes responsible for the production of behavior are computationally quite shallow, such that a distal interpretation of these processes and their attendant representations can be successfully projected from the outside in. Our common-sense conception of the causes of intentional behavior may encourage such an assumption, but it has little basis in fact. Computational considerations of the sort mentioned in Chapter 3.5 militate against it. We can, if we wish, continue to talk of propositional attitudes as relations to representations of this state of affairs on the presumption that any account of the computational realization of the attitudes will advert to certain representations, but the notion of representing a particular (distal) state of affairs is here being used so loosely that virtually any representation or any collection of representations that represents *inter alia* a particular state of affairs counts as a representation of just that particular state of affairs. But if the notion of representing a particular state of affairs is being used in so loose a fashion, then there is really nothing in the claim that propositional attitudes are relations to representations that rises to the level of a substantive empirical claim about the intrinsic nature of propositional attitudes. Nor is there anything here that rises to the level of a substantive empirical claim about the computational architecture that realizes propositional attitudes. All that we have is a claim to the effect that possession of propositional attitudes involves representations in some quite vague and unspecified sense of this expression. It is entirely consistent with this loose interpretation of representing a particular state of affairs that there be no distally interpretable representations at all, or that the representations to which the possessors of propositional attitudes are related are, as Braddon-Mitchell and Jackson (1996: 168 ff.) suggest, more analogous to maps than sentences, so that the individuation of such representations, on any plausible computational construal of their individuation conditions, would have little or no bearing on the individuation of propositional attitudes.

If the proposed measurement-theoretic account is correct in taking propositional attitudes to be aptitudes for the characteristic effects that we associate with propositional attitudes, then an account of the intrinsic nature of the attitudes is *also* going to have to explain their capacity to cause the characteristic effects that they do. This explanation will also take the form not of a philosophical analysis of the attitudes, but rather of an empirical account of underlying computational processes responsible for the causal efficacy that we associate with the attitudes. Such an account will explain how it is these processes produce these effects in the circumstances in which they do.

The issues here are important, so let me try to put these points in another way: On the proposed measurement-theoretic account, propositional attitudes are aptitudes for certain characteristic effects. But to say this is not to say anything about the psychological states responsible for our having these aptitudes that are the attitudes. Aptitudes are, as it were, person-level attributes of individuals, for which there is of course some sub-personal, presumably computational explanation. We have the aptitudes that we do in virtue of being in certain psychological states, and among these states are surely certain representational states, perhaps even certain computational data structures. But the aptitudes are not to be identified with any particular representational states, since these very same aptitudes could presumably be realized in all sorts of different computational ways, in different computational architectures, by means of different representational resources. The aptitudes that are the attitudes are one thing, the computational states and processes that realize them something else altogether. Now there is of course the question of just how these aptitudes are realized in creatures like ourselves, and an account of the intrinsic nature of the attitudes will presumably answer this question, inasmuch as the attitudes are the aptitudes that they are simply in virtue of these realizing states and processes.

Maybe it will turn out that there is a fairly straightforward account of how the aptitudes that are the attitudes are realized computationally (and perhaps neurophysiologically). Only empirical research will tell. But it might turn out that these aptitudes are, to use Dennett's phrase, innocently emergent from the computational mechanisms that realize them, so that at the end of the day we would have two disparate accounts of human cognition, one a personal level account couched in terms of propositional attitudes, the other a subpersonal level account couched in terms of computational structures, states, and processes, though without any clear account of how the attitudes are realized computationally. In such an event, we would have no particular reason to think of the attitudes themselves as relations to representations, even in the very loose sense described above, even if, as seems likely, creatures like ourselves have propositional attitudes only in virtue of having certain broadly representational psychological states.

7.3. PROPOSITIONAL ATTITUDES IN EMPIRICAL COMPUTATIONAL COGNITIVE SCIENCE: A MINIMALIST ACCOUNT OF THE COMPUTATIONAL ENTAILMENTS OF PROPOSITIONAL ATTITUDE ATTRIBUTIONS

The Received View, we saw in Chapter 2, makes specific claims both about the nature of cognitive capacities and cognitive processes and about the constitutive role of the propositional attitudes in such capacities and processes. Specifically, the view claims that the possession of a molar cognitive capacity consists in the possession of a number of subcapacities whose causal interaction constitutes the molar capacity, where (i) the subcapacities in question are capacities for processing computationally certain mental representations, (ii) the representations in question are 'explicit' in the sense of being computationally, if not physically, discrete formal structures that have determinate semantic contents, and (iii) these representations express the propositional contents of (certain of) their possessor's propositional attitudes. Thinking, and indeed cognition more generally, is claimed to be a computational, and more specifically inferential, process defined over one or more of these representations that eventuates in the production of either another representation or a behavior. Cognitive capacities and cognition, so conceived, thus accord to propositional attitudes an essential constitutive role in the basic computational structure of an individual's mind, its capacities, and its processes. The intended methodological moral is clear: if cognitive scientists wish to discern the computational structure of the mind, its capacities, and its processes, they can hardly do better than study the explanatory role of propositional attitudes attribution in common-sense propositional attitude psychology, since it is here that one will see clearly revealed the crucial role of propositional attitudes in cognition.

The proposed measurement-theoretic account of propositional attitudes disputes the notion that propositional attitude psychology is quite the methodological philosopher's stone that proponents of the Received View take it to be. According to the measurement-theoretic account, to attribute a propositional attitude is just to attribute an aptitude for the characteristic effects that we associate with that attitude. It is not to say anything more about the character of propositional attitudes that eventuate in those effects than simply that they are states apt to cause those effects. Nor is it to say anything about the nature of any computational processes that may produce these effects. There is no direct entailment from the propositional attitudes attributed to a subject to any computational cognitive architectural description of that individual. Propositional attitude attributions do not therefore provide a window into cognitive structure and cognitive processing. At most they provide a window into the individual's aptitude for producing the effects characteristic of the possessed attitudes.

As a characterization of an individual's aptitude for such effects, propositional attitude attributions are clearly attributions of internal psychological states, but they abstract away from all details concerning the nature of the computational states and processes that underlie them. By way of illustration, consider once again the Chomskian claim discussed at length in Chapter 3.5 that to know a natural language is *inter alia* to know a grammar for that language. The grammar that the linguist hypothesizes a speaker to have 'internalized', Chomsky emphasizes, is *not* a model for a speaker (Chomsky 1965: 9); it does *not* prescribe the character or functioning of such a model (ibid.); rather it describes 'abstract conditions that unknown mechanisms must meet' (Chomsky 1980a: 197). Against Dummett who claimed that a theory of meaning 'is not concerned to describe any inner psychological mechanisms' (Dummett 1976: 70), Chomsky insists that 'Dummett's theory of meaning *is* a "psychological hypothesis," though one that abstracts away from many questions that can be raised about inner mechanisms' (1980a: 111; emphasis mine). Dummett's theory is a psychological hypothesis because it specifies *conditions* that the 'inner psychological mechanisms' are alleged to meet, and in so doing describes in abstract terms those mechanisms. Grammars, Chomsky argues, are psychological hypotheses in precisely the same sense: they specify conditions that inner psychological mechanisms of the speaker/hearer are alleged to meet. A grammar does this, Chomsky argues (1980a: 82), by specifying the pairing of sounds and meanings that these inner mechanisms are alleged to compute.

To the extent that a characterization of an individual's propositional attitudes is a characterization of that individual's aptitude for producing the characteristic effects of those attitudes, i.e., to produce in specified circumstances certain behaviors and other thoughts, such a characterization is effectively an informal characterization of the *function* that this individual computes in the course of exercising whatever happens to be the cognitive capacity responsible for these effects. Specification of the function computed

in the exercise of a cognitive capacity is, as many computational psychologists
have emphasized, a crucial step in the development of a psychological theory
of that capacity; indeed, if Marr (1982) is correct, specification of the
function computed—what he called the 'theory of the computation'—is *the*
crucial step in the development of such a theory, since in the absence of
such a specification, the inquiry into computational mechanisms is in most
cognitive domains hopelessly unconstrained. Chomsky endorses claims by
Marr (e.g., 1982: 28) that linguistic theory is such a theory of computation,
i.e., that it is concerned with the pairing of sounds and meanings computed by
speaker/hearers and not with the 'theory of the algorithm', i.e., the algorithms
or computational mechanisms by which that pairing is computed:

> We may consider the study of grammar and UG to be at the level of the theory of the
> computation. But the same is true of some work in artificial intelligence . . . . I don't
> see any useful distinction between 'linguistics' and 'psychology,' unless we choose to
> use the former term for the study of the theory of computation in language, and the
> latter for the theory of the algorithm.
>
> (Chomsky 1980b: 48–9)

Thus, grammars, which Chomsky takes to be a specification of a speaker's
linguistic *knowledge*, provide a 'theory of the computation' for the computational mechanisms of language processing, and as such specify the function(s)
computed by speakers in the course of such processing.[9]

Marr himself does not, like Chomsky, explicitly identify propositional
attitude descriptions of some cognitive capacity as providing a specification
of the theory of computation for that capacity; however, in developing the
theory of the computation for early vision, Marr and his collaborators do
often avail themselves of the intentional idiom, describing the visual system
as 'knowing this', 'assuming that', and so on. Indeed, Marr begins his 1982
book by describing the task of the visual system as that of enabling us to 'know
what's where' in our immediate environment. So clearly Marr does presume
that informal propositional attitude descriptions do have a significant role
to play in the development of a theory of the computation, a theory that
eventuates in a specification of the function(s) computed in the course of

---

[9] The grammar is a theory of the computation for the computational mechanisms of language
processing only in the sense of specifying the pairing of sounds and meanings effected by those
mechanisms. The grammar, which specifies (intensionally) a function from lexical items into
sound-meaning pairs, does not otherwise characterize the functions that speakers compute from
sounds to meanings, or vice versa. For further discussion, see Matthews (2006).

the exercise of a cognitive capacity. Newell (1981) seems to have a similar picture of the role and utility of what he terms the 'knowledge-level', the level at which one describes what an intelligent agent or symbol system knows, believes, wants, etc.—in short, its propositional attitudes:

The knowledge level permits predicting and understanding behavior without having an operational model of the processing that is actually being done by the agent. The utility of such a level would seem clear, given the widespread need in life's affairs for distal prediction, and also the paucity of knowledge about the internal workings of humans. The utility is also clear in designing AI systems, where the internal mechanisms are still to be specified.

(Newell 1981: 11)

Knowledge-level descriptions, Newell emphasizes, specify the competence of a symbol system, its 'potential for generating action' (1981: 7); they specify what a symbol system 'should be able to do' (ibid.)—its aptitudes, as I would put it. But knowledge-level descriptions, Newell emphasizes, carry *no* structural information about how knowledge and goals are realized or how they are connected: 'the specification at the knowledge level is provided entirely by the *content* of the knowledge and the goals, *not by any structural way they are connected*' (ibid., emphasis mine). A given body of knowledge, specified at the knowledge level, is realized computationally, in Newell's view, by a symbol system that represents this body of knowledge by means of certain data structures and certain processes defined over these structures, but the knowledge-level description itself provides no information about how, computationally speaking, this is accomplished.

The proposed account of the attitudes as aptitudes finds support in the view expressed by Chomsky, Marr, and Newell as to the computational import of propositional attitude attributions: as characterizations of an individual's aptitude for behavior and thought, such attributions provide significant information regarding the functions that this individual is able to compute and which specify his/her cognitive competence. But these attributions provide little or no information regarding how the individual is able to do what he can do, how he is able to compute the function that he does in the course of exercising this competence. The proposed account also finds support in the actual practice of cognitive researchers, who use propositional attitude attributions in just the way described: propositional attitude descriptions are used to construct an intentional characterization of the competence to be explained, and then once that characterization is developed, researchers set about specifying a computational system that computes a function that generally satisfies that characterization. I say 'generally' because, the intentional characterization so developed typically involves considerable idealization and approximation, which in the usual case preclude any straightforward implementation. Thus, for example, in the case of parsing models for natural language that implement a particular grammar, the pairing of sounds and meanings (actually phonological and logical forms) computed by the parser invariably only approximates the pairing specified by the grammar. In some cases the pairing thus specified is computationally intractable under any plausible time constraints, even over the domain of sentences that speakers actually are capable of processing, in which case the pairing specified by the grammar is necessarily only an approximation of the one that speakers actually compute in the course of language processing (see Barton *et al.* 1987). But the methodological guidance provided by the grammar, which represents the speaker's linguistic competence, his knowledge of language, is generally good enough to make development of the grammar well worth the effort; indeed, in the usual case the computational model simply *cannot* be developed without first developing a grammatical description of the linguistic competence being modeled. This grammar, which specifies what a speaker is said to know, specifies a pairing of sentences with their structural descriptions that the computational psycholinguist can take as a specification of the mapping that the speaker effects in the course of language processing. And the rules and principles that constitute the grammar typically provide significant guidance to the sorts of computational structures and processes needed to compute this pairing, even if the parser does not incorporate the grammar as a component, specifically as the parsing grammar. The cleverness required of the computational theorist is to see just what combinations of available computational structures and processes will compute the desired pairing. Thus, the Marcus parser, as we explained, is able to assign the appropriate syntactic structure to sentences with passive morphology, not by actually moving constituents in the manner hypothesized by the EST grammar that the parser is intended to implement, but rather by means of a trace-dropping operation that achieves the same effect (see Chapter 3.5.5).

It is nevertheless somewhat misleading to suggest that to specify the propositional attitudes that constitute a cognitive capacity is to specify the function computed in the course of exercising that capacity, even under significant approximation and idealization, since a specification of the former will invariably *underspecify* a precise mathematical specification of the latter. The point can be illustrated by a nice example drawn from Gallistel's (1990) discussion of the dead reckoning capacity of the Tunisian desert ant *Cataglyphis bicolor*, which Gallistel describes as follows:

On the featureless Tunisian desert, a long-legged, fast-moving ant leaves the protection of the humid nest on a foraging expedition. It moves across the desert in tortuous loops, running first this way, then that, but gradually progressing ever farther away from the life-sustaining humidity of the nest. Finally it finds the carcass of a scorpion, uses its strong pincers to gouge out a chunk nearly its own size, then turns to orient to within one to two degrees of the straight line between itself and the nest entrance, a 1-millimeter-wide hole, 40 meters distant. It runs a straight line for 43 meters, holding its course by maintaining its angle to the sun. Three meters past the point at which it should have encountered the entrance, the ant abruptly breaks into the search pattern by which it eventually locates it. A witness to this homeward journey finds it hard to resist the inference that the ant on its search for food possessed at every moment a representation of its position relative to the entrance to the nest, a spatial representation that enabled it to compute the solar angle and distance of the homeward journey from wherever it happened to encounter food.

(Gallistel 1990: 1)

Gallistel cites experiments that show that in its return run to the nest, the ant does not rely on any sort of chemical trail laid down by itself or other ants, it does not rely on any sort of sensory beacon emanating from the nest, and it does not rely on known landmarks (at least, not until the ant is quite close to the nest). So how, Gallistel asks, does the ant '*know* where to head and how far to go'? (1990: 59, italics mine) The ant knows this, he says, because at every moment in its foraging trajectory it knows both its current heading and its position relative to the entrance of the nest, so that when it decides to return to the nest it knows in which direction to turn and how far to run. It knows these things because it relies exclusively on dead reckoning, a kind of navigation well-known to mariners, which presumes that over the course of its trajectory the ant continuously computes its current heading, its current speed, and, assuming that it can integrate these two variables, its current displacement from the nest.[10]

We can thus state what the ant must *know* if it is to exhibit the behavior that it does, but notice that we are not as yet able to specify the mathematical

---

[10] The ant's computation of its displacement relative to the nest is remarkably accurate: 'a distance error on the order of 10 per cent and an angular error on the order of $1°$ over violently twisting and turning courses that cover linear distances of as much as a kilometer' (Gallistel 1990: 65).

function that the ant computes, other than simply to say that it continuously computes its current heading, current speed, and current displacement from the nest. Crucial to a precise specification of the function computed by the ant is a specification of the frames of reference with respect to which each of these three variables are represented. Most crucially, to specify the function by which the ant computes its displacement from the nest, we must know or make an assumption about how the ant represents displacement. As Gallistel explains, 'a decision that must be made at the outset of constructing a computational model of dead reckoning is whether the computations are to be carried out within Cartesian or polar coordinates' (1990: 71). For until one makes such a decision, one cannot specify the displacement function that the ant computes. And, of course, until one decides how the ant represents displacement, and hence what function is being computed, one can hardly speculate as to the computational processes that the ant uses to compute displacement.

Gallistel argues that there are good empirical reasons for thinking that the ant uses a Cartesian coordinate system, but whatever the facts are here, the general point is this: propositional attitude descriptions specify the function computed in the course of the exercise of a cognitive capacity only to the extent that those descriptions specify in empirically justified, mathematically precise terms the pairing of inputs with outputs that the computed function effects. In the case of human language processing, a grammatical specification of a speaker's knowledge is tantamount to a specification of the function computed in the course of language processing, because the grammar does specify in reasonably precise mathematical terms the pairing of sentences with the associated structural descriptions that speakers are presumed to recover in the course of language processing (or at least the grammar provides a specification that can be rendered fairly easily in such terms). Something similar is true in the case of the propositional attitude descriptions deployed by Marr and his collaborators in their accounts of the visual system. But in many cases, arguably most cases, propositional attitude descriptions do *not* specify with sufficient mathematical precision the pairing of inputs with outputs. These descriptions in fact underspecify, or specify in ways that demand considerable mathematical 'precisification', the functions computed in the course of exercising the cognitive capacity in question. Nevertheless, these descriptions provide a useful starting point and methodology for developing the theory of the computation for a particular cognitive capacity. The theorist begins with an informal specification of the knowledge and assumptions that constitute the competence that a subject exhibits in the course of exercising a particular cognitive capacity. The theorist then refines and precisifies this specification on the basis of available empirical evidence, little by little developing a precise propositional attitude characterization of the function(s) computed in the course of the exercise of the capacity. Thus, for example, a cognitive ethologist such as Gallistel may develop, as in fact he does, a precise propositional attitude characterization of the knowledge that the desert ant possesses at any point along its foraging trajectory, e.g., it *knows* that its nest is located at position (θ,d), where θ is the angular displacement of the nest relative to the sun, and d is the distance to the nest. Similarly, a researcher such as Ullman (1979) may begin by describing that component of the visual system responsible for recovering structure from motion by saying that the visual system *assumes* that objects are rigid in translation, but then through a series of refinements based on empirical evidence develop a quite precise specification of just what this assumption comes to, specifically, that the visual system computes a function, in this case the so-called 'structure from motion' algorithm, the output of which, if it delivers one, is accepted as veridical, where the output will in fact be veridical just in case objects providing the visual input to the algorithm are rigid in translation.

7.4. FURTHER IMPLICATIONS OF THE PROPOSED ACCOUNT

Over the course of the last couple of decades, discussions of propositional attitudes have become closely intertwined with a number of philosophical views and projects. Most notable among these views are intentional realism and intentional content essentialism, while among these projects are the so-called naturalization project for intentionality, the Gricean intentional-based semantics project, and more recently the Schiffer/Fodor translational semantics project. In this final section of the chapter, I examine briefly the implications of the proposed measurement-theoretic account for these views and projects.

7.4.1. Intentional Realism and the Naturalization Project

Proponents of the Received View describe themselves as 'intentional realists', by which they mean that they are committed not simply to the claim that propositional attitudes exist but also to the claim that such states actually have semantically evaluable intentional contents. These philosophers have expended considerable effort over the last two decades trying to develop a semantic theory—a 'psychosemantics', as they call it—for the mental representations to which possessors of propositional attitudes are said to be related. They have undertaken this project, because they realize that if, as the Received View holds, the intentional (semantic) properties of propositional attitudes are inherited from the intentional properties of the mental representations which express the contents of these attitudes, then any account of the former is going to demand an account of the latter in the form of a semantic theory for these mental representations. And given the view's announced concern to establish the materialist *bona fides* of propositional attitudes, it is going to be an adequacy condition on such a theory that it be 'naturalistic', i.e., that the theory not advert to any intentional or semantic notions, since to do so would undercut the effort to establish these *bona fides*. The project of providing a naturalistic psychosemantics has come to be called the 'naturalization project'.

The proposed measurement-theoretic account is, like the Received View, thoroughly realist about propositional attitudes, but it is not realist about the supposed intentional contents of propositional attitudes. Such intentionality as propositional attitudes have is an intentionality, i.e., a 'directedness' or an 'aboutness', that they have in virtue of their behavioral relation to the states of affairs specified by the IUFs that are their representatives. It is not a semantic intentionality of the sort that the Received View imagines. Thus, it is not part of the proposed account that propositional attitudes actually have semantic properties, any more than it is part of a measurement-theoretic account of physical magnitudes that they actually have numerical properties. In both cases, the properties in question are properties of our conventional ways of representing propositional attitudes and physical magnitudes (though, of course, as we have seen, our success in so representing propositional attitudes and physical magnitudes depends upon their having certain empirical prop- erties that can find an image in these representations). The assumption that propositional attitudes have such properties is simply the result of an uncrit- ical tendency to believe that because we cannot conceive of these properties except in terms of such properties and because in our surrogative reasoning about the attitudes we quantify over such properties, they must in fact have them. But if it is not part of the proposed account that propositional attitudes have semantic properties, and if it is not part of the proposed account that propositional attitudes are relations to mental representations that express the propositional contents of the associated attitudes, then the proposed account of propositional attitudes does not stand in need of a theory of intentional content for such representations. And there is no more need for a naturalization project to establish the materialistic *bona fides* of propositional attitudes than there is need for an analogous naturalization project with respect to numbers to establish the materialistic *bona fides* of the physical magnitudes. There is no reason whatever to suppose that propositional attitudes, which by assumption are causally efficacious in the production of behavior and thought, are not themselves thoroughly materialistic states of their possessors. To be sure, there may be a naturalistic psychosemantic project concerning the representations to which scientific cognitive computational theories advert, but that project has no intrinsic connection to propositional attitudes, and there is, as Cummins (1989) has argued, little reason to suppose that proposed theories of intentional content will find any application in that domain. Those concerned with this different project would do better to investigate what Cummins calls 'structural interpretational semantics', or perhaps better still what computational theorists have studied extensively under the guise of the 'semantics of programming languages'.

7.4.2. Intentional Content Essentialism

Many philosophers of mind hold the view not simply that propositional attitudes have intentional contents but that they have their contents essentially: it is not possible for a propositional attitude to have a content different from the one that it has and still be the same propositional attitude. Cummins (1989) expresses this view, which we might dub 'intentional content essentialism', as follows:

> The contents of thoughts—typical adult human thoughts, anyway—are quite amazingly unique and determinate. When I think the thought that current U.S. policy in Central America is ill-advised, the proposition that current U.S. policy is ill-advised is the *intentional content* . . . of my thought. The proposition that current U.S. policy in South Africa is ill-advised is not the intentional content of that thought (though it may be something I believe, and hence, the intentional content of a different one of my thoughts).

> (Cummins 1989: 137)

Intentional content essentialism, it should be noted, is not the claim that propositions, specifically the propositions expressed by the *that*-clauses of attitude attributions, have their contents essentially, which of course they do. It is rather the claim that propositional attitudes themselves have intentional contents and furthermore have them essentially.

Intentional content essentialism presumably derives its intuitive plausibility from our ability, in the usual case, to 'express' our propositional attitudes verbally: our sentential expressions of our attitudes have propositional contents, and almost without exception the only sentences that we are prepared to offer and accept as expressing any particular one of our attitudes are ones that share the same propositional content. So if we are inclined, as intentional content essentialists are, to think of propositional attitudes themselves, and not simply their linguistic expressions, as having propositional contents, then it is a short step to concluding that they have their contents essentially.

The proposed measurement-theoretic account of the attitudes eschews intentional content essentialism in all its forms, for on this account propositional attitudes, strictly speaking, do not have propositional contents, indeed contents of any sort. At least nothing about propositional attitudes requires that they, as opposed to their natural language representatives, have contents. Yet because the proposed account is realist about the attitudes, it *does* hold that a subject's propositional attitudes are *determinate*. They are determinate in the sense that when someone has a propositional attitude, there is some particular, determinate propositional attitude state that this person is in. Specifically, that state is a determinate aptitude for, among other things, the characteristic behavior that manifests that state, *including*, it must be emphasized, certain determinate verbal expressions of the attitude (which themselves typically have determinate propositional contents). Thus, for example, if Cummins believes that current US policy in Central America is ill-advised, then that is what Cummins believes, and he will be apt *inter alia* to express this belief with a particular form of words, say the English sentence *current US policy in Central America is ill-advised* (which expresses a proposition to this effect). The 'amazing' *uniqueness* that Cummins attributes to intentional contents is presumably attributable to the fact that the possessor of a propositional attitude will typically have some specific way of expressing the attitude in question, e.g., as the belief that 'current U.S. policy in Central America is ill-advised'. A subject may accept other sentential expressions of his propositional attitude, but in the usual case all such expressions will share a single propositional content. Of course, a subject's having some particular, determinate propositional attitude is fully compatible with their being any number of different natural language representatives of that propositional attitude, some of which the subject may even fail to recognize as expressions of his attitude.

7.4.3. Propositional Attitude-Based Semantics Programmes

Formal semantic theories undertake to explain the semantic values (meanings, truth conditions, etc.) of complex expressions in a language as a function of the semantic values of the expressions' primitives (in conjunction with their syntactic structure and perhaps the context of utterance). In so doing, they propose to explain the semantic compositionality of natural language. More than a few philosophers have found such theories deeply unsatisfying inasmuch as they simply presuppose but do not explain the semantic properties of the primitives. These philosophers crave a more 'full-blooded' theory of meaning, one that would in some fashion explain the semantic properties of linguistic expressions in non-semantic terms. Especially influential have been various theories that propose to explain the meaning of expressions in terms of their use by speakers, in particular in terms of their use by speakers who use these expressions with the intention of producing certain characteristic effects in their audience (e.g., recognition of the speaker's intent, belief as to what the speaker intends to communicate). Grice (1989), for example, has famously proposed to reduce linguistic meaning to speaker's meaning, and then speaker's meaning to the possession of certain propositional attitudes, specifically to the intention on the part of the speaker to produce certain propositional attitudes in an audience by means of an utterance. The proposed measurement-theoretic account of the attitudes in no way impugns these propositional attitude-based semantic programmes for the simple reason that these programmes do not presuppose any particular account of propositional attitudes; in particular, these programmes do not presuppose a relational account of the attitudes, much less the Received View. It is enough simply that speakers can have the sorts of propositional attitudes that the account attributes to them. If anything, the proposed measurement-theoretic account is one that proponents of these programmes should embrace, precisely because it does not, like the Received View, leave them in the uncomfortable position of resting their account on semantically evaluable entities that demand their own semantics in order to establish the materialistic *bona fides* of propositional attitudes and hence of linguistic meaning.

7.4.4. Schiffer's and Fodor's Translational Semantics Programme

Many philosophers of language, most notably neo-Davidsonians (e.g., Lepore 1997, Larson and Segal 1995), have argued that learning a natural language is *inter alia* a matter of learning a formal compositional truth-conditional semantics that is then used in the course of language processing. Schiffer (1987) and Fodor (1990a) have both argued against such a role for semantic theory in language understanding—Schiffer on the grounds that natural languages don't have a compositional semantics, Fodor on the grounds that language understanding does not require knowledge of a semantic theory for the language in question. They have proposed instead that language acquisition and use involves the acquisition of a computational procedure—in Fodor's terms, a 'translation manual'; in Schiffer's terms, a partial recursive function—that maps heard utterances in one's natural language into the mentalese sentences that expresses the truth conditions of these utterances. Schiffer and Fodor dub the resulting account a 'translational' or 'perceptual' semantics for natural language in order to emphasize the translational, specifically perceptual character of the processes by which speakers come to understand what someone said in uttering a sentence.

There are reasons to doubt that Schiffer and Fodor have successfully argued for the thesis that language understanding doesn't require knowledge of a semantic theory (see Matthews 2004). Arguably, the compositional semantics envisioned by neo-Davidsonians is a *knowledge-level* specification of the computational procedure that Schiffer and Fodor take speakers to acquire and use. In other words, the semantics provides what Chomsky would call an intensional specification of the function computed by this computational procedure (see Section 7.3 above). The proposed measurement-theoretic account of the attitudes does not directly impugn Schiffer's and Fodor's envisioned account of language understanding, but it does challenge the description that they offer of the processes that map heard utterances into representations of what was said. Their account presupposes the basic tenets of the Received View, and as such runs together knowledge-level and computational descriptions of these processes. Thus, for example, Schiffer describes the hypothesized partial recursive function as mapping beliefs about heard utterances into beliefs about what was said, which clearly presupposes that these beliefs are represented in such fashion that they fall respectively within the domain and range of this function. Carefully separating these different levels of descriptions would make clear how impoverished their imagined account of language understanding really is. In the absence of the sort of specificity and detail that currently only a compositional truth-conditional semantics can provide, Schiffer and Fodor actually have little or nothing to say about the processes that underlies language understanding, little or nothing to say even about the character of the function that maps heard utterances into beliefs about what is said.

7.5. SUMMARY REMARKS

The proposed measurement-theoretic account of the attitudes offers a minimalist construal of propositional attitudes. The account argues that the predicates by which we attribute propositional attitudes, indeed our common-sense practice of attitude attribution, is consistent with a construal of propositional attitudes as simply states apt to produce their characteristic effects. On this minimalist construal, propositional attitudes are causally efficacious in the production of behavior and other mental states, but they do not have the semantic and inferential properties that philosophers, especially proponents of the Received View, have generally presumed them to have. At least they do not have them necessarily. The presumption that they have such properties arises from attributing to propositional attitudes properties and relations that are in fact possessed only by the particular sort of natural language representatives of the attitudes that we have evolved.

The proposed measurement-theoretic account leaves intact our common-sense attitude attribution and predictive/explanatory practice. It leaves intact our common-sense notion that the attitudes are causally efficacious in producing what we take to be their characteristic effects. It even leaves intact our common-sense notion of the intentionality of the attitudes, viz., that beliefs are beliefs *about* certain states of affairs and desires are desires *for* certain states of affairs, though the gloss that the account offers of this notion is one that cashes out the intentionality of the attitudes in *behavioral* rather than semantic terms; specifically, it cashes it out in terms of propositional attitudes being aptitudes for behavior which is focused on these states of affairs in ways that are specific to the attitude type. The proposed account does, however, have important consequences for certain currently popular philosophical doctrines and projects. Because propositional attitudes do not have the semantic properties that proponents of the Received View take them to have, we cannot be intentional realists in quite the way that they imagine; specifically, we cannot be realists about the semantic properties of propositional attitudes. They don't have contents in this sense. We can hardly be intentional content essentialists either. And because propositional attitudes don't have semantic properties, there is no need for a semantic theory for the mental representations that supposedly express the contents of propositional attitudes, and hence no need for the so-called naturalization project. This to my way of thinking is all to the good, for it is pretty clear that despite much philosophical effort over the last two decades this project has gone nowhere.

Other philosophical views and projects remain largely untouched by the proposed account. The task of providing a truth-conditional semantics for propositional attitude attributions remains largely unaffected, though if the proposed account is correct, then propositional attitude predicates must be construed as a kind of measurement predicate, and hence an understanding of attitude attributions requires both a semantics for these attributions and a measurement theory for the representatives in terms of which the truth conditions for attitude attributions are given. Attitude-based semantics programmes such as those proposed by Grice, on the one hand, and Fodor and Schiffer, on the other, can be pursued unaffected, though in the case of the Fodor and Schiffer's perceptual/translational semantics programme, it will have to be revised to eliminate its unnecessary commitments to the Received View.

The proposed account does not challenge the important role that propositional attitude attributions and propositional attitude psychology play in contemporary cognitive psychology, but it does challenge the particular role that some philosophers, especially proponents of the Received View, have claimed for it. The account attributes to attitude attributions precisely the very minimal structural/architectural commitments that the actual role of such attributions in cognitive computational modeling would predict: propositional attitude attributions serve to specify, albeit under significant idealization and with considerable imprecision, the functions computed in the course of cognitive processing, but such attributions provide no information on the computational structures or architectures that compute this function. The proposed account thus entails no change in actual cognitive scientific practice, only in how some philosophers have imagined that practice.

References

Armstrong, D. (1968) *A Materialist Theory of Mind* (London: Routledge & Kegan Paul).

Ascher, N. (1993) *Reference to Abstract Objects* (Kluwer: Dordrecht).

Bach, K. (1997) 'Do Belief Reports Report Beliefs?', *Pacific Philosophical Quarterly* 78: 215–41.

Barton, G., Berwick, R., and Ristad, E. (1987) *Computational Complexity and Natural Language* (Cambridge, MA: MIT Press).

Beckermann, A. (1996) 'Is There a Problem About Intentionality?', *Erkenntnis* 51: 1–23.

Bermudez, J. (2003) *Thinking without Words* (Oxford: Oxford University Press).

Berwick, R. (1985) *The Acquisition of Syntactic Knowledge* (Cambridge, MA: MIT Press).

—— and Weinberg, A. (1984) *The Grammatical Basis of Linguistic Performance* (Cambridge, MA: MIT Press).

Block, N. (1978) 'Troubles with Functionalism', in W. Savage (ed.), *Perception and Cognition: Issues in the Foundations of Psychology, Minnesota Studies in the Philosophy of Science*, vol. 9 (Minneapolis: University of Minnesota Press), 261–35. Reprinted in Block (ed.), *Readings in the Philosophy of Psychology, Vol. I* (Cambridge, MA: Harvard University Press, 1980).

—— (1981) *Readings in the Philosophy of Psychology, Vol. II* (Cambridge, MA: Harvard University Press).

Bonatti, L. (1998) 'Why It Took So Long to Bake Mental-Logic Cake: Historical Analysis of the Recipe and Its Ingredients', in Braine and O'Brien (1998a), 7–22.

Braddon-Mitchell, D. and Jackson, F. (1996) *Philosophy of Mind and Cognition* (Oxford: Blackwell).

Braine, M. (1978) 'On the Relation between the Natural Logic of Reasoning and Standard Logic', *Psychological Review* 85: 1–21.

—— and O'Brien, D. (1998a) *Mental Logic* (Hillsdale, NJ: Lawrence Erlbaum Associates).

—— —— (1998b) 'How to Investigate Mental Logic and the Syntax of Thought', in Braine and O'Brien (1998a), 45–62.

—— —— (1998c) 'The Theory of Mental-Propositional Logic: Description and Illustration', in Braine and O'Brien (1998a), 79–90.

—— —— Noveck, I., Samuels, M., Lea, R., Fisch, S., and Yang, Y. (1998) 'Further Evidence for the Theory: Predicting Intermediate and Multiple Conclusions in Propositional Logic Inference Problems', in Braine and O'Brien (1998a), 145–98.

Braine, M., Reiser, B., and Rumain, D. (1998) 'Evidence for the Theory: Predicting the Difficulty of Propositional Logic Inference Problems', in Braine and O'Brien (1998a), 91–144.

Bresnan, J. and Kaplan, R. (1982) 'Introduction: Grammars as Mental Representations of Language', in Bresnan (ed.), *The Mental Representation of Grammatical Relations* (Cambridge, MA: MIT Press), pp. xvii–lii.

Campbell, N. (1928) *An Account of the Principles of Measurement and Calculation* (London: Longmans).

Carnap, R. (1947) *Meaning and Necessity* (Chicago: University of Chicago Press).

Cheng, P. and Holyoak, K. (1985) 'Pragmatic Reasoning Schemas', *Cognitive Psychology* 17: 391–416.

Chomsky, N. (1959) 'Review of Skinner's *Verbal Behavior*', *Language* 35: 26–58.

_____ (1965) *Aspects of the Theory of Syntax* (Cambridge, MA: MIT Press).

_____ (1980a) *Rules and Representations* (New York: Columbia University Press).

_____ (1980b) 'Rules and Representations', *Behavior and Brain Science* 3: 1–61.

_____ (2000) *New Horizons in the Study of Language and Mind* (Cambridge: Cambridge University Press).

Churchland, P. (1979) *Scientific Realism and the Plasticity of Mind* (Cambridge: Cambridge University Press).

_____ (1981) 'Eliminative Materialism and the Propositional Attitudes', *Journal of Philosophy* 67: 67–90.

Cosmides, L. (1989) 'The Logic of Social Exchange: Has Natural Selection Shaped How Humans Reason? Studies with the Wason Selection Task', *Cognition* 31: 187–276.

Crimmins, M. (1992) *Talk about Belief* (Cambridge, MA: MIT Press).

_____ and Perry, J. (1989) 'The Prince and the Phone Booth: Reporting Puzzling Beliefs', *The Journal of Philosophy* 86: 685–711.

Cummins, R. (1983) *The Nature of Psychological Explanation* (Cambridge, MA: MIT Press).

_____ (1989) *Meaning and Mental Representation* (Cambridge, MA: MIT Press).

Davidson, D. (1968) 'On Saying That', *Synthese* 19: 130–46.

_____ (1989) 'What is Present to the Mind', in J. Brandl and W. Gombocz (eds.), *The Mind of Donald Davidson* (Amsterdam: Editions Rodopi), 3–18.

Davies, M. (1987) 'Tacit Knowledge and Semantic Theory: Can a Five Percent Difference Matter?', *Mind* 96: 441–62.

Dennett, D. (1977) 'Critical Notice: The Language of Thought by Jerry Fodor', *Mind* 86: 265–80. Page references to reprint as 'A Cure for the Common Code', in *Brainstorms* (Cambridge, MA: MIT Press, 1981), 90–108.

_____ (1987) 'Beyond Belief', in *The Intentional Stance* (Cambridge, MA: MIT Press), 116–211.

Díez, J. (1997) 'A Hundred Years of Numbers: An Historical Introduction to Measurement Theory 1887–1990', *Studies in the History and Philosophy of Science* 28: 167–85, 237–65.

Dretske, F. (1988) *Explaining Behavior: Reasons in a World of Causes* (Cambridge, MA: MIT Press).

Dummett, M. (1976) 'What is a Theory of Meaning? (II)', in G. Evans and J. McDowell (eds.), *Truth and Meaning* (London: Oxford University Press), 67–137.

Egan, F. (1991) 'Propositional Attitudes and the Language of Thought', *Canadian Journal of Philosophy* 21: 379–88.

—— (1995) 'Folk Psychology and Cognitive Architecture', *Philosophy of Science* 62: 179–96.

—— (2003) 'Naturalistic Inquiry: Where Does Mental Representation Fit In?', in L. Antony and N. Hornstein (eds.), *Chomksy and His Critics* (London: Blackwell), 89–104.

Field, H. (1978) 'Mental Representation', *Erkenntnis* 9: 13–61. Reprinted in Block (1981), 78–112.

—— (1981) Postscript to his 'Mental Representation', in Block (1981), 112–14.

Fiengo, R. and May, R. (1996) 'Interpreted Logical Form: A Critique', *Rivista di Linguistica* 8: 349–73.

Fodor, J. (1974) 'Special Sciences', *Synthese* 28: 121–45. Reprinted in Fodor, *Representations* (Cambridge, MA: MIT Press, 1981), 127–45.

—— (1975) *The Language of Thought* (New York: Crowell).

—— (1978) 'Propositional Attitudes', *Monist* 61. Page references to reprint in Fodor, *Representations* (Cambridge, MA: MIT Press, 1981), 177–203.

—— (1979) 'Three Cheers for Propositional Attitudes', in R. Cooper and E. Walker (eds.), *Sentence Processing* (Hillsdale, NJ: Lawrence Erlbaum). Page references to reprint in Fodor, *Representations* (Cambridge, MA: MIT Press, 1981), 100–23.

—— (1981) 'Some Notes on What Linguistics Is About', in Block (1981), 197–207.

—— (1983) *Modularity of Mind* (Cambridge, MA: MIT Press).

—— (1987) *Psychosemantics* (Cambridge, MA: MIT Press).

—— (1990a) 'Review of Stephen Schiffer's *Remnants of Meaning*', *Philosophy and Phenomenological Research* 50. Reprinted in Fodor (1990b), 177–91.

—— (1990b) *A Theory of Content and Other Essays* (Cambridge, MA: MIT Press).

Fodor, J., Bever, T., and Garrett, M. (1974) *The Psychology of Language* (New York: McGraw-Hill).

Fodor, J. and McLaughlin, B. (1990) 'Connectionism and the Problem of Systematicity', *Cognition* 35: 183–204.

Fodor, J. and Pylyshyn, Z. (1988) 'Connectionism and Cognitive Architecture: A Critical Analysis', *Cognition* 28: 3–71.

Gallistel, C. (1990) *The Organization of Learning* (Cambridge, MA: MIT Press).

Gallistel, C. (2006) 'The Nature of Learning and the Functional Architecture of the Brain', in Q. Ling, *et al.* (eds.), *Psychological Science Around the World, Vol. 1. Proceedings of the 28th International Congress of Psychology* (Hove, East Sussex: Psychology Press), 63–71.

Graves, C., Katz, J., Nishiyama, Y., Soames, S., Stecker, R., and Tovey, P. (1973) 'Tacit Knowledge', *Journal of Philosophy* 70: 318–30.

Grice, P. (1989) *Studies in the Way of Words* (Cambridge, MA: Harvard University Press).

Harman, G. (1973) *Thought* (Princeton: Princeton University Press).

Haugeland, J. (1978) 'The Plausibility of Cognitivism', *Behavioral and Brain Science* 2: 215–60.

Helmholtz, H. (1887) 'Zahlen und Messen, erkenntnistheoretisch betrachtet', translated as 'Counting and Measuring from an Epistemological Viewpoint', in his *Epistemological Writings* (Dordrecht: Reidel, 1977), 72–114.

Hodges, W. (1993) *Model Theory* (New York: Cambridge University Press).

Hölder, O. (1901) 'Die Axiome der Quantität und die Lehre vom Mass', *Berichte über die Verhandlungen der königliche sächsischen Akademie der Wissenschaften zu Leipzig Math.-Phys. Classe* 53: 1–64.

Holyoak, K. and Cheng, P. (1995) 'Pragmatic Reasoning from Multiple Points of View: A Response', *Thinking and Reasoning* 1: 373–88.

Horgan, T. and Graham, G. (1991) 'In Defense of Southern Fundamentalism', *Philosophical Studies* 62: 107–34.

Hornik, K., Stinchcombe, M., and White, H. (1989) 'Multilayer Feedforward Networks Are Universal Approximators', *Neural Networks* 2: 359–66.

Jackson, F. and Pettit, P. (1990) 'In Defense of Folk Psychology', *Philosophical Studies* 59: 31–54.

Johnson-Laird, P. (1975) 'Models of Deduction', in R. Falmagne (ed.), *Reasoning: Representation and Process in Children and Adults* (Hillsdale, NJ: Lawrence Erlbaum Associates).

_____ (1983) *Mental Models* (Cambridge, MA: Harvard University Press).

_____ and Byrne, R. (1991) *Deduction* (Hillsdale, NJ: Lawrence Erlbaum Associates).

_____ _____ (1993) 'Mental Models or Formal Rules?', *Behavioral and Brain Sciences* 16: 368–80.

King, J. (2002) 'Designating Propositions', *Philosophical Review* 111: 341–71.

Kirsch, D. (1990) 'When Is Information Explicitly Represented', in P. Hanson (ed.), *Information, Content and Meaning* (Vancouver: UBC Press), 340–65.

Krantz, D., Luce, D., Suppes, P., and Tversky, A. (1971) *Foundations of Measurement, Vol. I* (New York: Academic Press).

Kripke, S. (1979) 'A Puzzle about Belief', in A. Margalit (ed.), *Meaning and Use* (Dordrecht: Reidel), 239–83.

Larson, R. and Ludlow, P. (1993) 'Interpreted Logical Forms', *Synthese* 95: 305–55.

——and Segal, G. (1995) *Knowledge of Meaning* (Cambridge, MA: MIT Press).

Lepore, E. (1997) 'Conditions on Understanding Language', *Proceedings of the Aristotelian Society* 19: 41–60.

Lewis, D. (1972) 'Psychophysical and Theoretical Identifications', *Australasian Journal of Philosophy* 50: 249–58.

Loar, B. (1988) 'Social Content and Psychological Content', in R. Grimm and D. Merrill (eds.), *Contents of Thought* (Tucson: University of Arizona Press).

Loewer, B. and Rey, G. (1991) *Meaning in Mind: Fodor and His Critics* (Oxford: Blackwell).

Ludlow, P. (2000) 'Interpreted Logical Forms, Belief Attribution, and the Dynamic Lexicon', in K. Jaszczolt (ed.), *The Pragmatics of Propositional Attitude Reports* (Oxford: Elsevier Science), 31–42.

Lycan, W. (1981) 'Form, Function, and Feel', *Journal of Philosophy* 78: 24–50.

Marcus, M. (1980) *A Theory of Syntactic Recognition for Natural Language* (Cambridge, MA: MIT Press).

Marr, D. (1982) *Vision* (New York: Freeman).

Matthews, R. (1990) 'The Measure of Mind', Report No. 57/1990, Research Group on Mind and Brain, ZiF (Bielefeld).

——(1991a) 'Is There Vindication through Representationalism?', in Loewer and Ray (1991), 137–50.

——(1991b) 'Psychological Reality of Grammars', in A. Kasher (ed.), *The Chomskyan Turn* (London: Blackwell), 182–99.

——(1994) 'The Measure of Mind', *Mind* 103: 131–46.

——(1997) 'Can Connectionists Explain Systematicity?' *Mind & Language* 12: 154–77.

——(2004) 'Does Linguistic Competence Require Knowledge of Language?', in A. Barber (ed.), *Epistemology of Language* (Oxford: Oxford University Press), 187–213.

——(2006) 'Knowledge of Language and Linguistic Competence', *Philosophical Issues* 16: 200–20.

Miller, G. and Chomsky, N. (1963) 'Finitary Models of Language Users', in R. Luce, R. Bush, and E. Galanter (eds.), *Handbook of Mathematical Psychology* (New York: John Wiley), 419–91.

Moltmann, F. (2003) 'Propositional Attitudes without Propositions', *Synthese* 135: 77–118.

Mundy, B. (1986) 'On the Theory of Meaningful Representation', *Synthese* 67: 391–437.

Mundy, B. (1987) 'The Metaphysics of Quantity', *Philosophical Studies* 51: 29–54.

Narens, L. (1985) *Abstract Measurement Theory* (Cambridge, MA: MIT Press).

Newell, A. (1980) 'Physical Symbol Systems', *Cognitive Science* 4: 135–83.

Newell, A. (1981) 'The Knowledge Level', *AI Magazine* (Summer), 1–20.

O'Brien, D. (1998) 'Mental Logic and Irrationality: We Can Put a Man on the Moon, So Why Can't We Solve Those Logical Reasoning Problems?', in Braine and O'Brien (1998a), 23–43.

Perry, J. (1979) 'The Problem of the Essential Indexical', *Nous* 13: 3–21.

Pietroski, P. (1996) 'Fregean Innocence', *Mind and Language* 11: 338–70.

Prior, A. (1971) *Objects of Thought* (Oxford: Clarendon Press).

Pylyshyn, Z. (1984) *Computation and Cognition* (Cambridge, MA: MIT Press).

Quine, W. (1960) *Word and Object* (Cambridge, MA: MIT Press).

Ramsey, P. (1927) 'Facts and Propositions', in *Foundations: Essays in Philosophy, Logic, Mathematics and Economics* (London: Routledge, 1978).

Richard, M. (1990) *Propositional Attitudes: An Essay on Thoughts and How We Ascribe Them* (Cambridge: Cambridge University Press).

Rips, L. (1983) 'Cognitive Processes in Propositional Reasoning', *Psychological Review* 90: 38–71.

_____ (1994) *The Psychology of Proof: Deductive Reasoning in Human Thinking* (Cambridge, MA: MIT Press).

Roberts, F. (1979) *Measurement Theory* (Reading, MA: Addison-Wesley).

Russell, B. (1913) *Theory of Knowledge*. The unfinished 1913 manuscript, ed. E. Eames (London: Unwin Hyman Ltd. 1984; repr. Routledge, 1993).

Schiffer, S. (1987) *Remnants of Meaning* (Cambridge, MA: MIT Press).

_____ (1992), 'Belief Ascription', *Journal of Philosophy* 89: 499–521.

Schwarzchild, R. and Wilkinson, K. (2002) 'Quantifiers in Comparatives: A Semantics of Degree Based on Intervals', *Natural Language Semantics* 10: 1–41.

Skinner, B. (1985) 'Cognitive Science and Behaviorism', *British Journal of Psychology* 76: 291–301.

Stabler, E. (1983) 'How Are Grammars Represented?', *Behavioral and Brain Sciences* 6: 185–94.

Stalnaker, R. (1984) *Inquiry* (Cambridge, MA: MIT Press).

_____ (1991) 'The Problem of Logical Omniscience I', *Synthese* 89. Reprinted in *Context and Content* (Oxford: Oxford University Press, 1999), 241–54.

Sterelny, K. (1990) *The Representational Theory of Mind* (London: Blackwell).

Stevens, S. (1946) 'On the Theory of Scales of Measurement', *Science* 103: 667–80.

Stich, S. (1978) 'Beliefs and Subdoxastic States', *Philosophy of Science* 45: 499–518.

Suppes, P. (1951) 'A Set of Independent Axioms for Extensive Quantities', *Portugaliae Mathematica* 10: 163–72.

_____ and Zinnes, J. (1963) 'Basic Measurement Theory', in R. Luce, D. Krantz, and E. Galanter (eds.) *Handbook of Mathematical Psychology, Vol. I* (New York: Wiley and Sons), 1–76.

——Krantz, D., Luce, D., and Tversky, A. (1989) *Foundations of Measurement, Vol. II* (New York: Academic Press).

Swoyer, C. (1987) 'The Metaphysics of Measurement', in J. Forge (ed.), *Measurement, Realism and Objectivity* (Dordrecht: Reidel), 235–90.

——(1991) 'Structural Representation and Surrogative Reasoning', *Synthese* 87: 449–508.

Ullman, S. (1979) *The Interpretation of Visual Motion* (Cambridge, MA: MIT Press).

Whyte, J. (1990) 'Success Semantics', *Analysis* 50: 149–57.

——(1991) 'The Normal Rewards of Success', *Analysis* 51: 65–73.

Index